ARIEL ASCENDING

ARIEL ASCENDING

WRITINGS ABOUT SYLVIA PLATH

Edited by Paul Alexander

HARPER & ROW, PUBLISHERS, New York
Cambridge, Philadelphia, San Francisco, London
Mexico City, São Paulo, Singapore, Sydney

1817

Copyright acknowledgments follow page 218.

ARIEL ASCENDING. Copyright © 1985 by Paul Alexander. All rights reserved. Printed in the United States of America. No part of this book may be used or reproduced in any manner whatsoever without written permission except in the case of brief quotations embodied in critical articles and reviews. For information address Harper & Row, Publishers, Inc., 10 East 53rd Street, New York, N.Y. 10022. Published simultaneously in Canada by Fitzhenry & Whiteside Limited, Toronto.

FIRST EDITION

Designer: Sidney Feinberg

Library of Congress Cataloging in Publication Data

Main entry under title:

Ariel ascending.

   1. Plath, Sylvia—Addresses, essays, lectures.
2. Poets, American—20th century—Biography—Addresses, essays, lectures. I. Alexander, Paul, 1955–
PS3566.L27Z57 1985   811'.54 [B]   84–47616
ISBN 0-06-015333-4   85 86 87 88 89 10 9 8 7 6 5 4 3 2 1
ISBN 0-06-091175-1 (pbk.)   85 86 87 88 89 10 9 8 7 6 5 4 3 2 1

I would like to thank the University of Houston for support and assistance in the completion of this book; I am indebted, in particular, to Charles E. Bishop, John Leslie, Elizabeth Cooper, and Clinton B. Jones.

Contents

Introduction

Sylvia Plath worked as a professional writer for only about seven years, from mid-1955 just after her graduation from Smith College until her suicide in February 1963. During her brief career, however, Plath produced an enormous bulk of material, explored almost every possible genre. She wrote several commissioned nonfiction pieces for American and British magazines and for the BBC; perhaps as many as seventy short stories, some published in popular magazines, the majority still unpublished at the time of her death; a verse play, *Three Women;* and a children's story, *The Bed Book.* She maintained an exhausting correspondence through letters with a variety of people, most notably her mother, and by the end of her life, after years of diary-keeping, had produced an extensive journal. During these seven years she also wrote *The Bell Jar,* a novel, and brought to some final state over two hundred and fifty poems. In the last months of her life she was at work on a second novel, *Falcon Yard* —a draft of which, in fact, she had finished before she had written *The Bell Jar*—but one night in July 1962 in a moment of anger she destroyed the only copy of that manuscript by fire.

Besides the commissioned nonfiction pieces and a number of individual poems which appeared in magazines and journals in the United States and England, Sylvia Plath had published at the time of her death only one collection of poems under her own name, *The Colossus and Other Poems* (by Heinemann in England in 1960, by Knopf in the United States in 1962), and, under the pseudonym Victoria Lucas, *The Bell Jar* (by Heinemann in England in January 1963). Consequently, when she died at age thirty, Sylvia Plath was regarded by most serious readers of literature simply as someone about to break onto the scene, another young poet with obvious potential. She was, in fact, still at that stage in her career where acceptance of her work for publication was not at all certain, so much so that in the months immediately preceding her death, as she sent out her latest poems (the poems which would eventually be collected to make *Ariel*), she received a steady stream of rejection slips in which, time and again, editors warned her that the emotion in these new poems was overpowering the form, that her verse was out of control, that she was mining a destructive art. They were much more reluctant to publish these harsh, often biting poems over the restrained but academically sound poems she had written only years before, the poems which for the most part made up *The Colossus.*

It was her suicide in February 1963—and the details of that suicide—which melted this resistance. With an interest in the final days of her life came an interest in the poems she was writing in those final days and, as a consequence, in the months following her death her work garnered more recognition than it ever had before. On February 17 *The Observer* ran four poems, selected by A. Alvarez, then that publication's poetry editor, from poems she had written in the final weeks of her life. In April *London Magazine* ran seven poems and *The Atlantic Monthly* two. On August 3 *The New Yorker* printed seven poems—as many as the magazine had run in the seven previous years she had published there. In October *Encounter* ran ten poems, *The Review* nine. Since only a handful of these poems had been accepted for publication before Plath's death, the majority of them were acquired from her estate through her husband, Ted Hughes, who assumed the role of literary executor after her suicide and from that time on oversaw the publication of virtually all of her work.

During the last half of 1963 and on into 1964 a groundswell of fascination arose concerning Sylvia Plath's final poems, for these poems, it seemed—on the surface at least—contained the necessary bits and pieces of information needed to explain the intense unhappiness Sylvia Plath had endured for the last six months of her life. It was only logical for these poems published individually to be collected into one volume and the resulting *Ariel,* assembled by Hughes and based in part on an arrangement of the manuscript Plath herself had made before she died, appeared in England and in the United States in 1965.

The attention Sylvia Plath's work received in the two years following her death was nothing compared to that which resulted from *Ariel*. *The Colossus* had gone basically unnoticed by reviewers. During the eighteen months following its publication, *Ariel*, on the other hand, was reviewed by most major newspapers and magazines. Sylvia Plath's visibility peaked in the summer of 1966 when *Ariel* was profiled in *The Atlantic Monthly*, *The New York Times*, *Harper's*, *Newsweek*, and *Time*, where "Daddy" was reprinted. The story of Sylvia Plath's brief life and tragic death, sketched repeatedly in these and other reviews and profiles, often became an integral part of the discussion of the *Ariel* poems. It seemed no doubt essential, for here, apparently, in her final poems Sylvia Plath not only achieved an obvious breakthrough in language and voice but had also detailed the gradual mental deterioration of a woman who was confounded by her own motherhood, who was out of love, who was obsessed with the notion of death—a woman who ostensibly resembled Sylvia Plath. It is always odd when a writer's work is published posthumously but Sylvia Plath's final poems, strikingly unified and forceful in this single volume, were even more unusual since they appeared to document almost systematically the events which resulted in her own death. Not surprisingly, to *Ariel*'s initial critics the craft and skill behind the poems did not seem as important as their subject matter and the circumstances surrounding their publication.

With an audience for Sylvia Plath's work firmly established, Faber & Faber printed a new edition of *The Bell Jar* in England in 1966. This time, however, through a note on the inside front cover, the book was identified as Sylvia Plath's. Suddenly, the novel—which centers around the mental breakdown, shock treatment, and dramatic suicide attempt of a young woman during the summer between her junior and senior years in college, a novel deemed a "considerable achievement" by the *Times Literary Supplement* when it was published under the name Victoria Lucas—was read as Plath's autobiographical novel. The mental anguish of the protagonist in *The Bell Jar* appeared to predict the extreme unhappiness of the narrator of the *Ariel* poems in a very clear way. The two books together explained a great deal. Sylvia Plath's decline in the last months of her life was not without precedent. She had encountered a similar period of unhappiness some ten years before and lived through it.

For a number of reasons the Plath edition of *The Bell Jar* was not published in the United States until 1971 when it was reissued by Harper & Row. To this edition an appendix was added which contained eight original Plath pen-and-ink drawings and a biographical afterword by Lois Ames, an essay which for the first time revealed some of the more private details of Sylvia Plath's life. In 1971 two other books of poems, *Crossing the Water* and *Winter Trees*, appeared in England. Ted Hughes tagged the poems in *Crossing the Water* "transitional poems" since they were written basically before *Ariel* and after *The Colossus* and reflect Plath's departure from the objective style she had all but perfected in the early part of her career and the more innovative subjective style she was pursuing in the latter part. *Winter Trees* was made up of poems left out of *Ariel* and the verse play *The Women*. *Crossing the Water* was published in the United States in 1971, *Winter Trees* in 1972.

Also in 1971 the first half of A. Alvarez's memoir of Sylvia Plath appeared in London in *The Observer*. The article (reprinted here under the title used when it was first published several months later in the United States in *The New American Review* and when it subsequently served as the prologue to Alvarez's study of suicide, *The Savage God*) was then entitled "The Road to Suicide" and vividly described the months and weeks just prior to Sylvia Plath's death. The first installment was so troublesome in its exactness that *The Observer* did not run the second half of the piece.

Just after the publication of Sylvia Plath's middle poems, with much of her poetic canon complete and some facts of her life and death well established, an enormous amount of Plath and Plath-related material began to be published in the United States and England, a trend which continued on through the decade. Critical essays on her work appeared in literary journals, longer studies were brought out in book form, remembrances by friends showed up in popular magazines, and her poems were excerpted widely. Nancy Hunter Steiner's memoir, *A Closer Look at Ariel*, came out in 1973, followed by Edward Butscher's pseudo-literary biography in 1976. Also Aurelia Plath, Sylvia Plath's mother, collected and edited a volume containing a portion of Plath's letters to her in *Letters Home*, and Harper & Row published Plath's short fiction and prose pieces, *Johnny Panic and the Bible of Dreams*. Most recently Ted Hughes edited Sylvia Plath's *The Collected Poems* which won, almost twenty years after her death, the 1982 Pulitzer Prize for Poetry, and that same year the Dial Press published *The Journals of Sylvia Plath*, a sampling of her voluminous journal.

One might ask, then—and the question would be legitimate—why a book such as *Ariel Ascending* should be assembled in the first place. What could possibly be accomplished by adding one more document to an already overwhelming number of documents concerning Sylvia Plath? The answer to that question would be much easier if the subject of these essays were another writer. Anthologies of this sort should reflect the current critical thinking on the author in question; *Ariel Ascending* does, but it accomplishes, I hope, something else as well, and that "something else" is what blurs the issue of why this book was undertaken, even if only slightly. Because of the unusual circumstances surrounding the publication of her work due to her suicide, because much of the work published *is* about her life in the form of journals and letters, and because a good portion of the creative work appears on the surface at least to be autobiographical, many readers and critics of Sylvia Plath, instead of evaluating the quality of her poetry and prose, have studied her work in hopes of explaining more completely the facts and details of her personal life and of unearthing in her writing some motives for the way she chose to end it. Consequently, Sylvia Plath has been portrayed as the champion of feminist causes, even though in her own life she was anything but a feminist; as the ultimate confessional poet, even though she wrote in a highly subjective voice for only a small portion of her career; and, most sadly, as a "legend" or "cult figure," roles she would have regarded with certain disdain. So *Ariel Ascending* was begun with the intention of providing not only a current critical look at Sylvia Plath but also—by including essays which avoid sensationalizing her life and death and instead examine the craft of her poetry and prose—a sort of milestone to indicate a more appropriate way of regarding Sylvia Plath.

This is not to say that no serious intellectual pieces have been written on Sylvia Plath (it has always been a question of proportion) and, in fact, several of the more striking pieces included in this collection are reprints selected from a growing body of fine scholarly essays addressing Plath's work. My first task, therefore, was to decide which of these previously published pieces I would include in the volume. Some choices suggested themselves immediately: Joyce Carol Oates's knowledgeable discourse on Plath as lyric poet;

Helen Vendler's study of the various phases of Plath's poetry; Elizabeth Hardwick's startlingly perceptive overview of Plath's career
and the effects certain events in her life had on her development as
a writer; A. Alvarez's unsettling but poignant portrait of Plath as
woman, mother, artist. Simultaneously, I also began to secure original essays from some of the foremost writers, poets, and critics
working today, to give the book a more timely quality, to offer
essays written not simply to be "new" but written to reflect an
intense yet objective way of examining Plath's work. The result is
several pieces as moving and informed as any written on Sylvia
Plath: Stanley Plumly's finely developed meditation on Plath's career as a poet; Grace Schulman's examination of a pivotal group of
Plath's early poems; Rosellen Brown's consideration of Plath as
short-prose writer; Vance Bourjaily's thorough study of Plath's artistic accomplishment in *The Bell Jar.*

Months passed and when I finally brought the bulk of these
essays together I was then faced with arranging them in some sensi-
ble order. Since many of the pieces, in one way or another, address
similar issues, I decided I would not divide the book into the expected sections but instead present them as one continuous sequence, even though, when one reads the anthology as a whole,
certain subtle demarcations do become clear. The book's initial
essays, for instance, focus predominantly on Sylvia Plath's poetry.
Some are built on close readings of individual poems, others on
tracing general trends in her poetry. Following these essays Elizabeth Hardwick's piece serves as a sort of transition from the first part
of the book to the last. The next four essays examine Sylvia Plath's
fiction, her short stories in passing but mostly *The Bell Jar,* while the
final five pieces in the book deal with broader tendencies in Sylvia
Plath's work and do not limit themselves to discussing any specific
period or genre. All of the essays in this collection, however, raise
the single most important question one can ask about any writer:
how good is the work and will it last?

When I first considered what I wanted to say in the introduction
to this book I drew a complete blank. For weeks, day after day, I
littered my study with false starts, threw out, in some cases, whole
drafts of possible introductions. I had never before experienced such
a difficult time writing one single piece. I felt a number of awkward-

nesses about it: that the book belonged as much to Sylvia Plath as it did to me and, consequently, that anything I might say by way of introduction would necessarily ring false; that the essays in the collection should, individually and collectively, stand alone and speak for themselves; that introductions by their nature represent a false form and are often misleading. But my mind kept drifting back to the question with which I ended the previous section and ultimately it occurred to me that any introduction I should write must somehow answer that question, for in some unnamable way I knew I undertook this project initially to help determine a particular answer to that particular question. Considering this, I then remembered a decade ago when I was an undergraduate student in a literature class, a class which required me to read, for the first time seriously, the volume *Ariel.* As I studied the book that semester I was deeply moved by the protagonist's intense anguish, by the bitter humor and the all-too-ephemeral joy she employed to cope with that anguish. Today I am still deeply moved by many of the poems— "Elm," "Cut," "Ariel," "Fever 103°," "Morning Song"—and since that time I have found, as I read Plath's work many times over, that I admire other of her achievements perhaps as much as I do the *Ariel* poems: the fierce craftsmanship and subtle understatement of numerous early poems, the translucent transformations of several middle poems, *The Bell Jar*'s eerie humor and powerful character portrait, the poignance of her best short stories and personal essays. The answer to that question—how good is the work and will it last?— has seemed so obvious to me, seems so obvious to me now. Throughout her writing career Sylvia Plath showed clear signs of a constantly maturing genius which culminated in a group of poems written from that impulse to make private images into public metaphors in a vital and distinctive way. Her accomplishments are paralleled only by that handful of writers in any generation in any century which sets for its end the unachievable and achieves it. This is how we should regard Sylvia Plath and why I entitled this anthology what I did: she was a writer of enormous talent whose work, years later, still aspires, arrests, ascends.

—PAUL ALEXANDER

ARIEL ASCENDING

Helen Vendler

An Intractable Metal

The Collected Poems of Sylvia Plath finally appeared in 1982, almost twenty years after Plath's suicide, on February 11, 1963. Nothing in the introduction, written by her former husband, the British poet Ted Hughes, quite explains the long delay in the publication of this collection. Before Plath died, she had prepared the volume called *Ariel* for the press, but the "*Ariel* eventually published in 1965 was a somewhat different volume from the one she had planned," Hughes tells us; it incorporated poems she had planned to keep for a subsequent book, and "omitted some of the more personally aggressive poems from 1962"—those concerning her husband's infidelity, which led to the dissolution of the marriage and to Plath's move from Devon to London. Her daughter, Frieda, was two at the time of the move; her son, Nicholas, not yet a year old. Less than a month after his first birthday, Plath was dead. She had managed to live and to write after previous attempts at suicide, but, like Cesare Pavese (to cite a comparable case), she continually needed to find reasons *not* to kill herself, rather than a reason to do so.

Until recently, most of the writing about Plath has been psychologically or politically motivated. The time of her fame coincided with a widespread acceptance of the Freudian myths of selfhood (which she also embraced) and with the rise of women's liberation. Plath's life seemed a textbook illustration of the "Electra complex" (as she herself called it, schooled by her therapists and her college reading in psychology), and she also seemed an instance of the damage done to gifted women by social convention. Plath's language—a heady cross of *Kinder, Küche,* Freud, and Frazer—found an audience that already knew and shared its world of reference. An

1

electric current jumped between *Ariel* and a large (mostly female) set of readers; and from then on, the poetry of Plath became a part of the feminist canon. *Crossing the Water* and *Winter Trees* were published in 1971; they, together with *The Colossus* (the only volume published in Plath's lifetime, in 1960) and *Ariel,* made up the Plath poetic canon until *The Collected Poems.*

Plath scholars know most of the work published therein. Ted Hughes and his sister Olwyn have been publishing, bit by bit, small groups of the poems in limited editions in England (all royalties are assigned to the two children). The poems not previously published in any form were mostly very early; the few later ones in this category were undistinguished. For the general reader, however, *The Collected Poems* conveyed for the first time the whole of Plath's work, arranged chronologically by date of composition. Fifty very early poems are printed in an appendix; the chronological arrangement begins with the year 1956, when Plath, who was born in 1932, was twenty-three. But the memorable poems do not begin until she turns twenty-four—after her marriage, in June 1956. She had six years of mature writing before she died, at thirty. Those years included her second year as a Fulbright fellow at Newnham College, Cambridge; a year of teaching at Smith, where she had been an undergraduate; a year in Boston, where she audited Robert Lowell's writing class at Boston University; and her return to England. In London, after she and Hughes had decided to give up teaching and to live as writers, she had, in succession, a child, a three-month miscarriage, and an appendectomy. There she also wrote her autobiographical novel, *The Bell Jar* (published in England under the pseudonym Victoria Lucas). In 1961, she and Ted Hughes moved from London to Devon, and she had their second child. Then came the separation from Hughes which produced a remarkable spate of writing: in the thirty-one days of October 1962, Plath finished twenty-five poems (while in the entire year of 1960—which included the last three months of her first pregnancy, the birth of her daughter, and her first months of motherhood—she wrote only twelve).

The events of Plath's life during these years—though some, like the transatlantic move, are slightly unusual—are on the whole those that many women have lived through, not excepting marital disappointments, the discovery of infidelity, and finding oneself a single mother. These events, banal to everyone except the one experiencing them, have been the occasion in the twentieth century of any number of banal poems. As subjects, they are as well-worn as the subject of parents (Plath's other topic). What is striking, and satisfying, about reading Plath's poems is how well she holds her own, and how firmly she transforms the topics she masters—how her best poems maintain themselves in passion without lacking a strict, informing intelligence. In some of the poems (notably the early ones), intelligence averts its eyes from feeling or overcontrols feeling; later, the balance sometimes tips in the other direction, and Plath becomes merely vituperative or spiteful, angrily refusing the acuteness of reflection present in her best work. Her piercing strength when intelligence and feeling cooperate is not easily forgotten.

Plath seems very young now to any older reader, and her career seems cruelly self-aborted. Remembering ourselves at thirty, we wish she could have had the years of living that would inevitably have provided her with new views of her past and, in consequence, new views of herself. Her suicide, for all her attempt to dress it in Greek necessity, seems an unhappy accident—a failure of social resource, a failure of medicine (a hospital bed could not be found for her), and even a failure of weather (she hated the cold, and died in London's coldest winter in years). We are more conscious now of the physiological causes of (and remedies for) depression, thanks to poets like Lowell who have expressed considerable irony about the sedulous efforts of therapists to ascribe to environmental causes what turns out to be a lack of lithium.

By the time she died, Plath had written at least two scenarios of her life. In the first scenario, her father, Otto (an entomologist who died, when she was eight, of willfully uncared-for diabetes), is a doting parent, a hero, and a god, and she is his mourning daughter; her mother, Aurelia, is a heroine who keeps Plath and her brother alive by working as a teacher of secretarial skills. (Plath's devotion to her mother and Aurelia Plath's to her daughter appear in the incessant letters they exchanged; some of Sylvia's were collected in *Letters Home,* published in 1975.) In the second scenario, Otto Plath becomes an incestuously seductive father, a Nazi, and a vampire; and Sylvia is his victim, a Jew in his concentration camp. Aurelia Plath in this scenario is a tentacular mother, a barnacle obsessively clinging to her daughter, a "blubbery Mary." Plath's scenarios about Ted Hughes underwent comparable changes, as he metamorphosed from fertility god into monster; and Plath's fictions about herself changed, too—from the fruitful bride of the sun, "quick with seed," bearing a king as she crouches in the grass, she turns into Lady Lazarus, who eats men like air. Eventually, if Plath had managed to stay alive, all the scenarios would probably have revised themselves; she would have seen her parents in yet another guise, and perhaps her husband, too. Certainly she would have seen both herself and her children differently. As she writes about them, her children are infants, pure and poignant, untroubled by their mother's anxieties:

> Your clear eye is the one absolutely beautiful thing.
> I want to fill it with color and ducks,
> The zoo of the new
>
> Whose names you meditate . . .
>
> ("Child")

When, in the future, they became contrary and baffling adolescents, Plath would have needed to find another fiction for them, and for herself.

The one thing that recommends Plath to us most strongly now is her ability to change her mind when she saw a new truth. She was on the lookout for new truths; never one to receive the world passively, she hunted for accuracy and excoriated herself for her failures. She changed her mind, when it was necessary, in a violent way, repudiating her previous position with all the force of her daunting energy. She had no Keatsian capacity for maintaining two contrary truths at once. But it is not impossible that in middle age she might have come to entertain her scenarios as plural truths, to find some of the equilibrium granted, late, to Lowell, who ended by seeing his parents less harshly. Sylvia Plath, when she died, had at last begun to recognize a monstrousness in herself. If her father was a vampire, so was she. She had also begun to realize that "there is no terminus," no point at which the world is arranged for good, with all its truths established:

> There is no terminus, only suitcases
> Out of which the same self unfolds like a suit
> Bald and shiny, with pockets of wishes,
> Notions and tickets, short circuits and folding mirrors.

This realization could be the chief principle of interest in life—more wishes, more notions, more tickets—but to Plath, in her tiredness, it seemed a nightmare.

What is regrettable in Plath's work is not the domestic narrow-ness of her subject matter (Emily Dickinson and George Herbert made faultless poetry out of matter as putatively "narrow") but the narrowness of tone. She has wit and sardonic irony; she has blank despair; and she has neutral judgment and observation, and even, at the end, tenderness. But she veers from zero to one hundred like a dangerously swinging needle; she has none of the ravishing variety of tone that colors Herbert's colloquies with God. Plath has another narrowness, too—her scrupulous refusal to generalize, in her best poems, beyond her own case. She will not speak about the human condition, in the way Emily Dickinson emboldened herself to. Dic-kinson had an acute, generalizing mind as well as an eye for minute particulars; in Plath we miss the sudden, illuminating widening of perspective that Dickinson learned from Emerson. Plath was stub-bornly truthful, and she may have felt herself the exception rather than the rule. But her sense of herself as exceptional prevented her from seeing herself as one of many.

There are two hundred and twenty-four mature poems in *The Collected Poems,* and those after *The Colossus* are better (as most critics have said) than those composed for that volume. Plath assidu-ously worked and worked on poetry, as she had worked on aca-demic subjects; no poet has worked harder. Either marriage and childbearing alone or the encouragement and help of Ted Hughes —or, more probably, both—changed her style. She discovered ways to make lines seem inevitable, not only in sound but also (her most interesting discovery) in looks. She had worked hard at imitating Dylan Thomas, and had early mastered certain coarse sound effects. But in a late line like "The shadows of ringdoves chanting, but easing nothing," she has given up on a bald imitation of Thomas and has found her own voice. Some of the binding devices in such a line are familiar—the parallel of "chanting" and "easing," the repetition of words of two syllables. But what is more unusual is the matching of "nothing," though it is syntactically not parallel, with "chanting" and "easing." Such ear-rhymes are a true binding and a false binding at once, setting the words aslant. The last half of the word "shad-ows"—"dows"—almost matches the "doves" of "ringdoves" in the same witty way. Plath's later style is full of such cunning; her eye-rhymes (often without any aural equivalent like that in "doves" and "dows") continue vigorously to the end of her career, and replace her earlier, self-conscious overwriting for the ear. We require of a poem that the words spring toward each other in magnetic attraction, but we are offended when the trick is done obviously. Plath's later rapprochements seem almost casual by contrast with her obtrusive early rhymes and rhythms, but they are far more premeditated. She began keeping drafts, Hughes tell us. Eventually, they may be published, and testify to the angle of revision she favored. The later poems, at their best, bear witness to Plath's pains-taking work to make their parts fall into place and lock.

When Plath began to be able to find adequate language for her feelings, she redid a great number of her earlier themes. Here is early (pre-1956) Plath writing about the moon, always for her the pre-sider:

> The choice between the mica mystery
> of moonlight or the pockmarked face we see
>   through the scrupulous telescope
> is always to be made: innocence
> is a fairy-tale; intelligence
>   hangs itself on its own rope.
>   ("Metamorphoses of the Moon")

"Intelligence hangs itself on its own rope" is a formulation better than what turns up in most college verse, but the language of this poem is Audenesque, prematurely "disillusioned," and arch. (Auden must have been the recommended intellectual model at college in those days; he is equally present in early Rich.) Only the end sounds particularly vigorous; "the mica mystery of moonlight" (in a poem alliteratively named "Metamorphoses of the Moon") shows off Plath's easy alliteration, which in fact does *not* draw the words together but pushes them apart, by calling attention to its own flashiness.

This is from "The Moon and the Yew Tree," written in 1961, just before Plath's twenty-ninth birthday:

> The moon is no door. It is a face in its own right,
> White as a knuckle and terribly upset.
> It drags the sea after it like a dark crime; it is quiet
> With the O-gape of complete despair. . . .

The complacency of the earlier poem is replaced by a distraught but tenacious appropriation of both the world and earlier poetry. (The "gape" is from the gape of Niobe mourning her children in Keats's

"Endymion.") This appropriation comes as much from the poet's staring at the moon and staring at a particular line of Keats as from her staring at herself. In any case, the merely fashionable is cast aside, and Plath now seeks out her own affinities—helped, it seems clear, by Hughes.

Plath's phrasemaking went from strength to strength in her last two years, and it is a steady instruction to see her exact eye (with "no preconceptions," as she said of a mirror) attempt to take in reality afresh. An owl cries "from its cold indigo," and the chill lies in the matching c-o-d-i-d-i-g-o, where the "c" and the "g" are only variants of one sound. Under Plath's clinical gaze, her lungs are "two gray, papery bags"; at a funeral, as the open grave yawns, "for a minute the sky pours into the hole like plasma"; the buzz of bees in a bee box is a "furious Latin"; the glittering snow is "marshaling its brilliant cutlery" (a theft from Emily Dickinson); the darkness of a storeroom is "the black bunched in there like a bat," and the compression of "bunched" hides a beast waiting to spring; the flesh of a cut thumb is, as a detached eye takes a cool look, "red plush"; glistening worms are "sticky pearls" (with the shock coming from the sudden endowing of the inorganic word "pearls" with gluey life); a calla lily displays "cold folds of ego" (the "cold indigo" trick again, but with the added surprise of a pairing like "sticky pearls"); and on the farm in winter Plath sees "the barbarous holly with its viridian/Scallops, pure iron," matching the holly leaf's shape with scallops, viridian with iron, and erecting a stiff, bristling fence of "r"s—"barbarous," "viridian," "pure," "iron." These are all virtuoso phrases, and no poetry could be made up of such things exclusively, but they reassure us that in her most violent moments Plath's eye and ear could remain undisturbedly, and even laboriously, accurate.

Plath used to berate herself for not remembering everything in detail—a room she had seen, or what a person had been wearing— and in her journal she noted things down with meticulous exactness. She apparently deceived all of Cambridge into seeing her as a gushing, if intelligent, American coed, but it is to her credit that she could not deceive herself. "That is the latent terror, a symptom: it is suddenly either all or nothing; either you break the surface shell into the whistling void or you don't," she wrote in the journal in 1956. The terse, diagnostic language authorizes the experience even to those of us who may not have had it: "The horror is the sudden folding up and away of the phenomenal world, leaving nothing. Just rags. Human rooks which say: Fraud."

The poems of Plath's last years find a way of giving illustration to that folding up of the phenomenal world. For her, the poems also filled the void: "If I sit still and don't do anything, the world goes on beating like a slack drum, without meaning," she says in the journal. The best of her poems illustrate both the fullness and the emptiness of the universe: how it is filled with complicated, rich, obdurate, and significant forms—yew trees, gothic letters, blackberries—and how these forms are shadowed by others, diaphanous, elusive, obscuring, and blank, whether moonlight, fog, cloud, or ocean. This dialectic of forms is brought at times to an almost supernatural beauty. For example, under the threatening veils of "a sky/Palely and flamily/Igniting its carbon monoxides" there open the poppies in October:

> O my God, what am I
> That these late mouths should cry open
> In a forest of frost, in a dawn of cornflowers.
> ("Poppies in October")

That is from a poem written on her thirtieth birthday, the same day as "Ariel," with its equally riveting balance of "substanceless blue" and "the red/Eye, the cauldron of morning."

A bleaker version of form appears in "Blackberrying," where the organic is both beautiful and disgusting:

> I come to one bush of berries so ripe it
> is a bush of flies,
> Hanging their bluegreen bellies and their
> wing panes in a Chinese screen.

A "last hook" in the downward path through the blackberry brambles takes Plath from the overdetermined berry/fly bushes to the obscure emptiness of the sea:

> A last hook brings me
> To the hills' northern face, and the face is orange rock
> That looks out on nothing, nothing but a great space
> Of white and pewter lights, and a din like silversmiths
> Beating and beating at an intractable metal.

The resistance of experience to meaning, expressed here in the word "intractable," appears in comparable words all through Plath's poetry: I note, at random, "indefatigable," "irrefutable," "irreplaceable," "irretrievable," "inaccessible," "invisible," "untouchable," "inexorable," "unbreakable," "impossible," "indeterminate," "unintelligible," "indigestible," "unidentifiable," "incapable," and "ineradicable"—a family of barriers to soul, mind, and body. Against those glassy barriers Plath heroically went about her business of constructing meaning, both psychic and literary. She knew enough to choose "The Colossus," a poem about this wearing struggle, as the title poem of her first book. The poem resembles the anxiety dreams Plath had as a child, about tasks too large ever to be done adequately. She addresses, in the poem, the broken statute of her father:

> I shall never get you put together entirely,
> Pieced, glued, and properly jointed.
> . . . .
> Thirty years now I have labored
> To dredge the silt from your throat.
> I am none the wiser.
>
> Scaling little ladders with gluepots and pails of Lysol
> I crawl like an ant in mourning
> Over the weedy acres of your brow
> To mend the immense skull-plates and clear
> The bald, white tumuli of your eyes.

The many poems about Plath's father, including the famous bee poems (Otto Plath had written a book called *Bumblebees and Their Ways*), take up many myths of explanation, including Freudian diagrams, folk myths, fairy tales, and religious analogies. While we may all need such myths to approach the mystery of family relations, Plath not only, with new insights, replaced one myth with another but also changed her style to fit the myth. The sacrificial victim of the bee poems speaks in a style of obedient, paralyzed sentences, in a dead-toned drama. Occasionally, it modulates to melodrama ("I have a self to recover, a queen"), but in style that melodrama is never satisfactorily voiced in the bee sequence. It awaits its cold and controlled derangement in "Lady Lazarus" and in "Daddy," where style turns to slashing caricature of Freudian self-knowledge:

> Every woman adores a Fascist,
> The boot in the face, the brute
> Brute heart of a brute like you.
>   ("Daddy")

Gone are the elegant vicissitudes of rhyme, slant rhyme, and syllabics, and all the genteel college writing-class conventions:

> But they pulled me out of the sack,
> And they stuck me together with glue.
> And then I knew what to do.
> I made a model of you,
> A man in black with a Meinkampf look
>
> And a love of the rack and the screw.
> And I said I do, I do.
>
> ("Daddy")

This "Threepenny Opera" style is an effect usable only once; the violence done to the self here (provoked by the violence Plath suffered under the shock of Hughes's desertion) is the substance of the jeering style. Plath lashes out at her former idolatry of her father and at her subsequent idolatry of her husband, but she also demolishes the noble myths of her own earlier poems, turning the Freudian-Hellenic colossus into a "Ghastly statue with one gray toe/Big as a Frisco seal . . . "

"Lady Lazarus," written in the same feverish thirtieth-birthday month that produced "Daddy" and "Ariel," is a mélange of incompatible styles, as though in a meaningless world every style could have its day: bravado ("I have done it again"), slang ("A sort of walking miracle"), perverse fashion commentary ("my skin/Bright as a Nazi lampshade"), melodrama ("Do I terrify?"), wit ("like the cat I have nine times to die"), boast ("This is Number Three"), self-disgust ("What a trash/To annihilate each decade"). The poem moves on through reductive dismissal ("The big strip tease") to public announcement, with a blasphemous swipe at the *ecce homo* ("Gentlemen, ladies/These are my hands/My knees"), and comes to its single lyric moment, recalling Plath's suicide attempt in the summer before her senior year at Smith:

> I rocked shut
>
> As a seashell.
> They had to call and call
> And pick the worms off me like sticky pearls.

Almost every stanza of "Lady Lazarus" picks up a new possibility for this theatrical voice, from mock movie talk ("So, so, Herr Doktor./So, Herr Enemy") to bureaucratic politeness ("Do not think I underestimate your great concern") to witch warnings ("I rise with my red hair/And I eat men like air"). When an author makes a sort of headcheese of style in this way—a piece of gristle, a piece of meat, a piece of gelatin, a piece of rind—the disbelief in style is countered by a competitive faith in it. Style (as something consistent) is meaningless, but styles (as dizzying provisional skepticism) are all.

Poems like "Daddy" and "Lady Lazarus" are in one sense demonically intelligent, in their wanton play with concepts, myths, and language, and in another, and more important, sense not intelligent at all, in that they willfully refuse, for the sake of a cacophony of styles (a tantrum of style), the steady, centripetal effect of thought. Instead, they display a wild dispersal, a centrifugal spin to further and further reaches of outrage. They are written in a loud version of what Plath elsewhere calls "the zoo yowl, the mad soft/ Mirror talk you love to catch me at." And that zoo yowl has a feral slyness about it, which rises to a heated hatred in the poems about Hughes and about Plath's rivals (as she saw them)—her mother, Hughes's sister Olwyn, and Hughes's mistress. The distress of these poems unbalanced them aesthetically. When Plath turns her loathing back on herself, she instantly resumes control of structure, and the newly stoic poems recover shape and power: "The heart shuts,/ The sea slides back/The mirrors are sheeted."

Plath's cold verdict on her own choices admits the irreconcilables in her psychic constitution: "Perfection is terrible, it cannot have children." Her drive toward perfection (of which she had such a clear and distinct idea, and toward which she slaved) was incompatible—or so it seemed to her in her depleted state—with the act that had, along with poetry, brought her real happiness: the bearing of children. The verdict of the poems is against perfection and for children. This conviction enlarged and deepened her last poems, in which she alternated, pitiably, between a deathly resignation and a despair that envied the narcissistically appetitive flowers:

> The claw
> Of the magnolia,
> Drunk on its own scents,
> Asks nothing of life.
> ("Paralytic")

There is more outrage and satire and hysteria in some of the last poems than there is steady thought, especially steady thought evinced in style. Plath, for whatever reason, could not rise to the large concerns of tragedy in a Keatsian way. Her unevenness recalls Hart Crane, but she did not have Crane's open generosity of vision. She did possess—and it gives her a claim on us—a genius for the transcription in words of those wild states of feeling which in the rest of us remain so inchoate that we quail under them, speechless.

Stanley Plumly

What Ceremony of Words

Resoluteness
Simplified me . . .

"Her attitude to her verse was artisan-like: if she couldn't get a table out of the material, she was quite happy to get a chair, or even a toy. The end product for her was not so much a successful poem, as something that had temporarily exhausted her ingenuity." This comment by Ted Hughes, in 1981, in his well-known introduction to *The Collected Poems*, must have come as a surprise to many of Sylvia Plath's readers. Still nearly twenty years after her death, the notion that the poet of suicidal imperatives might be as committed to form, right up to the end of her career, as she appeared to be committed to content must have seemed secondary or at least beside the point. The poet who could begin her last poem with the knowledge that "The woman is perfected./Her dead/Body wears the smile of accomplishment" had surely transcended the duller duties of the artisan. Yet until the last year of Plath's life, March to February, her poems have none of the cold confessional, frenetic, lean, somebody's-done-for, apocalyptic drive of that sad time. Instead, they reveal a poetry preoccupied with the inventions of rhythm, pattern, and an emphatic, sometimes excessive aural sense of the way words bond within the line or sentence. They reveal a poetry in constant preparation for the next move, the next place to be— whether it meant slanting the rhyme, divesting the stanza of a scheme, or opening the poem to the indictment of immediate experience.

Perhaps those who preferred the "autobiography of a fever" in *Ariel*—Robert Lowell's phrase—were thinking of some of the golden writing that appeared in magazines in the late Fifties, writing that could sound like

13

> Through fen and farmland walking
> With my own country love
> I saw slow flocked cows move
> White hulks on their day's cruising;
> Sweet grass sprang for their grazing.
>   ("Song for a Summer's Day")

Or perhaps they had in mind some of the formula writing that appeared in *The Colossus,* the table-chair-toy writing of the craftsman, so elaborate and insistent that even in "Black Rook in Rainy Weather," one of her strongest early poems, the abcde//abcde pattern of rhyme survives for seven stanzas. Elaborations of the labor of poetry tend to be the rule before 1959, the labor of apprenticing, so much so that John Frederick Nims could speak, in his review of *Ariel,* of the "drudgery" of the first book. What distinguishes Plath, though, from other budding formalists of the time is that she worked to invent forms rather than fill them. Aside from the obligatory school-girl sonnets and villanelles and sestinas, there are very few traditional forms in her career. She was always inventing, contriving, conjuring. Form was something she could create, even repeat; it could mean passage to the next poem, and to the future. Those who found *Ariel* profoundly different from the work that preceded it could have looked back, for formal guidance and anticipation, to "Mushrooms," the last poem written for the first book—

> Overnight, very
> Whitely, discreetly,
> Very quietly
>
> Our toes, our noses
> Take hold on the loam,
> Acquire the air.

And before that to "Moonrise" ("Death whitens in the egg and out of it./I can see no color for this whiteness./White: it is a complexion of the mind."). And before that to "The Thin People" ("Empty of complaint, forever/Drinking vinegar from tin cups: they wore// The insufferable nimbus of the lot-drawn/Scapegoat. . . ."). And before that to a small piece of a poem entitled "Resolve"—

> Day of mist: day of tarnish
>
> with hands
> unserviceable, I wait
> for the milk van

the one-eared cat
laps its gray paw—

of which these are the first few lines, written in 1956. Cat's paws, thin people, and mushrooms are obviously not the issue here. The predominant mode of *Ariel* is couplets and triplets, and the short line, stanzas of psychological shorthand, of the quick take, the hook. Whatever the difference on the scale of pain the poems of the last year represent, they had models for their making, antecedents for their craft.

If *Ariel* was, and has been since, worshiped for its perceived confessional content, its doom images, its words-torn-from-the-death-flesh heart of experience, worshiped for poems, in Lowell's phrase, that "play Russian roulette with six cartridges in the cylinder," it is also a book justly celebrated for its powerful and poignant testimony—at the nerve end and at the cutting edge—of a life that became simply too vulnerable. At its best it survives the "O-gape of complete despair" by the sheer discipline of its art. But we need accept neither the cynicism of Hugh Kenner, who maintains that "all Plath's life, a reader had been someone to manipulate," nor the anxiety of A. Alvarez, who speculates that "it is as though she had decided that, for her poetry to be valid, it must tackle head-on nothing less than her own death," to question assumptions about the nature of Plath's achievement and the position her most famous book holds within the perspective of her *Collected Poems.* What concerns me, as it has concerned others, is that the biography and autobiography, *The Bell Jar* and the letters, the rumor and the psychoanalysis not displace the beauty and triumph of the range of her art. Whatever "confessional" means to the poetry to which it is too often ill-ascribed, it is first of all a kind of journalism, a reductive label intended to *get at* something in the work, something of publicity value. It is about the news in a poem, its gossip. With the names and the dates in place, it would paraphrase, extrapolate the projected psychological content, not unlike the theme-mongering sometimes promoted in the academy. Except that it would not be looking for ideas but intimacy, the dream-data, the midnight or dawn compulsions. It would turn poetry into the prose of therapy. And it would fantasize the poet as victim and the domestic and daily terrors of the world as villain, chief of which is the paradigm of the lost or bad parent. "We suggest that a pattern of guilt over imagined incest informs all of Plath's prose and poetry. When Otto Plath died of natural causes in a hospital on November 2, 1940, he might just as well have been a lover jilting his beloved."[1] Whether the critic here is right or wrong is not the issue; the issue is that Plath's guilt is irrelevant to the good reading of her poems. Not that we need to see her poetry in isolation or in a vacuum, but independent of tabloid vagaries and mythic pretentions. The life in her poetry is a transformation, not an imitation. Its terms and its struggles are acted out within the form, within the crux and often crisis of form. "Daddy" may or may not be light verse, as Plath herself once suggested. It is certainly less confessional than it is persona writing —intoxicating, relentless, allegorical, and, finally, dark. It is patently ironical, and nearly Swiftian in its satire. "Lady Lazarus" may or may not be a signature poem, but it is far too close to being a parody of the poet as suicide and the publicity of suicide to be confessional. Taken straight, beware, beware, it is only funny, or worse, bald angry. The fact that these poems too have antecedents in earlier work ("Daddy" as far back as the rhythms of "The Disquieting Muses"—"I learned, I learned, I learned elsewhere,/From muses unhired by you, dear mother"; "Lady Lazarus" as far back as the gothicism of "All the Dead Dears"—"This lady here's no kin/Of mine, yet kin she is: she'll suck/Blood and whistle my marrow clean") implies that even angst requires strategy and preparation in order to be effective, especially under the pressures of the extreme. They are both crafty poems, with histories to their craft. Nazi lampshades and Meinkampf looks, vampirism and witchery are part of the planning, among the buttons pushed. Plath did not suddenly become a poet with such poems or with the publication of *Ariel*, nor did she become a success at the moment of her death. She worked hard at a craft for which she had the gift for a good ten years.

We can run a search for the Medusan imagery or plead a case for Yeatsian cosmology, we can concentrate on the "Sivvy" poems (mother) or on the beekeeper poems (father), we can read her as a romantic or as a precipitant expressionist, we can locate influences as different as Theodore Roethke and Wallace Stevens. We can, in the long postmortem, see her as Esther Greenwood or as Lady Lazarus, daughter or mother, supplicant or applicant, sinned against or sinning. We can place her in history or alone with her ambitions. We can test Plath's work, in other words, in any number of ways alternate to the trials and errors of confessionalism. And we have. But where is there room, in the various critical/biographical approaches, for the unforced visual quality of "Departure," written in 1956 and included in *The Colossus,* where is there room for the aural power and density of "Blackberrying," written in the early fall of 1961 and excluded from *Ariel*—among the assumptions about her content and the "staticky/Noise of the new," among the attractions of violence, both sentimental and rhetorical, where is the notice, in Keats's word, of Plath's capacity for *disinterestedness,* her ability to be at one with or disappear into the richness of the text?

At one level, "Departure" looks to be not much more than a sharply focused study, in brilliant painter's terms, of a fishing village, Benidorm, along the Spanish coast: table and chair work, even though the concretion of images generates especial energy.

> The figs on the fig tree in the yard are green;
> Green, also, the grapes on the green vine
> Shading the brickred porch tiles.
> The money's run out.
>
> How nature, sensing this, compounds her bitters.
> Ungifted, ungrieved, our leavetaking.
> The sun shines on unripe corn.
> Cats play in the stalks.
>
> Retrospect shall not soften such penury—
> Sun's brass, the moon's steely patinas,
> The leaden slag of the world—
> But always expose
>
> The scraggy rock spit shielding the town's blue bay
> Against which the brunt of outer sea
> Beats, is brutal endlessly.
> Gull-fouled, a stone hut
>
> Bares its low lintel to corroding weathers:
> Across the jut of ochreous rock
> Goats shamble, morose, rank-haired,
> To lick the sea-salt.

The sea, the coastal territory, "water striving to reestablish its mirror/Over the rock," will become central and stock figures in Plath's work right to the end. In this poem, perhaps the first purely realized of her early pieces, a poem fairly free of the self-conscious and compacting busyness of a great deal of the writing at this time, the sea and environs represent the antagonist, the life principle. They make it possible for the object world itself to become the subject, because unlike the majority of the popular writing starring the first-person singular Plath, this piece mutes the position of the speaker to simple motivational status—resignation. "The money's run out.//Ungifted, ungrieved, our leavetaking." What shines in the real eye is correlative nature. True, in its own small way, it is a natural world that could hardly be called neutral—what is not kinetic is vitally colorful—but neither is it parceled into the raw examples of what become, later, psychic fractures. This "quick" study reads whole, it pays attention, directly, to detail—the green figs and grapes, the cats in the unripe corn—and without editorial help allows the details to develop and complicate the moment on their own. The half-serious line "Retrospect shall not soften such penury" permits the poet her chance to project: from that line the images go up in volume and increase in intensity. The simple fact of penury and the need to move on, the poem's motivation, force a growth in strategy—the eye can no longer just see, it must interpret.

This is the way in which, in the logic and psychologic of the structure, brass and steely patinas, nature compounds her bitters. The corroding weathers of the rest of the poem are consequences of powers within the poem, leading all the way back to the flat report that the money's run out. Nothing in this poem, therefore, is imposed from outside its world. Its lines of clear delineation and projection come from within what is immediately established, as in any good story. Compare the longer, softer rhythms of the first three lines to the same length of work in the last two stanzas; once the money's gone (penury), the rhythms turn tighter, much more consonantal, and abrupt. Thus we know, in the plot of things, why the prosody has changed, and we know, by the time the sea is brutal endlessly, that something serious is at stake without the speaker having to promote her cause. Later, of course, by 1962, what is at stake will take on absolute proportions. By then the poems will have acquired so much external life, such an autobiographic force-field, that it will seem difficult to judge whether a particular poem has created sufficient self-reference not to depend on the author's prose therapies.

"Departure" represents a psychological landscape (seascape). It is as well an accurate rendering: it begins and ends *inside* the picture, within the framing warmth of the fig trees and the harshness of the sea-salt. Its otherness is the object, and objective, world, but also natural, chronological, alive. A few years into the future, Plath will write, along with "Mussel Hunter at Rock Harbor," "Tulips," and "Last Words," one of her finest poems of that narrative, objective category in which the line-into-sentence is extended in time, and connects and continues fully enough to fill the white space—her "wide" poems, as one observer puts it. "Blackberrying" rests somewhere between the beating of the outer sea of "Departure" and the Devon coast of "Sheep in Fog," where the "hills step off" into whiteness. It certainly rests between them "stylistically," between the clearly delineated shapes and solids of the older poem and the spare, poetry-as-absence surrealism of one of her last.

Nobody in the lane, and nothing, nothing but blackberries,
Blackberries on either side, though on the right mainly,
A blackberry alley, going down in hooks, and a sea
Somewhere at the end of it, heaving. Blackberries
Big as the ball of my thumb, and dumb as eyes
Ebon in the hedges, fat
With blue-red juices. These they squander on my fingers.
I had not asked for such a blood sisterhood; they must love me.
They accommodate themselves to my milkbottle, flattening their
    sides.

Overhead go the coughs in black, cacophonous flocks—
Bits of burnt paper wheeling in a blown sky.
Theirs is the only voice, protesting, protesting.
I do not think the sea will appear at all.
The high, green meadows are glowing, as if lit from within.
I come to one bush of berries so ripe it is a bush of flies,
Hanging their bluegreen bellies and their wing panes in a Chinese
    screen.
The honey-feast of the berries has stunned them; they believe in
    heaven.
One more hook, and the berries and bushes end.

The only thing to come now is the sea.
From between two hills a sudden wind funnels at me,
Slapping its phantom laundry in my face.
These hills are too green and sweet to have tasted salt.
I follow the sheep path between them. A last hook brings me
To the hills' northern face, and the face is orange rock
That looks out on nothing, nothing but a great space

> Of white and pewter lights, and a din like silversmiths
> Beating and beating at an intractable metal.

Eliot is fond of referring to the "aural imagination," the ability of the language to transform the image in the process of its pronouncement. Valéry speaks, in his notebooks, of the language within language. And Rilke says that "if a thing is to speak to you, you must regard it for a certain time as *the only one that exists.*" "Blackberrying," it seems to me, brings together the best vocal and most effective visual impulses in Plath's poetry. It gives the speaker her role without sacrificing the poem's purchase on the actual impinging natural world. It enlarges rather than reduces. Its ceremony comes from one of the poet's most disguised sources, the small moment, the domestic life. ("Mushrooms," the poems for her children, the poppy poems all share, for example, a sense of size, even though they derive from objects and experiences small and diurnal in scale.) "Blackberrying" likewise isolates the action to the job at hand, and to the story line. But unlike the sound and image effects of poems better known, this one is not driving nails, sawing on one Orphic string, or ritualizing an extreme psychological state. No question that at the point of entry the reader is tested: either accept the muscular terms of the poem or stay out. Timed in the present progressive, it opens in motion, in saturation, incantatory. We are led, immediately, in hooks, down a blackberry alley, where a sea, somewhere at the end of it, is heaving. The impression is one of tunneling, of being drawn into and through narrow, yet thick space. All the senses are crowded, even exchanged ("Blackberries/Big as the ball of my thumb, and dumb as eyes/Ebon in the hedges, fat . . ."). What is remarkable is the way Plath, in shifting the context of the blackberries from container (alley) to contained (milkbottle), intensifies the feel of claustrophobia. Once the berries are in the bottle—"they squander on my fingers . . . they must love me"—they flatten their sides in order to accommodate; they, in effect, choke on the space. It is a brilliant telescoping and projecting and resolving of the speaker's "going down in hooks," and is prepared by a stanzaic pattern of free verse that allows the middle lines to fill before breaking at emphatic (sea/Blackberries/eyes/fat) hooks in the sentence. The credibility and vitality of the movement of the full stanza, however, are validated by what will carry the rest of the poem— Plath's skill at creating aural equivalents, images that gain their first power from their hearing. The first line, for instance, though one of the least apparent "imaged" in the poem, still manages to effect a strong visual pull by letting "nobody in the lane" be picked up and quickly reinforced by "nothing, nothing" only to bump, abruptly, into "but blackberries." It is a line of wonderful subtraction by addition, the content filling the needs of the form. This same sense of abutment structures the remaining stanza. By repeating and paralleling the word "blackberries" three strategic times, Plath makes, in effect, a single alley-and-hook sentence down to the last two and a half lines. Then, like a stepping-off of periods, she shuts off with three full stops, each a little longer in coming than the one before. This vertical rhythm is what pacing in a poem, and music in poetry, is all about.

If the enclosures of the alley and milkbottle help organize the experience in the beginning stanza, the plan of the whole poem becomes obvious by the second. The cloister opens to the overarching sky, and by the third stanza to the open sea. This Devon landscape-to-seascape is right out of Hardy—nobody in the lane, far from the madding crowd. In just the time it takes to get from the blackout, blackberry close of the alley, where we can hear the great source "heaving," to the "high, green meadows," over which go birds that are "bits of burnt paper wheeling in a blown sky," we realize the speaker is being pulled along, compelled. The mimetic language is becoming denser, a little waxy—"the choughs in black, cacophonous flocks." The first three lines of the second stanza, in fact, press their vocalization, their repetitions of sounds—"protesting, protesting"—about as far as they dare, leading the poet to counter the buildup, as she does everywhere in the poem, with a flat, declarative notice, in this case, that "I do not think the sea will appear at all." Two of the longest lines Plath ever wrote appear at the end of this stanza. They make a kind of couplet, coming out of one of the poem's best balanced lines:

> I come to one bush of berries so ripe it is a bush of flies,
> Hanging their bluegreen bellies and their wing panes in a Chinese
> screen.
> The honey-feast of the berries has stunned them; they believe in
> heaven.

Looking ahead to the denials in the forms of the later work, we can appreciate the fecundity here, not simply in the fullness of the image of the berries, but in the progression of the idea of the berries—berries, flies, bellies, wing panes, honey-feast, heaven. And the berries that have been blue-red juices so squandered on fingers they must love me are now the honey-feast of flies that believe in heaven. This is the countryside of health; the speaker's senses are sated. There is uncharacteristic generosity in this writing *sans* the sometimes characteristic rhetoric. There is giving-over to the world, to the natural world, to the life outside, beyond the nerve ends of the self. Giving over, however, does not mean giving up. "The only thing to come now is the sea," announces the speaker at the start of the last stanza. She emerges, as into a sense of light, from the winding sheep path, from the high meadows, from the blackberry alley, with the wind, the open wind, suddenly blowing its phantom laundry in her face. The close, interior dimensions of where she has come from in order to get here, having been called by the clues of the heaving of wind on water and overhead, having picked her way —of all tests—through blackberries, have brought her, one last hook, to the edge, the north face.

Plath's position at the end of "Blackberrying" is a reading of her position for the remainder of her life leading up to the "edge" of her last poem. "We have come so far, it is over." Here, however, at this full and apparently open moment, looking toward the complementary, fantasy coast of Brittany (another "Finisterre"), it is not over. The sea may be "beating an intractable metal" and the speaker may be looking out at "a great space," but this climactic image, as psychologically as it is actually audible, underscores the rich, insulating presence of the whole of this writing. Nearly every line risks the heavy hand that has marked too many of her narrative-nature poems: the clogged consonance, the alliterative tattoo, the aureate weight of the diction. Yet the insistent winding path of its structure (the movement from the blind and sensual alley to the meadow sighting of bird flocks and flies to the vulnerability of the dissociative mind confronting the intractable) and the absorption of the speaker into the flow of the action (though she is the actor, she is led) help keep the language of "Blackberrying" on the line and insures that the incantatory effects result from the inwardness of the experience, from even the threat of the experience. The images of the Chinese screen and the metal of silversmiths, as opposed to the homely milkbottle, may seem extracurricular to the landscape of the poem, but they are as much a part of the transformation as are the choral features of nothing, nothing, protesting, protesting, beating, beating. These images are projections; their dimensions get their measure within the text. If the speaker, ontologically, is as cut off by the white and pewter lights and the din of the silversmiths as she has been by the opacity of the blackberries and the bush of flies, perhaps we have come back to the "nothing" in the last stanza for a reason. Her condition, throughout the poem, is static, in a dark that is blind and in a light that is blinding. It is the blackberrying itself that is the motion, the active principle. But it is more than a motive: it is the act of the lyric form answering itself at every turning, every *ing*, making of the emotion an enclosure.

"Blackberrying" is high rhetorical style compared to the great majority of poems that finally made it into the posthumous *Ariel*. Only "The Moon and the Yew Tree" and "Tulips" suggest its density of texture, though in tone they both better approximate the "light of the mind" of what became a very strange and luminous book. If Valéry is right, that form in poetry is the voice in action, then Plath was obviously in some debate as to what her true voice was: the poet of riches or the poet of austerity, the poet of connection or the poet of the quick cut. It is a formal debate inherent in her career, declaration or denial. To her credit, she allowed the debate to become a dialectic, allowed the energy of the argument to produce rather than paralyze the work at hand. Nevertheless, by the end of her life—the last year, year and a half—it is clear that the poetry of absence, "words dry and riderless," is the rule. So much so that almost every good poem in the manner of

> Axes
> After whose stroke the wood rings,
> And the echoes!
> Echoes traveling
> Off from the center like horses
> ("Words")

turns into an *ars poetica,* an address of and to her art. Which is to say that concomitant with the struggle for life is her struggle with the form her passion wished to take. Poems as superficially variant in subject as "Words" and "Sheep in Fog" and the incomparable "Ariel" share this interest in a self-reflexive, self-defining purity of purpose, and each chooses the expressive terms of "indefatigable hoof-taps" ("Words") and "hooves, dolorous bells" ("Sheep in

Fog") to enact the purification. "Ariel" is, of course, Plath's singular and famous example of the form completely at one with its substance, the language exactly the speedy act of its text. The point for the poet is obvious: "How one we grow,/Pivot of heels and knees." The speaker thus becomes as much Ariel as the horse, and together they become the one thing, the poem itself, "the arrow,//The dew that flies/Suicidal, at one with the drive." The run from stasis in darkness into the red eye of morning is a miraculous inhabiting, in which the natural and referential world dissembles, blurs into absence, to the point that the transformation of the horse and rider can become absolute. "Something else//Hauls me through air . . ." In seconds, she is a white Godiva, unpeeling dead hands and stringencies, then, almost simultaneously, she is foam to wheat, and at that freeing instant, in terror or in esctasy, the child's cry melts in the wall. "Ariel" is as close to a poetry of pure, self-generating, associative action as we could hope for, as if the spirit, at last, had found its correlative, had transcended, in the moment, memory. Mallarmé once speculated that the ideal poem would be "a reasonable number of words stretched beneath our mastering glance, arranged in enduring figures, and followed by silence." This is generic enough to account for a lot of symbolist writing. It certainly accounts for the nigger-eye berries that cast dark hooks.

Plath did not live long enough to sort out a form that could negotiate between the enclosing rhetoric of a "Blackberrying" and the absolute, open language of an "Ariel." Likely she would have never needed to. Likely this "third" form is a wished-for integration of personality, the healing of fracture. For me, though, the writing near the end is not up to the discipline of "Ariel," and feels instead a little starved, anorectic. Such writing may be accurate of the state of her soul, but it is beyond the perfection of her art, the perfection that "Blackberrying," in September of 1961, and "Ariel," in October of 1962, individually represent. Here is a poet who could either project into the landscape or internalize it so as to disappear; she could both narrate and configure experience. In either case, she was committed to the transforming powers of the art, emblems of a life outside her own. Putting the "blood sisterhood" of "Blackberrying" beside the red-eyed cauldron sunrise of "Ariel," we can begin to see that behind the separate masks, all the masks of her good poems, there is a unity, an integrity, and an integrating of imagination— that whatever the hammer-splittings of the self, behind the sad mask of the woman is the mind and heart of someone making transcendent poems. To the extent that Plath is "artisan-like" is the extent to which she is whole. Beginning in the fall of 1961, she will have written the truest symbolist poetry we have had since Hart Crane, and before him since Dickinson.

NOTE

1. *The Confessional Poets* by Robert Phillips (Southern Illinois University Press: Carbondale, 1973), p. 128.

The Death Throes of Romanticism: The Poetry of Sylvia Plath

I am not cruel, only truthful—
The eye of a little god . . .
—Plath, "Mirror"

Tragedy is not a woman, however gifted, dragging her shadow around in a circle, or analyzing with dazzling scrupulosity the stale, boring inertia of the circle; tragedy is cultural, mysteriously enlarging the individual so that what he has experienced is both what we have experienced and what we need not experience—because of his, or her, private agony. It is proper to say that Sylvia Plath represents for us a tragic figure involved in a tragic action, and that her tragedy is offered to us as a near-perfect work of art, in her books *The Colossus* (1960), *The Bell Jar* (1963), *Ariel* (1965), and the posthumous volumes published in 1971, *Crossing the Water* and *Winter Trees.*

   This essay is an attempt to analyze Plath in terms of her cultural significance, to diagnose, through Plath's poetry, the pathological aspects of our era that make a death of the spirit inevitable—for that era and all who believe in its assumptions. It is also based upon the certainty that Plath's era is concluded and that we may consider it with the sympathetic detachment with which we consider any era that has gone before us and makes our own possible: the cult of Plath insists she is a saintly martyr, but of course she is something less dramatic that this, but more valuable. The "I" of the poems is an artful construction, a tragic figure whose tragedy is classical, the result of a limited vision that believed itself the mirror held up to nature—as in the poem "Mirror," the eye of a little god who imagines itself without preconceptions, "unmisted by love or dislike." This is the audacious hubris of tragedy, the inevitable reality-challenging statement of the participant in a dramatic action he does not know is "tragic." He dies, and only we can see the purpose of his death—to illustrate the error of a personality who believed itself godlike.

The assumptions of the essay are several: that the artist both creates and is created by his art, and that the self—especially the "I" of lyric poetry—is a personality who achieves a kind of autonomy free not only of the personal life of the artist but free, as well, of the part-by-part progression of individual poems; that the autobiograph- ical personality is presented by the artist as a testing of reality, and that its success or failure or bewilderment will ultimately condition the artist's personal life; that the degree to which an audience accepts or rejects or sympathetically detaches itself from a given tragic action will ultimately condition the collective life of an era; and that the function of literary criticism is not simply to dissect either cruelly or reverentially, to attack or to glorify, but to illustrate how the work of a significant artist helps to explain his era and our own. The significance of Plath's art is assumed. Her significance as a cultural phenomenon is assumed. What needs desperately to be seen is how she performed for us, and perhaps in place of some of us, the concluding scenes in the fifth act of a tragedy, the first act of which began centuries ago.

Narcissi

D. H. Lawrence said in *Apocalypse* that when he heard people complain of being lonely he knew their affliction: ". . . they have lost the Cosmos." It is easy to agree with Lawrence, but less easy to understand what he means. Yet if there is a way of approaching Plath's tragedy, it is only through an analysis of what Plath lost and what she was half-conscious of having lost:

> I am solitary as grass. What is it I miss?
> Shall I ever find it, whatever it is?
> *(Three Women)*

We must take this loss as a real one, not a rhetorical echoing of other poets' cries; not a yearning that can be dismissed by the robust and simple-minded among us who, like that formidably healthy and impossible Emerson, sought to dismiss the young people of his day "diseased" with problems of original sin, evil, predestination, and the like by contemptuously diagnosing their worries as "the soul's mumps, and measles, and whoopingcoughs" ("Spiritual Laws"). Emerson possessed a consciousness of such fluidity and explorative intelligence that any loss of the cosmos for him could seem nothing more serious than an adolescent's perverse rebelliousness, at its most profound a doubt to be answered with a few words.

These "few words" in our era are multiplied endlessly—all the books, the tradition at our disposal, the example of a perpetually renewed and self-renewing nature—and yet they are not convincing to the Sylvia Plaths of our time. For those who imagine themselves as filled with emptiness, as wounds "walking out of hospital," the pronouncements of a practical-minded, combative, "healthy" society of organized individuals are meaningless. Society, seen from the solitary individual's viewpoint, is simply an organization of the solitary, linked together materially—perhaps, in fact, crowded together but not "together," not vitally related. One of Plath's few observations about larger units of human beings is appropriately cynical:

And then there were other faces. The faces of nations,
Governments, parliaments, societies,
The faceless faces of important men.

It is these men I mind:
They are so jealous of anything that is not flat! They are
    jealous gods
That would have the whole world flat because they are.
                                              (Three Women)

And, in rapid associative leap that is typical of her poetry—and typical of a certain type of frightened imagination—Plath expands her sociological observation to include the mythical figures of "Father" and "Son," who conspire together to make a heaven of flatness: "Let us flatten and launder the grossness from these souls" (Three Women). The symbolic figures of "Father" and "Son" do not belong to a dimension of the mind exclusive, let alone transcendent, of society; and if they embody the jealous assumptions of an imagined family of "parent" and "child," they are more immediate, more terrifyingly present, than either.

"Nations, governments, parliaments, societies" conspire only in lies and cannot be trusted. Moreover, they are male in their aggression and their cynical employment of rhetoric; their counterparts cannot be women like Plath, but the creatures of "Heavy Women," who smile to themselves above their "weighty stomachs" and meditate "devoutly as the Dutch bulb," absolutely mute, "among the archetypes." Between the archetypes of jealous, ruthless power, represented by the Father/Son of religious and social tradition, and the archetypes of moronic fleshly beauty, represented by these smug mothers, there is a very small space for the creative intellect, for the employment and expansion of a consciousness that tries to transcend such limits. Before we reject Plath's definition of the artistic self as unreasonably passive, even as infantile, we should inquire why so intelligent a woman should assume these limitations, why she should not declare war against the holders of power and of the "mysteries" of the flesh—why her poetry approaches but never crosses over the threshold of an active, healthy attack upon obvious evils and injustices. The solitary ego in its prison cell is there by its own desire, its own admission of guilt in the face of even the most crazily ignorant of accusers. Like Eugene O'Neill, who lived into his sixties with this bewildering obsession of the self-annihilated-by-Others, Plath exhibits only the most remote (and rhetorical) sympathy with other people. If she tells us she may be a bit of a "Jew," it is only to define herself, her sorrows, and not to involve our sympathies for the Jews of recent European history. Of course, the answer is that Plath did not like other people; like many who are persecuted, she identified in a perverse way with her own persecutors, and not with those who, along with her, were victims. But she did not "like" other people because she did not essentially believe that they existed; she knew intellectually that they existed, of course, since they had the power to injure her, but she did not believe they existed in the way she did, as pulsating, breathing, suffering individuals. Even her own children are objects of her perception, there for the restless scrutiny of her image-making mind, and not there as human beings with a potentiality that would someday take them beyond their immediate dependency upon her, which she sometimes enjoys and sometimes dreads.

The moral assumptions behind Plath's poetry condemned her to death, just as she, in creating this body of poems, condemned it to death. But her moral predicament is not so pathological as one may think, if conformity to an essentially sick society is taken to be—as many traditional moralists and psychologists take it—a sign of normality. Plath speaks very clearly a language we can understand. She is saying what men have been saying for many centuries, though they have not been so frank as she, and, being less sensitive as well, they have not sickened upon their own hatred for humanity: they have thrived upon it, in fact, "sublimating" it into wondrous achievements of material and mechanical splendor. Let us assume that Sylvia Plath acted out in her poetry and in her private life the deathliness of an old consciousness, the old corrupting hell of the Renaissance ideal and its "I"-ness, separate and distinct from all other fields of consciousness, which exist only to be conquered or to inflict pain upon the "I." Where at one point in civilization this very masculine, combative ideal of an "I" set against all other "I"s —and against nature as well—was necessary in order to wrench man from the hermetic contemplation of a God-centered universe and prod him into action, it is no longer necessary, its health has become a pathology, and whoever clings to its outmoded concepts will die. If romanticism and its gradually accelerating hysteria are taken as the ultimate ends of a once-vital Renaissance ideal of subject/object antagonism, then Plath must be diagnosed as one of the last romantics; and already her poetry seems to us a poetry of the past, swiftly receding into history.

The "I" that is declared an enemy of all others cannot identify with anyone or anything, since even nature—or especially nature— is antagonistic to it. Man is spirit/body but, as in the poem "Last Words," Plath states her distrust of the spirit that "escapes like steam/In dreams, through the mouth-hole or eye-hole. I can't stop it." Spirit is also intellect, but the "intellect" exists uneasily inside a prison house of the flesh; a small, desperate, calculating process (like the ego in Freud's psychology) that achieves only spasmodic powers of identity in the constant struggle between the id and the superego or between the bestial world of fleshly female "archetypes" and hypocritical, deathly male authorities. This intellect does not belong naturally in the universe and feels guilt and apprehension at all times. It does not belong in nature; nature is "outside" man, superior in brute power to man, though admittedly inferior in the possibilities of imagination. When this intellect attempts its own kind of creation, it cannot be judged as transcendent to the biological processes of change and decay, but as somehow conditioned by these processes and, of course, found inferior. Why else would Plath call a poem about her own poetry "Stillborn" and lament the deadness of her poems, forcing them to compete with low but living creatures?—"They are not pigs, they are not even fish . . ." It is one of the truly pathological habits of this old consciousness that it puts all things into immediate competition: erecting Aristotelian categories of "x" and "non-x," assuming that the distinction between two totally unconnected phases of life demands a kind of war, a superior/inferior grading.

For instance, let us examine one of Plath's lighter and more "positive" poems. This is "Magi," included in *Crossing the Water*. It summons up literary affiliations with Eliot and Yeats, but its vision is exclusively Plath's and, in a horrifying way, very female. Here, Plath is contemplating her six-month-old daughter, who smiles "into thin air" and rocks on all fours "like a padded hammock." Imagined as hovering above the child, like "dull angels," are the Magi of abstraction—the intellectual, philosophical concepts of Good, True, Evil, Love, the products of "some lamp-headed Plato." Plath dismisses the Magi by asking, "What girl ever flourished in such company?" Her attitude is one of absolute contentment with the physical, charming simplicities of her infant daughter; she seems to want none of that "multiplication table" of the intellect. If this poem had not been written by Sylvia Plath, who drew such attention to her poetry by her suicide, one would read it and immediately agree with its familiar assumptions—how many times we've read this poem, by how many different poets! But Plath's significance now forces us to examine her work very carefully, and in this case the poem reveals itself as a vision as tragic as her more famous, more obviously troubled poems.

It is, in effect, a death sentence passed by Plath on her own use of language, on the "abstractions" of culture or the literary as opposed to the physical immediacy of a baby's existence. The world of language is condemned as only "ethereal" and "blank"—obviously inferior to the world of brute, undeveloped nature. Plath is saying here, in this agreeable-mannered poem, that because "Good" and "Evil" have no meaning to a six-month-old infant beyond the facts of mother's milk and a belly ache, they have no essential meaning at all—to anyone—and the world of all adult values, the world of complex linguistic structures, the world in which Plath herself lives as a normal expression of her superior intellect, is as "loveless" as the multiplication table and therefore must be rejected. It is extraordinary that the original romantic impulse to honor and appreciate nature, especially mute nature, should dwindle in our time to this: a Sylvia Plath willfully admitting to herself and to us that she is inferior to her own infant! The regressive fantasies here are too pathetic to bear examination, but it is worth suggesting that this attitude is not unique. It reveals much that is wrong with contemporary intellectuals' assessment of themselves: a total failure to consider that the undeveloped (whether people or nations) are not sacred because they are undeveloped, but sacred because they are part of nature, that and the role of the superior intellect is not to honor incompletion, in itself or in anything, but to help bring about the fulfillment of potentialities. Plath tells us that a six-month-old infant shall pass judgment on Plato; and in the poem "Candles" she asks, "How shall I tell anything at all/To this infant still in a birth-drowse?" It is impossible, of course, for her to tell the infant anything, if she assumes that the infant possesses an intuitive knowledge superior to her own. And yet, and yet . . . she does desire to "tell" the infant and us. But her "telling" cannot be anything more than a half-guilty assertion of her own impotence, and she will ultimately condemn it as wasteful. The honoring of mute nature above man's ability to make and use language will naturally result in muteness; this muteness will force the individual into death, for the denial of language is a suicidal one and we pay for it with our lives.

Back from the maternity ward, resting after her painful experience, the most "positive" of Plath's three women is reassured when she looks out her window, at dawn, to see the narcissi opening their white faces in the orchard. And now she feels uncomplex again; she is relieved of the miraculous pain and mystery of childbirth and wants only for herself and for her child "the clear bright colors of the nursery,/The talking ducks, the happy lambs." She meditates:

> I do not will [my baby] to be exceptional.
> It is the exception that interests the devil.
> . . . .
> I will him to be common.

It seems to us pitiful that Plath should desire the "common"—should imagine that her loving words for her infant are anything less than a curse. But her conviction that "the exception interests the devil" is very familiar to us, an expression of our era's basic fear of the intellect; the centuries-old division between "intellect" and "instinct" has resulted in a suicidal refusal to understand that man's intelligence is instinctive in his species, simply an instinct for survival and for the creation of civilization. Yet the "loving of mute-ness" we find in Plath is understandable if it is seen as a sensitive revulsion against the world of strife, the ceaseless battle of the letter "I" to make victories and extend its territory. Even the highest intelligence, linked to an ego that is self-despising, will utter curses in the apparent rhythms of love:

> right now you are dumb.
> And I love your stupidity,
> The blind mirror of it. I look in
> And find no face but my own . . .
> ("For a Fatherless Son")

The narcissi of the isolated ego are not really "quick" and "white" as children (see "Among the Narcissi") but victimized, trampled, and bitter unto death. Plath's attitude in these gentler poems about her motherhood is, at best, a temporary denial of her truly savage feelings—we are shocked to discover her celebration of hatred in "Lesbos" and similar poems, where she tells us what she really thinks about the "stink of fat and baby crap" that is forcing her into silence, "hate up to my neck."

The poems of hatred seem to us very contemporary, in their jagged rhythms and surreal yoking together of images, and in their defiant expression of a rejection of love, of motherhood, of men, of the "Good, the True, the Beautiful." If life really is a struggle for survival, even in a relatively advanced civilization, then very few individuals will win; most will lose (and nearly all women are fated to lose); something is rotten in the very fabric of the universe. All this appears to be contemporary, but Plath's poems are in fact the clearest, most precise (because most private) expression of an old moral predicament that has become unbearable now. And its poignant genesis is very old indeed:

> And now I was sorry that God had made me a man. The beasts, birds, fishes, etc., I blessed their condition, for they had not a sinful nature; they were not to go to hell after death. . . .
> (John Bunyan, *Grace Abounding* "I"/"i")

Male/Female: Nature as Object and as Nightmare

All this involves a variety of responses, though behind them is a single metaphysical belief. The passive, paralyzed, continually surfacing and fading consciousness of Plath in her poems is disturbing to us because it seems to summon forth, to articulate with deadly accuracy, the regressive fantasies we have rejected—and want to forget. The experience of reading her poems deeply is a frightening one: it is like waking to discover one's adult self, grown to full height, crouched in some long-forgotten childhood hiding place, one's heart pounding senselessly, all the old rejected transparent beasts and monsters crawling out of the wallpaper. So much for Plato! So much for adulthood! Yet I cannot emphasize strongly enough how valuable the experience of reading Plath can be, for it is a kind of elegant "dreaming-back," a cathartic experience that not only cleanses us of our personal and cultural desires for regression, but explains by way of its deadly accuracy what was wrong with such desires.

The same can be said for the reading of much of contemporary poetry and fiction, fixated as it is upon the childhood fears of annihilation, persecution, the helplessness we have all experienced when we are, for one reason or another, denied an intellectual awareness of what is happening. For instance, the novels of Robbe-Grillet and his imitators emphasize the hypnotized passivity of the "I" in a world of dense and apparently autonomous things; one must never ask "Who manufactured these things? Who brought them home? Who arranged them?"—for such questions destroy the novels. Similarly, the highly praised works of Pynchon, Barthelme, Purdy, Barth (the Barth of the minimal stories, not the earlier Barth), and countless others are verbalized screams and shudders to express the confusion of the ego that believes itself—perhaps because it has been told so often—somehow out of place in the universe, a mechanized creature if foolish enough to venture into Nature; a too-natural creature for the mechanical urban paradise he has inherited but has had no part in designing. The "I" generated by these writers is typically a transparent, near-nameless personality; in the nightmarish works of William Burroughs, the central consciousness does not explore a world so much as submit pathetically to the exploration of himself by a comically hostile world, all cartoons and surprising metamorphoses. Plath's tentative identity in such poems as "Winter Trees," "Tulips," and even the robustly defiant "Daddy" is essentially a child's consciousness, seizing upon a symbolic particularity (tulips, for instance) and then shrinking from its primary noon, so that the poems—like the fiction we read so often today—demonstrate a dissolution of personality. As Jan B. Gordon has remarked in a review of *Winter Trees,* Plath's landscapes become pictorial without any intermediate stage, so that we discover ourselves "in *una selva oscura* where associations multiply endlessly, but where each tree looks like every other one."[1] That is the danger risked by those minimal artists of our time whose subject is solely the agony of the locked-in ego: their agonies, like Plath's landscapes, begin to look alike.

But if we turn from the weak and submissive ego to one more traditionally masculine, activated by the desire to name and to place and to conquer, we discover a consciousness that appears superficially antithetical:

> Average reality begins to rot and stink as soon as the act of individual creation ceases to animate a subjectively perceived texture.
>
> > (Vladimir Nabokov, from an interview)

> The obscure moon lighting an obscure world
> Of things that would never be quite expressed,
> Where you yourself were never quite yourself
> And did not want nor have to be,
>
> Desiring the exhilarations of changes:
> The motive for metaphor, shrinking from
> The weight of primary noon,
> The A B C of being . . .
> > (Wallace Stevens, "The Motive for Metaphor")

Where in Plath (and in countless of our contemporaries) the ego suffers dissolution in the face of even the most banal of enemies, in such writers as Nabokov and Stevens the ego emerges as confident and victorious. Yet we see that it is the same metaphysics—the same automatic assumption that there is an "average" reality somehow distinct from us, either superior (and therefore terrifying) or inferior (and therefore saved from "rot" and "stink" only by our godly subjective blessing). This is still the old romantic bias, the opposition between self and object, "I" and "non-I," man and nature. Nabokov and Stevens have mastered art forms in which language is arranged and rearranged in such a manner as to give pleasure to the artist and his readers, excluding any reference to an available exterior world. Their work frees the ego to devise and defend a sealed-off universe, inhabited chiefly by the self-as-artist, so that it is quite natural to assume that Nabokov's writing is about the art of writing and Stevens's poems about the art of writing; that the work gives us the process of creativity that is its chief interest. Again, as in Plath, the work may approach the threshold of an awareness of other inhabitants of the human universe, but it never crosses over because, basically, it cannot guarantee the existence of other human beings: its own autonomy might be threatened or at least questioned. The mirror and never the window is the stimulus for this art that, far from being overwhelmed by nature, turns from it impatiently, in order to construct the claustrophobic *Ada* or the difficult later poems of Stevens, in which metaphors inhabit metaphors and the "weight of primary noon" is hardly more than a memory. The consciousness discernible behind the works of Nabokov and Stevens is like that totally autonomous ego imagined—but only imagined—by Sartre, which is self-created, self-named, untouched by parental or social or cultural or even biological determinants.

Since so refined an art willfully excludes the emotional context of its own creation, personality is minimal; art is all. It is not surprising that the harsh, hooking images of Plath's poetry should excite more interest, since Plath is always honest, perhaps more honest than we would like, and her awareness of a lost cosmos involves her in a perpetual questioning of what nature is, what the Other is, what does it want to do to her, with her, in spite of her . . . ? Nabokov and Stevens receive only the most incidental stimuli from their "average reality" and "obscure world," but Plath is an identity reduced to desperate statements about her dilemma as a passive witness to a turbulent natural world:

> There is no life higher than the grasstops
> Or the hearts of sheep, and the wind
> Pours by like destiny, bending
> Everything in one direction.
> . . . .
> The sheep know where they are,
> Browsing in their dirty wool-clouds,
> Gray as the weather.
> The black slots of their pupils take me in.
> It is like being mailed into space,
> A thin, silly message.
> ("Wuthering Heights")

And, in "Two Campers in Cloud Country," the poet and her companion experience a kind of comfort up in Rock Lake, Canada, where they "mean so little" and where they will wake "blank-brained as water in the dawn." If the self is set in opposition to everything that excludes it, then the distant horizons of the wilderness will be as terrible as the kitchen walls and the viciousness of hissing fat. There is never any integrating of the self and its experience, the self and its field of perception. Human consciousness, to Plath, is always an intruder in the natural universe.

This distrust of the intellect in certain poets can result in lyric-meditative poetry of an almost ecstatic beauty, when the poet acknowledges his separateness from nature but seems not to despise or fear it:

> O swallows, swallows, poems are not
> The point. Finding again the world,
> That is the point, where loveliness
> Adorns intelligible things
> Because the mind's eye lit the sun.
> (Howard Nemerov, "The Blue
> Swallows")

Nemerov shares with Stevens and Plath certain basic assumptions: that poems are "not the point" in the natural universe, and that the poet, therefore, is not in the same field of experience as the swallows. Poetry, coming from the mind of man, not from the objects of mind's perception, is somehow a self-conscious, uneasy activity that must apologize for itself. In this same poem, the title poem of Nemerov's excellent collection *The Blue Swallows*, the poet opposes the "real world" and the "spelling mind" that attempts to impose its "unreal relations on the blue swallows." But despite Nemerov's tone of acquiescence and affirmation, this is a tragic assumption in that it certainly banishes the poet himself from the world: only if he will give up poetry and "find again the world" has he a chance of being saved. It is a paradox that the poet believes he will honor the objects of his perception—whether swallows, trees, sheep, bees, infants—only by withdrawing from them. Why does it never occur to romantic poets that they exist as much by right in the universe as any other creature, and that their function as poets is a natural function? —that the adult imagination is superior to the imagination of birds and infants?

In art this can lead to silence; in life, to suicide.

The Deadly Mirror: The Risks of Lyric Poetry

Among the lesser known of Theodore Roethke's poems is "Lines Upon Leaving a Sanitarium," in which the poet makes certain sobering, unambiguous statements:

> Self-contemplation is a curse
> That makes an old confusion worse.
> . . . .
> The mirror tells some truth, but not
> Enough to merit constant thought.

Perhaps it is not just Plath's position at the end of a once-energetic tradition and the circumstances of her own unhappy life that doomed her and her poetry to premature dissolution, but something in the very nature of lyric poetry itself. What of this curious art form that, when not liberated by music, tends to turn inward upon the singer, folding and folding again upon the poet? If he is immature to begin with, of what can he sing except his own self's immaturity, and to what task can his imagination put itself except the selection of ingenious images to illustrate this immaturity? Few lyric poets, beginning as shakily as the young Yeats, will continue to write and rewrite, to imagine and reimagine, in a heroic evolution of the self from one kind of personality to another. The risk of lyric poetry is its availability to the precocious imagination, its immediate rewards in terms of technical skill, which then hypnotize the poet into believing that he has achieved all there is to achieve in his life as well as in his art. How quickly these six-inch masterpieces betray their creators! The early successes, predicated upon ruthless self-examination, demand a repeating of their skills even when the original psychological dramas have been outgrown or exhausted, since the lyric poet is instructed to look into his heart and write and, by tradition, he has only his self to write about. But poetry—like all art—demands that its subject be made sacred. Art is the sacralizing of its subject. The problem, then, is a nearly impossible one: how can the poet make himself sacred? Once he has exposed himself, revealed himself, dramatized his fantasies and terrors, what can he do next? Most modern poetry is scornful, cynical, contemptuous of its subject (whether self or others), bitter or amused or coldly detached. It shrinks from the activity of making the world sacred because it can approach the world only through the self-as-subject; and the prospect of glorifying oneself is an impossible one. Therefore, the ironic mode. Therefore, silence. It is rare to encounter a poet like Robert Lowell, who, beginning with the stunning virtuosity of his early poems, can move through a period of intense preoccupation with self *(Life Studies)* into a period of exploratory maneuvers into the personalities of poets quite unlike him *(Imitations)* and, though a shy, ungregarious man, write plays and participate in their productions *(The Old Glory)* and move into a kind of existential political-historical poetry in which the self is central but unobtrusive *(Notebook)*. Most lyric poets explore themselves endlessly, like patients involved in a permanent psychoanalysis, reporting back for each session determined to discover, to drag out of hiding, the essential problem of their personalities—when perhaps there is no problem in their personalities at all, except this insane preoccupation with the self and its moods and doubts, while much of the human universe struggles simply for survival.

If the lyric poet believes—as most people do—that the "I" he inhabits is not integrated with the entire stream of life, let alone with other human beings, he is doomed to a solipsistic and ironic and self-pitying art, in which metaphors for his own narcissistic predicament are snatched from newspaper headlines concerning real atrocities. The small enclosed form of the typical lyric poem seems to preclude an active sanctifying of other people; it is much easier, certainly, for a novelist to investigate and rejoice in the foreign/intimate nature of other people, regardless of his maturity or immaturity. When the novel is not addressed to the same self-analysis as the lyric poem, it demands that one look out the window and not into the mirror; it demands an active involvement with time, place, personality, pasts, and futures, and a dramatizing of emotions. The novel allows for a sanctification of any number of people, and if the novelist pits his "I" against others, he will have to construct that "I" with care and love; technical virtuosity is so hard to come by—had Dostoevsky the virtuosity of Nabokov?—that it begins to seem irrelevant. The novelist's obligation is to do no less than attempt the sanctification of the world!—while the lyric poet, if he is stuck in a limited emotional cul-de-sac, will circle endlessly inside the bell jar of his own world, and only by tremendous strength is he able to break free.

The implications of this essay are not that a highly self-conscious art is inferior by nature to a more socially committed art—on the contrary, it is usually the case that the drama of the self is very exciting. What is a risk for the poet is often a delight for his reader; controlled hysteria is more compelling than statements of Spinozan calm. When Thomas Merton cautioned the mystic against writing poems, believing that the "poet" and the "mystic" must never be joined, he knew that the possession of any truth, especially an irrefutable truth, cannot excite drama. It may be a joy to possess wisdom, but how to communicate it? If you see unity beneath the parts, bits, and cogs of the phenomenal world, this does not mean you can make poetry out of it—

> All leaves are this leaf,
> all petals, this flower
> in a lie of abundance.
> All fruit is the same,
> the trees are only one tree
> and one flower sustains all the earth.
> ("Unity," from *Manual Metaphysics*
> by Pablo Neruda; trans. Ben Belitt)

—not Neruda's best poetry.

By contrast, Plath's poems convince us when they are most troubled, most murderous, most unfair—as in "Daddy," where we listen in amazement to a child's voice cursing and rekilling a dead man, in a distorted rhythmic version of what would be, in an easier world, a nursery tune. An unforgettable poem, surely. The "parts, bits, cogs, the shining multiples" *(Three Women)* constitute hallucinations that involve us because they stir in us memories of our own infantile pasts and do not provoke us into a contemplation of the difficult and less dramatic future of our adulthood. The intensity of "Lesbos" grows out of an adult woman's denying her adulthood, her motherhood, lashing out spitefully at all objects—babies or husbands or sick kittens—with a strident, self-mocking energy that is quite different from the Plath of the more depressed poems:

> And I, love, am a pathological liar,
> And my child—look at her, face down on the floor,
> Little unstrung puppet, kicking to disappear—
> Why, she is schizophrenic,
> Her face red and white, a panic . . .
> . . . .
> You say I should drown my girl.

> She'll cut her throat at ten if she's mad at two.
> The baby smiles, fat snail,
> From the polished lozenges of orange linoleum.
> You could eat him. He's a boy.

Though Plath and her friend, another unhappy mother, obviously share the same smoggy hell, they cannot communicate, and Plath ends the poem with her insistence upon their separateness: "Even in your Zen heaven we shan't meet."

A woman who despises herself as a woman obviously cannot feel sympathy with any other woman; her passionate love/hate is for the aggressors, the absent husbands or the dead fathers who have absorbed all evil. But because these male figures are not present, whatever revenge is possible must be exacted upon their offspring. The poem "For a Fatherless Son" is more chilling than the cheerful anger of "Daddy" because it is so relentless a curse. And if it hints of Plath's own impending absence, by way of suicide, it is a remarkably cruel poem indeed. Here the mother tells her son that he will presently be aware of an absence, growing beside him like "A death tree . . . an illusion,/And a sky like a pig's backside. . . ." The child is temporarily too young to realize that his father has abandoned him, but

> One day you may touch what's wrong
> The small skulls, the smashed blue hills, the godawful hush.

This is one of the few poems of Plath's in which the future is imagined, but it is imagined passively, helplessly; the mother evidently has no intention of rearranging her life and establishing a household free of the father or of his absence. She does not state her hatred for the absent father, but she reveals herself as a victim, bitter and spiteful, and unwilling to spare her son these emotions. Again, mother and child are roughly equivalent; the mother is not an adult, not a participant in the world of "archetypes."

So unquestioningly is the division between selves accepted, and so relentlessly the pursuit of the solitary, isolated self by way of the form of this poetry, that stasis and ultimate silence seem inevitable. Again, lyric poetry is a risk because it rarely seems to open into a future: the time of lyric poetry is usually the present or the past. "This is a disease I carry home, this is a death," Plath says in *Three Women,* and, indeed, this characterizes most of her lines. All is brute process, without a future; the past is recalled only with bitterness, a stimulus for present dismay.

When the epic promises of "One's-self I sing" is mistaken as the singing of a separate self, and not the universal self, the results can only be tragic.

Crossing the Water

Plath understood well the hellish fate of being Swift's true counterpart, the woman who agrees that the physical side of life is a horror, an ungainly synthesis of flesh and spirit—the disappointment of all the romantic love poems and the nightmare of the monkish soul. Since one cannot make this existence sacred, one may as well dream of "massacres" or, like the Third Voice in the play *Three Women*, express regret that she had not arranged to have an abortion: "I should have murdered this," she says in a Shakespearean echo, "that murders me." "Crossing the water"—crossing over into another dimension of experience—cannot be a liberation, an exploration of another being, but only a quiet movement into death for two "black, cut-paper people":

> Cold worlds shake from the oar.
> The spirit of blackness is in us, it is in the fishes.
> . . . .
> Are you not blinded by such expressionless sirens?
> This is the silence of astounded souls.
> ("Crossing the Water")

In most of the poems and very noticeably in *The Bell Jar*, Plath exhibits a recurring tendency to dehumanize people, to flatten everyone into "cut-paper people," most of all herself. She performs a kind of reversed magic, a desacralizing ritual for which psychologists have terms—reification, rubricization. Absolute, dramatic boundaries are set up between the "I" and all others, and there is a peculiar refusal to distinguish between those who mean well, those who mean ill, and those who are neutral. Thus, one is shocked to discover in *The Bell Jar* that Esther, the intelligent young narrator, is as callous toward her mother as the psychiatrist is to her, and that she sets about an awkward seduction with the chilling precision of a machine—hardly aware of the man involved, telling us very little about him as an existing human being. He does not really exist, he has no personality worth mentioning. Only Esther exists.

"Lady Lazarus," risen once again from the dead, does not expect a sympathetic response from the mob of spectators that crowd in to view her, a mock-phoenix rising from another failed suicide attempt: to Plath there cannot be any connection between people, between the "I" who performs and the crowd that stares. All deaths are separate, and do not evoke human responses. To be really safe, one must be like the young man of "Gigolo," who has eluded the "bright fish hooks, the smiles of women," and who will never age because —like Plath's ideal self—he is a perfect narcissus, self-gratified. He has successfully dehumanized himself.

The cosmos is indeed lost to Plath and her era, and even a tentative exploration of a possible "God" is viewed in the old terms, in the old images of dread and terror. "Mystic" is an interesting poem, on a subject rare indeed to Plath, and seems to indicate that her uneasiness with the "mill of hooks" of the air—"questions without answer"—had led her briefly to thoughts of God. Yet whoever this "God" is, no comfort is possible because the ego cannot experience any interest or desire without being engulfed:

> Once one has seen God, what is the remedy?
> Once one has been seized up
>
> Without a part left over,
> Not a toe, not a finger, and used,
> Used utterly . . .
> What is the remedy?

Used: the mystic will be exploited, victimized, hurt. He can expect no liberation or joy from God, but only another form of dehumanizing brutality. Plath has made beautiful poetry out of the paranoia sometimes expressed by a certain kind of emotionally disturbed person who imagines that any relationship with anyone will overwhelm him, engulf and destroy his soul. (For a brilliant poem about the savagery of erotic love between lovers who cannot quite achieve adult autonomy or the generosity of granting humanity to each other, see Ted Hughes's "Lovesong" in *Crow,* not inappropriate in this context.)

The dread of being possessed by the Other results in the individual's failure to distinguish between real and illusory enemies. What must be in the human species a talent for discerning legitimate threats to personal survival evidently never developed in Plath—this helps to explain why she could so gracefully fuse the "evil" of her father with the historical outrages of the Nazis, unashamedly declare herself a "Jew" because the memory of her father persecuted her. In other vivid poems, she senses enemies in tulips (oxygen-sucking tulips?—surely they are human!) or sheep (which possess the unsheeplike power of murdering a human being) or in the true blankness of a mirror, which cannot be seen as recording the natural maturation process of a young woman but must be reinterpreted as drawing the woman toward the "terrible fish" of her future self. Plath's inability to grade the possibilities of danger is reflected generally in our society and helps to account for peculiar admissions of helplessness and confusion in adults who should be informing their children: if everything unusual or foreign is an evil, if everything new is an evil, then the individual is lost. The political equivalent of childlike paranoia is too obvious to need restating, but we have a cultural equivalent as well that seems to pass unnoticed. Surely the sinister immorality of films like *A Clockwork Orange* (though not the original English version of the Burgess novel) lies in their excited focus upon small, isolated, glamorized acts of violence by nonrepresentative individuals, so that the unfathomable violence of governments is totally ignored or misapprehended. Delmore Schwartz said that even the paranoid has enemies. Indeed he has enemies, but paranoia cannot allow us to distinguish them from friends.

In the summer of 1972 I attended a dramatic reading of Plath's *Three Women*, given by three actresses as part of the International Poetry Conference in London. The reading was done in a crowded room, and unfortunately the highly professional performance was repeatedly interrupted by a baby's crying from another part of the building. Here was—quite accidentally—a powerful and perhaps even poetic counterpoint to Plath's moving drama. For there, in the baby's cries from another room, was what Plath had left out: the reason for the maternity ward, the reason for childbirth and suffering and motherhood and poetry itself.

What may come to seem obvious to people in the future—that unique personality does not necessitate isolation, that the "I" of the poet belongs as naturally in the universe as any other aspect of its fluid totality, above all that this "I" exists in a field of living spirit of which it is one aspect—was tragically unknown to Plath, as it has been unknown or denied many. Hopefully, a world of totality awaits us, not a played-out world of fragments; but Sylvia Plath acted out a tragically isolated existence, synthesizing for her survivors so many of the sorrows of that dying age—romanticism in its death throes, the self's ship, *Ariel*, prematurely drowned.

> It is so beautiful, to have no attachments!
> I am solitary as grass. What is it I miss?
> Shall I ever find it, whatever it is?
>   *(Three Women)*

NOTE

1. *Modern Poetry Studies*, vol. 2, no. 6, p. 282.

John Frederick Nims

The Poetry of Sylvia Plath

A TECHNICAL ANALYSIS

It is true that Sylvia Plath was struck by a lightning from the spirit. But it is also true that she had spent much of her life forging speech of a metal to conduct the lightning without being instantly fused. There is little that can be said about how to get struck by lightning but a good deal that can be said about how to forge a resistant metal.

I might begin by saying to young writers: forget *Ariel* for a while; study *The Colossus*. Notice all the stanza forms, all the uses of rhythm and rhyme; notice how the images are chosen and related; how deliberately sound is used. It is no accident, for instance, that there are seven identical drab "a"s in "salt flats,/Gas tanks, factory stacks—that landscape" ("Suicide off Egg Rock"). Remember that *The Bell Jar* tells us she "wrote page after page of villanelles and sonnets," and this in one semester of one class. Perhaps for writers this is the gist of the Plath case: without the drudgery of *The Colossus,* the triumph of *Ariel* is unthinkable.[1]

There are writers who think poetry comes gushing the moment they turn on the warm water faucet of their spontaneity. But Sylvia Plath, in some prefatory remarks for a recording, dismissed such indulgence with acidity: "I think my poems come immediately out of the sensuous and emotional experiences I have, but I must say I *cannot* sympathize with these cries from the heart that are informed by nothing except, you know, a needle or a knife, or whatever it is. I believe one should be able to control and manipulate experiences, even the most terrifying, like madness, like being tortured . . . and should be able to manipulate these experiences with an informed and intelligent mind."[2]

"Control," "manipulate," "informed," "intelligent mind"—

46

these are the key words. It does not follow that a poem never "comes" easily (though this is rare); but it comes only along circuits laboriously prepared, generally for years in advance.

One of the more frivolous ways of judging poetry is in terms of contemporary significance. My plan is to discuss the work of a good modern poet in terms of those things which have made up the physical body of poetry in all times and places, and which indeed never change. Things which could be illustrated from any of the great poets of our tradition: Sappho, Catullus, the Archpoet, Bernart de Ventadour, Villon, San Juan de la Cruz, Goethe, Leopardi, Valéry, Rilke, or the poets in English we presumably know better. Looking at the works of the ten poets I mention, I am struck by how timeless, how undated their essential quality is.

Poetry, if it is anything, is a real voice in a real body in a real world. The world does not change as much as we think; and the body, with its voice-producing mechanism, changes probably not at all. The timeless excellence of Sylvia Plath lies in what she has in common with such poets as I have mentioned: the sense of language and of metaphor; the throat-produced sounds of her poetry; the physical rhythms that invigorate it.

Metaphor (I use the word here to include simile and all metaphoric ways of seeing) was for Aristotle "by far the greatest thing . . . which alone cannot be learned; it is the sign of genius." Some contemporary theorists are against it, although to reject metaphor is not only to enervate poetry but to hog-tie the human mind.

The qualities of a good metaphor would seem to be two: when A is compared to B, B is a thing at first sight surprisingly (and delightfully or shockingly) remote from A; and B is a thing at least as common, as available, as A. Or probably more common, since the purpose of metaphor is to see more clearly.

Sylvia Plath seems to me more brilliant at metaphor than others popularly grouped with her as confessional poets. In her poetry almost all of the metaphors are on target, having the excellences I mentioned (and often a third I can only suggest now: A is not only like B in one salient respect, but also picks up a supercharge of meanings proper to B but impregnating A also, as in the *smile-book* image below). In *The Colossus* we find "The pears fatten like little buddhas"; a corpse is "black as burnt turkey"; "Sun struck the water like a damnation" and "Everything glittered like blank paper"; dead moles are "shapeless as flung gloves . . . blue suede" and they have "corkscrew noses"; a dead snake lies "inert as a shoelace" and the maggots are "thin as pins"; burnt wood has the "char of karakul." In *Ariel*, it is said of a newborn baby that "Love set you going like a fat gold watch," and of its voice, "The clear vowels rise like balloons." Family smiles in a photograph "catch onto my skin, little smiling hooks." The snow of Napoleon's retreat is "marshaling its brilliant cutlery"; a swarm of bees is "A flying hedgehog, all prickles."

She also shows a total control of the figures she uses. This is a matter of attention and tact: how soon can one drop a metaphor, or dissolve it for another? Bad writers sometimes superimpose images so carelessly that we get an amateur's double exposure, with grotesque or comic results. Even good writers nod.

Sylvia Plath shows a more conscientious commitment to her images. "Hardcastle Crags" begins:

> Flintlike, her feet struck
> Such a racket of echoes from the steely street,
>
> . . . .
>
>   that she heard the quick air ignite
> Its tinder and shake
>
> A firework of echoes . . .

"Flintlike," she begins; therefore the street is "steely" and the air a "tinder" that can "ignite" a "firework." Four stanzas later she is "a pinch of flame," and in the last stanza there is "Enough to snuff the quick/Of her small heat out." Beginning as flint, she ends as "mere quartz grit." In "The Colossus," an early sketch for "Daddy," imagery of a fallen statue is sustained throughout. This knitting or girdering of images is everywhere in *Ariel*: the underwater or water imagery in "Tulips" is only one of the more obvious examples. "Getting There" is all metaphor; "Daddy," "Lady Lazarus," and "Fever 103°" are richly and consistently figurative.

The sound of words—any page of Sylvia Plath shows her preoccupation with it. *The Colossus* displays a concern almost excessive, unless we see it as a preparation for *Ariel*. Sound is an element of poetry tricky to talk about, sense and nonsense here being so close together, and the line between so fine and wavering. The chapter on words in Herbert Read's *English Prose Style* makes sense: he believes that "vocal appropriateness" is "perhaps the most important aspect of the problem of style as determined by the choice of words." Precise meaning is not enough; words have a body as well as a mind, and sometimes the body matters more. Many poets would agree with Valéry that the poet's "inner labor consists less of seeking words for his ideas than of seeking ideas for his words and paramount rhythms." Many would not agree: look, they feel, I can't be bothered with these trifles when I've got these Important Things to Say. Rather like the hurdler complaining that the hurdles interfere with his stride.

Words are more expressive when they are somehow like what they mean: fast or slow or gruff or shrill, or produced by mouth and lip movements that mimic the dynamics of rejection, say, or the prolonging of a caress. That is why Catullus has given probably the best kiss in literature in his "Illo purpureo ore suaviata," in which not only are lip movements appropriate, but, in Latin prosody, the two round "o"s coming together fuse as one. These are effects beyond mere onomatopoeia—which we can find too in Plath when it is called for, as in "Night Shift," perhaps an exercise in the manner of "Swarte smekyd smethes." Her factory has less clangor, a more "muted boom":

> though the sound
> Shook the ground with its pounding.

There is much deliberately ugly sound in "Night Shift," especially in the way words echo noises from a preceding word: "A metal detonating/Native, evidently . . .//Indefatigable fact." More interesting than such onomatopoeia are those words whose sound is an analogy for, a little charade of, their meaning: *smudge* is smudgy to say; *globe* is a roundness in the mouth; *sling* hisses and then lets go. The thousands of hours Sylvia Plath spent with her thesaurus indicates she must have considered words as embodiments. And considered what happens when they go together: poets have a tendency to stay in the same key of sound, to set up patterns in it, so that what they write has a more unified and tougher texture than casual speech. Speech is a tweedy fabric; verse is a twill. Or poets work to avoid repeating a sound, when the repetition is meaningless, or meaninglessly ugly.

Look at any page of *The Colossus,* and you see expressive repetitions and patterns: "greased machines," "gristly-bristled," "wingy myths," "cuddly mother," "clumped like bulbs," "Lambs jam the sheepfold." In "Mushrooms," "Our toes, our noses/Take hold on the loam . . .//Soft fists insist on/Heaving the needles."

Generally, we can see a reason for such effects: in "clumped like bulbs" and "lambs jam," the sound itself is clumped or jammed.

Often Sylvia Plath repeats a sound several times: "Drinking vinegar from tin cups." Now, we can get very arch here and talk about "a thin metallic acidity puckering the lips"; but the most we can say sensibly is that the repetitions of the "in" sound are sort of tinny. Tin cups do go *click* or *clink* rather than *clank* or *clunk*. If we say that the bird that "flits nimble-winged in thickets" has his five short "i"s to suggest quickness, we have Plato with us: he too held that the short "i" is the quickest of the vowel sounds. It is easy to find monotony dramatized in "daylight lays its sameness on the wall," and to find a sense of unpleasant enclosure in "This shed's fusty as a mummy's stomach." And there are any number of lines somehow like what they mean: the great sow that is

> Mire-smirched, blowzy,
>
> Maunching thistle and knotweed on her snout-cruise
> ("Sow")

or the texture of rocky soil in

> What flinty pebbles the ploughblade upturns
> As ponderable tokens

in which the *ond* of *ponderable* must have encouraged the *godly* and *doddering* of the line that follows.

Sound effects in themselves are trivial, and facility with these will never write a poem. It can temper the metal, but it cannot provoke the heavens into striking. As it did strike in several of the *Ariel* poems. Sound effects here are less obtrusive than before; more subtle, more sparing, more saved for where they matter. But they are here: "Square as a chair," "strips of tinfoil winking," "starless and fatherless, a dark water." There are many in the bee poems: "were there not such a din in it" and "the unintelligible syllables." In "Lady Lazarus," there are such things as "the flesh/The grave cave ate." "Lesbos" opens with a vicious hiss. But "Nick and the Candlestick" is the real showpiece for sound:

> I am a miner. The light burns blue.
> Waxy stalactites
> Drip and thicken . . .

And what a contrast between the brilliant chill of

> Christ! they are panes of ice,
> A vice of knives . . .

and the pulpy warmth of these words to a baby:

> The blood blooms clean
>
> In you, ruby.

A sound device even more compelling in *Ariel* is the kind of rhyme used. There is something really new, though it is not easy to do anything new with a device so time-worn and so primitive. Primitive: children and simple people love it; so do composers of folk songs, authentic or pseudo. Only some of our more cerebral theorists, who write as if they had no bodies anyway, pish-tush it with prudery.

The rhymes we find in *The Colossus* are already at an advanced stage of their evolutionary history. We can assume that hundreds of earlier poems had exhausted, for the time, the poet's taste for full rhyme; it is with real surprise that we come across, in "Snake-charmer," *breast-manifest-nest.* By preference she rhymes more atonally. The same vowel sound but with different consonants after it: *fishes-pig-finger-history; worms-converge.* Different vowel sounds but with the same final consonant: *vast-compost-must; knight-combat-beat* (this is her most characteristic kind of rhyme in *The Colossus*). Unaccented syllables going with accented or unaccented: *boulders-wore; footsoles-babel.* She considers all final vowels as rhyming with all others: *jaw-arrow-eye* (perhaps suggested by the Middle-English practice in alliteration). Or she will mate sounds that have almost anything in common: *ridgepole-tangle-inscrutable.* The ties become so very loose that it is not always clear when they are intended. *Depths-silver-there*—can these be rhymes? They occur at the end of a poem in terza rima, which has been clearly in rhyme up to this triad. In "Suicide off Egg Rock" the final words of the twenty-four lines each pair somewhere—in her fashion—with another, but the pairings are not immediately caught by the ear in such a list of end-words as: *drizzled, flats, landscape, of, updraught, damnation, into, tattoo, children, spindrift, wave, gallop, sandspit, blindfold, garbage, forever, eyehole, brainchamber, pages, paper, corrosive, wastage, water, ledges* (the list is interesting as diction). Rhymes like these mean more to the writer than to any reader, who will miss many of them. One feels that Sylvia Plath had an obsession with rhyme, felt poetry *had* to have it, but at times made her compliance a token one. She knows the poems rhyme, even if we do not. Should we call this "token rhyme"? Or "ghost rhyme"—since it is like a revenant never completely exorcised? Or are all these things trifles to ho-hum away? It is clear that to her they were not.

In *Ariel*, the use of rhyme is very different. In some poems it is ghostlier than ever. But more often it is obvious: rhyme at high noon. The same sound may run on from stanza to stanza, with much identical rhyme. "Lady Lazarus" illustrates the new manner. The poem is printed in units of three lines, but the rhyme is not in her favorite terza-rima pattern. Six of the first ten lines end in an "n" sound, followed by a sequence in long "e," which occurs in about half of the next twenty-two lines. Then, after six more "n"s we have "l"s ending eleven of fourteen lines; and then several "r"s, leading into the six or more "air" rhymes that conclude the sequences. Almost Skeltonian: the poet seems to carry on a sound about as long as she can, although not in consecutive lines. "Compulsive rhyme," we might call this, for it seems fair to see it as deeper than a mere literary device, and as somehow related to needs of the exacerbated psyche. Most of the poems after "Lady Lazarus" rhyme on in this way (although the tendency is much fainter in "Berck-Plage"). "Lesbos" is bound together by compulsive rhyme, broken here and there by couplets that recall Eliot— and indeed this poem is her "Portrait of a Lady," and her "Prufrock," with even the breakers "white and black." In "Daddy" the compulsion to rhyme becomes obsession. Perhaps never in the history of poetry has the device carried so electric a charge. Breathing love and hate together, it coos and derides, even more insistent at the end of the poem than at the beginning, so that form refutes what content is averring. Over half of the lines end in the "oo" sound, and of these nearly half are the one word "you." This is rhyme with—and for!—a vengeance. The bee poems string together the same sort of compulsive rhyme: eight of the last ten lines of "The Arrival of the Bee Box" end in long "e." The extremely devious and intricate rhyme-work of *The Colossus*, then, has led to something almost excessively simple, something we might find monotonous if it were not so deeply significant.

All I have said about rhyme has implied something about stanza form. She writes almost always in stanzas or stanza-like units. Often in the later poems there is no relation between rhyme scheme and stanza form: each goes its separate way, with a kind of schizophrenic indifference to the other. Just as her rhyme, even when barely there, *is* there, so with the stanza: even when there seems no formal reason for the unit, she remains faithful to its appearance on the page. Probably here, as with rhyme, we have a source of discipline that is personal and internal: it is for her, not for us. Of the "pages of villanelles and sonnets" there is nothing in *The Colossus* except one sonnet, in nine-syllable lines. Only four of the poems are nonstanzaic, two of them barely so. There is one poem in rather free couplets. The fifty others are in stanzas of from three to nine lines. Her favorite form is terza rima, which makes up six of the twelve poems in three-line stanzas. In some of these she adds an extra complexity to the terza rima by having the second line short in the odd-numbered tercets, and the first and third lines short in the even-numbered ones, so that the poem seems to seesaw on the page. Among the longer stanza forms there is much intricacy and variation; she seems to be trying out as many tight forms as possible. "Black Rook in Rainy Weather" even follows the Provençal system of *rimas dissolutas:* each line rhymes with the corresponding lines of all the other stanzas.

In spite of several fine poems, *The Colossus* has the air of being an exercise book. *Ariel* is very different. The stanza forms are fewer and simpler, far more loosely bound by rhyme. Before, there was one poem in two-line units; now there are nine: everything is more concise. Of the nine, none rhyme as couplets; rhyme is present, but in no regular way. Ten poems are in three-line units; two of these look rather like "Sow" on the page, although with shorter lines. But none rhymes as terza rima. The five-line stanzas now have no formal rhyme scheme, although again they are rhyme-haunted. There are only two poems in longer stanza forms (of seven lines), and one nine-line poem about pregnancy (nine-ness: an earlier pregnancy poem had nine lines of nine syllables each).

And what of rhythm? In *The Colossus,* she seems practicing in the rhythms, as well as in everything else. Up until our own time, there have been chiefly two kinds of rhythm in English. The first predominated until Chaucer; it was based on the heavy stress-accent native to our language. The line was divided into two halves with two stresses in each (sometimes emphasized by alliteration); it did not matter how many unstressed syllables there were, nor where they were (pronunciation actually limits the possibilities). We find the rhythm everywhere in early poetry:

> Whére beth théy   befóren us wéren?

exactly as we find it centuries later in E. E. Cummings:

> he sáng his dídn't   he dánced his díd

and Sylvia Plath:

> Ìncense of deáth.   Your dáy approáches.

or

> Béasts of oásis,   a bétter tíme.

Ransom discusses it as the "folk line" or "dipodic line"; he finds it in Thomas Hardy:

> We stoód by a pónd   that wínter dáy

and uses it as the basis of his own "Bells for John Whiteside's Daughter":

> There was súch spéed   in her líttle bódy.

In *The Colossus,* there are ten poems that read themselves naturally, if freely, in the folk line. Perhaps the best are "Suicide off Egg Rock" and "Blue Moles."

As everyone knows, the other system was brought over from the Continent by Chaucer. There are still some who resent the foreign importation, although at least three fourths of the English poetry that matters has been written in it, not without success. The line has five pulsations, and in theory, if almost never in fact, all five are two-syllable pulsations, with the second syllables stronger than the first. We find it in Chaucer's pulsations:

> Hyd, Absolom, thy giltë tresses clere

exactly as in Cummings's

> all ignorance toboggans into know . . .

Basically, iambic is the *lub-dubb* of the heartbeat, perhaps the first sensation that we, months before our birth, are aware of. Nothing unnatural about that as a rhythm. It has always been common in human speech. Aristotle called it the most colloquial, or speechlike, of the rhythms, the one used most naturally in speechlike poetry because most commonly heard in real speech. R. P. Blackmur once said he had listened to recordings of poetry in thirty-odd languages, and in every one except Chinese could detect the iambic base. I make this defense because the rhythm is sometimes attacked today as unnatural. But there are still some, like Sylvia Plath, who would as soon listen to their own heart for rhythms as take dictation from a typewriter. In *The Colossus* she has eight poems in pure iambic pentameter (in the organic, not the metronomic sense), and nearly twenty others that use it freely or in combination with other line lengths. (Why, by the way, *penta*meter? Could it have anything to do with the physiological fact that our heart pulses five times, on an average, for every time we breathe?)

She also has fourteen poems in accentual count (this is a count, not a rhythm)—the system that organizes lines by number of syllables, with no regard for their stress or importance. This is finger counting, more foreign to the nature of spoken English than Chaucer's imported novelty. People under the stress of emotion may speak rhythmically, but they do not count their syllables. For emotion is stress in language; it is the stresses that have to pulsate if we are to have a living rhythm. And syllabic count is made up of undifferentiated elements, whereas a stress rhythm has two forces working against each other: not so much the systole and diastole of the accents as the impassioned dialogue between speech rhythm and meter, a dialogue full of anticipations, surprises, and sudden pacts. A tension between such polarities as make up our existence.

Such poets as Marianne Moore and W. H. Auden, however, have shaped many of their poems on a grid of syllabics; over these the living rhythms move. And there is always something to be said for exercises in the syllabic line. Once attuned to the accentual, one is easily carried away into a kind of automatic facility, so that the lines "flow" too easily. (It is the prevalence of bad iambics of course that has led its enemies into their blanket condemnation.) Writing in syllabics can be a salutary exercise in countering the sing-song— and this is the importance of the syllabics in *The Colossus*. They tend to be the colder poems: objective, intellectual, descriptive. Passion always brings the poet back to a heart-rhythm, as in "Witch Burning":

> My ankles brighten. Brightness ascends my thighs.
> I am lost, I am lost, in the robes of all this light.

Another advantage of syllabics is that they can be of value to the writer (if not to the reader) as an additional principle of control, a way of making it harder for oneself, of checking (as Valéry thinks we should) the logorrheas of "inspiration." And the syllabic poem can come alive if it has a physical rhythm overriding the finger count. What speaker of English can hear *as fifteen* the fifteen sylla-bles of a line in "Fern Hill," or would be bothered if Dylan Thomas skipped a couple? Yet we all hear the passionate stress-rhythm that overrides them. Something of the sort happens in Sylvia Plath's "Mushrooms":

> Nudgers and shovers
> In spite of ourselves.
> Our kind multiplies:
>
> We shall by morning
> Inherit the earth.
> Our foot's in the door.

These are five-syllable lines, but what catches the ear is not so much the fiveness as the traditional swing, as old as Homer at least, of dactyls and spondees, with a rest or two.

There is only one syllabic poem in *Ariel,* and it is not one of the better poems. Syllabics seem to have served their callisthenic pur-pose in *The Colossus;* when the poet comes to write her important work, she dismisses them. In *Ariel,* there is almost no metrical innovation—unless we think of the comma splice and its nervous impetus. But this is more a matter of syntax than of metrics. May I suggest that the best poets are not often the metrical innovators? This they leave for the fussbudgets. It is always easier to invent a new metrical system than to write a good poem in the existing one. New medium: new tedium—was Roethke, that devotee of the nur-sery rhyme, thinking of this when he wrote "Some rare new te-dium's taking shape"?

Far from making meter new, *Ariel* even marks what metrists might consider a severe regression. Apart from the syllabic "You're," everything can be accounted for by the most basic of English rhythms. Frost says that we have "virtually but two rhythms," strict iambic and loose iambic. These, and little else, we find in *Ariel,* often both in the same poem. The loose iambics work toward that most unfashionable of all feet, the anapest (or its mirror image, the dactyl). Probably not since the Assyrian came down like the wolf on the fold has there been so high a proportion of anapests

in an important collection of poems. Not that *Ariel,* in all the ways
that really matter, is not a highly original collection. But tampering
with the heartbeat of poetry is not a significant kind of originality;
all one is likely to get is verbal fibrillation. In *Ariel* at least, the more
original and significant the poem, the more traditional the rhythm.

The lines in *Ariel* are by no means always pentameter, although
they are so enough times to surprise us. Probably they are heard as
pentameter even when not printed so. One example: lines 2 to 10
of "Lady Lazarus" can be spaced, without violence to the cadence,
as

> One year in every ten / I manage it—
>
> A sort of walking miracle, my skin
> Bright as a Nazi lampshade, / My right foot
>
> A paperweight, / My face a featureless
> fine / Jew linen. // Peel off the napkin / O
> my enemy. Do I terrify?— // The nose . . .

And the poem comes back to that cadence everywhere, particularly
at moments of greatest intensity:

> Soon, soon the flesh / The grave cave ate will be
> At home on me // And I a smiling woman.

or

> The peanut-crunching crowd / shoves in to see // Them
> unwrap me hand and foot— / the big strip tease.

This is much more regular than the opening of Shakespeare's Sonnet 116: "Let me not to the marriage of true minds," which has only
one iambic foot in the five.

Many key lines are printed as pentameter:

> And like the cat I have nine times to die. . . .
> . . . .
> To last it out and not come back at all. . . .
> . . . .
> And pick the worms off me like sticky pearls. . . .
> . . . .
> For the eyeing of my scars, there is a charge. . . .

"Tulips" is more in the Fletcherian mode: more anapests, more extra
syllables:

> I didn't want any flowers, I only wanted
> To lie with my hands turned up and be utterly empty.
> How free it is, you have no idea how free—
> The peacefulness is so big it dazes you . . .

and the conclusion:

> The water I taste is warm and salt, like the sea,
> And comes from a country far away as health.

The poem "Ariel" looks more irregular, but it too never gets far
from an iambic base. Much of it could be spaced so that, metrically,
it would be no looser than Jacobean verse. "Lesbos," which opens
like an echo of Tourneur, is even more regular:

> Where they crap and puke and cry and she can't hear.
> You say you can't stand her, / The bastard's a girl.
> . . . .
> She'll cut her throat at ten if she's mad at two.
> . . . .
> Even in your Zen heaven we shan't meet.

Look anywhere—the poems of *Ariel* return to a solid pentameter
base again and again. Even when they do not, they tend to remain
loose iambic, whatever the line length:

> Obscene bikinis hide in the dunes . . .
> ("Berck-Plage")

> Love set you going like a fat gold watch.
> ("Morning Song")

> What a thrill—
> My thumb instead of an onion.
> The top quite gone
> Except for a sort of hinge . . .
> ("Cut")

> It is a heart,
> This holocaust I walk in,
> O golden child the world will kill and eat.
> ("Mary's Song")

I quote so much because I expect incredulity. "You mean Sylvia
Plath is so *square?*" In *Ariel*, square as a chair, technically. Which
is one reason the book seems so original. Except to the shallow and
the jaded, mere novelty is a bore: everything changes, said Valéry,

except the avant-garde. And while "Make it new" is very good advice, perhaps "Make it do" is even better. If one has the strength and the resources to. But the example of what Sylvia Plath actually achieved is more convincing than any remarks of mine.

In the famous and terrible "Daddy," the iambs are varied with anapests and spondees:

> no not
> Any less the black man who
>
> Bit my pretty red heart in two.
> I was ten when they buried you.
> At twenty I tried to die
> And get back, back, back to you.
> I thought even the bones would do.

"The Bee Meeting" has longer lines of the same units. It is only in the less impressive poems, those more in the manner of *The Colossus*, that we are not likely to be caught into the rhythm: in "Medusa," for example.

Although I have said very little about diction, numerous quotations have probably suggested the point I would make. In *The Colossus* the diction is always distinguished and elegant, but it is a written language more often than a spoken one. More literary than actual. There are lines not likely to come from a human throat:

> Haunched like a faun, he hooed
> From grove of moon-glint and fen-frost
> Until all owls in the twigged forest . . .
>   ("Faun")

But I open *Ariel* and have no trouble hearing:

> I have done it again.
> One year in every ten
> I manage it—
>   ("Lady Lazarus")

or

> Pure? What does it mean?
>   ("Fever 103° ")

or

> Somebody is shooting at something in our town . . .
>> ("The Swarm")

Not every line in *Ariel* passes this difficult voice test, but what we hear almost everywhere is a real voice in a real body in a real world. In *The Colossus,* the voice is often not vibrant; indeed, it is often not her own. Sometimes, as in "Ouija," it is the voice of Wallace Stevens, with "aureate poetry / In tarnished modes . . . / Fair chronicler of every foul declension." In "Spinster" it is the voice of Ransom, and in "Dark House" it is purest Roethke:

> All-mouth licks up the bushes
> And the pots of meat.
> He lives in an old well,
> A stony hole. He's to blame.
> He's a fat sort.

Dylan Thomas is present, and some others. These are marvelous exercises in imitation, and, like everything else she did, prepared her to speak for herself in *Ariel.* Perhaps as writer one finds oneself only after having tried to be another. "More than half a lifetime to arrive at this freedom of speech," said Eliot of Yeats's 1914 volume. "It is a triumph." Sylvia Plath did not have half a lifetime, but in a few years, in all the ways I have tried to describe, she prepared herself to endure and transmit, if only for a while, the fires of heaven.

NOTES

1. Since writing this, I have found that Peter Davison has made much the same point in "Inhabited by a Cry: The Last Poetry of Sylvia Plath" (*The Atlantic,* August 1966, pp. 76–77). He too considers *The Colossus* "advanced exercises"; and says of *Ariel:* "these poems would never have come into being without the long, deliberate, technical training that preceded them. We can only perform with true spontaneity what we have first learned to do by habit."

2. *The Poet Speaks,* Argo Record Co. No. RG 455, London (recorded October 30, 1962). Sylvia Plath reads "Lady Lazarus," "Daddy," and "Fever 103°," as well as commentary. Other readers are Ted Hughes, Peter Porter, and Thom Gunn.

Barbara Hardy

Enlargement or Derangement?

Passions of hate and horror prevail in the poetry of Sylvia Plath, running strongly counter to the affirmative and life-enhancing quality of most great English poetry, even in this century. We cannot reconcile her despairing and painful protest with the usual ideological demands of Christian, Marxist, and humanist writers, whether nobly and sympathetically eloquent, like Wordsworth, breezily simplified, like Dylan Thomas, or cunning in ethical and psychological argument, like W. H. Auden or F. R. Leavis. Her poetry rejects instead of accepting, despairs instead of glorying, turns its face with steady consistency toward death, not life. But these hating and horrified passions are rooted in love, are rational as well as irrational, lucid as well as bewildered, so humane and honorable that they are constantly enlarged and expanded. We are never enclosed in a private sickness here, and if derangement is a feature of the poetry, it works to enlarge and generalize, not to create an enclosure. Moreover, its enlargement works through passionate reasoning, argument, and wit. Its judgment is equal to its genius.

The personal presence in the poetry, though dynamic and shifting, makes itself felt in a full and large sense, in feeling, thinking, and language. In view of certain tendencies to admire or reject her so-called derangement as a revelatory or an enclosed self-exploration, I want to stress this breadth and completeness. The poetry constantly breaks beyond its own personal cries of pain and horror, in ways more sane than mad, enlarging and generalizing the particulars, attaching its maladies to a profoundly moved and moving sense of human ills. Working through a number of individual poems, I should like to describe this poetry as a poetry of enlargement, not derangement. In much of the poetry the derangement is scarcely present, but where it is, it is out-turned, working through reason and love.

I want to begin by looking at a poem from *Ariel* which shows how dangerous it is to talk about the "typical" Sylvia Plath poem, or even the "typical" late poem. I must make it clear that I do not want to rest my case on the occasional presence of life-enhancing poems, but to use one to explain what I mean by imaginative enlargement. "Nick and the Candlestick" (written October 1962) is not only a remarkable poem of love, but that much rarer thing—are there any others?—a fine poem of maternal love. It is a poem which moves toward two high points of feeling, strongly personal and particular, deeply eloquent of maternal feeling, and lucidly open to a Christian mythical enlargement. The first peak comes in the tenth stanza, and can perhaps be identified at its highest point in one word, the endearment "ruby," which is novel, surprising, resonant, and beautiful:

> Remembering, even in sleep,
> Your crossed position.
> The blood blooms clean
>
> In you, ruby.
> The pain
> You wake to is not yours.

The second peak comes at the end, in a strongly transforming conclusion, a climax in the very last line. It comes right out of all that has been happening in the poem but transforms what has gone before, carrying a great weight and responsibility, powerfully charged and completing a process, like an explosion or a blossoming:

> You are the one
> Solid the spaces lean on, envious.
> You are the baby in the barn.

The final enlargement is daring, both in the shock of expansion and in the actual claim it makes. She dares to call her baby Christ and in doing so makes the utmost claim of her personal love, but so that the enlargement does not take us away from this mother, this child, this feeling. This most personally present mother-love moves from the customary hyperbole of endearment in "ruby" to the vast claim. When we look back, when we read again, the whole poem is pushing toward that last line, "You are the baby in the barn." The symbol holds good, though at first invisibly, for the cold, the exposure, the dark, the child, the mother, the protection, and the redemption from share of pain. Each sensuous and emotional step holds for the mother in the poem and for Mary: this is the warmth of the mother nursing her child in the cold night; this is a proud claim for the child's beauty and the mother's tenderness; this is love and praise qualified by pain. Any mother loving her child in a full awareness of the world's horror—especially seeing it and feeling it—vulnerable and momentarily safe in sleep—is reenacting the feeling in the Nativity, has a right to call the child the "baby in the barn."

"Ruby" is a flash of strong feeling. It treasures, values, praises, admires, measures, contemplates, compares, rewards. Its full stretch of passion is only apparent when the whole poem is read, but even on first encounter it makes a powerful moment, and strikes us as thoroughly formed and justified at that stage. Like every part of the poem, even the less urgent-sounding ones, it refers backward and forward, and has also continuity not only within the poem but with larger traditions of amorous and religious language, in medieval poetry (especially *The Pearl*), in the Bible, in Hopkins. The fusion of the new and the old is moving. This baby has to be newly named, like every baby, and has its christening in a poem, which bestows a unique name, in creative energy, as ordinary christenings cannot, but with something too of the ritual sense of an old and common feeling. Sylvia Plath is a master of timing and placing, and the naming endearment comes after the physically live sense of the sleeping child, in the cold air, in the candlelight, in its healthy color. The mildly touched Christian reference in "crossed position" prepares for the poem's future. Its gentleness contrasts strongly, by the way, with the violence of very similar puns in Dylan Thomas, and confirms my general feeling that Sylvia Plath is one of the very few poets to assimilate Thomas without injury, in an entirely benign influence. Her sensuous precision is miles away from Thomas: "ruby" is established by the observation, "The blood blooms clean/ In you," and the comparison works absolutely, within the poem, though it has an especially poignant interest when we think of the usual aggressiveness and disturbance of redness in her other poems, where the blooming red of tulips or poppies are exhausting life-demands, associated with the pain of red wounds, or the heavy urgency of a surviving beating heart. Here it is a beloved color, because it is the child's, so in fact there is a constancy of symbolism, if we are interested. "Clean," like "crossed" and "ruby" has the same perfectly balanced attachment to the particularity of the situation— this mother, this baby—and to the Christian extension. "The pain/ You wake to is not yours" works in the same way, pointing out and in, though the words "out" and "in" do less than justice to the fusion here.

The perfected fusion is the more remarkable for being worked out in a various tone, which includes joking. Like the medieval church, or the Nativity play, it can be irreverent, can make jokes about what it holds sacred, is sufficiently inclusive and sufficiently certain. So we are carried from the fanciful rueful joke about "A piranha/Religion, drinking//Its first communion out of my live toes" to the final awe. Or from the casual profane protest, "Christ! they are panes of ice" to the crossed position, the pain not his, the baby in the barn. An ancient and audacious range.

If this is a love poem, it is one which exists in the context of the other *Ariel* poems, keeping a sense of terrors as well as glories, in imagery which is vast and vague: "the stars/Plummet to their dark address"; and topically precise and scientific: "the mercuric/Atoms that cripple drip/Into the terrible well." It is a poisoned world that nourishes and threatens that clean blood. Perhaps only a child can present an image of the uncontaminated body, as well as soul, and there is also present the sense of a mother's fear of physical contamination. The mercuric atoms are presumably a reference to the or-gano-mercury compounds used in agriculture, and the well seems to be a real well.

The poet loves and praises, but in no innocent or ideal glorying. This is a cold air in which the candle burns blue before yellow, nearly goes out, reminds us of the radiance in so many paintings of Mother and Child, but also of a real cold night, and of the miner's cold, his dark, his cave, his nightwork, his poisoned breathing. The intimacies and protections and colors are particular too: "roses," "the last of Victoriana," "soft rugs." The expansion moves firmly into and out of a twentieth-century world, a medieval poetry, ritual, and painting, and the earliest Christ-story, and this holds for its pains and its loving. It moves from light to dark, from love to fear. It moves beyond the images of mother-love, indeed begins outside in the first line's serious wit, "I am a miner." It uses—or, better, feels for—the myth of Redemption not in order to idealize the particulars but rather to revise and qualify the myth, to transplant it again cheerfully, to praise only after a long hard look at the worst. The love and faith and praise are there, wrung out and achieved against the grain, against the odds. She said of the poem, in a BBC broadcast: "A mother nurses her baby son by candlelight and finds in him a beauty which, while it may not ward off the world's ill, does redeem her share of it."

True, it is not typical. There are two other very loving poems of maternal feeling, "Riddle" and "You're," happy peals of conceits, but nothing else moves so, between these two extremities of love and pain, striking spark from such poles. "Nick and the Candlestick" is not proffered as an instance of togetherness, but as a lucid model of the enlargement I want to discuss.

At the heart of her poetry lies the comment that she herself made about this enlargement:

> I think my poems come immediately out of the sensuous and emotional experiences I have, but I must say I cannot sympathize with these cries from the heart that are informed by nothing except a needle or a knife or whatever it is. I believe that one should be able to control and manipulate experiences, even the most terrifying—like madness, being tortured, this kind of experience—and one should be able to manipulate these experiences with an informed and intelligent mind. I think that personal experience shouldn't be a kind of shut-box and mirror-looking narcissistic experience. I believe it should be generally relevant, to such things as Hiroshima and Dachau, and so on.[1]

A mere explicit statement that the poet believes personal experience of pain should not be a mirror or a shut box but should be relevant to Hiroshima and Dachau is plainly not an answer to the question of appropriateness. Nor would a mere listing of such references do much: the intelligent poet can after all attempt but fail to break open the shut box, may impose intellectually schematic associations with the larger world. Alain Resnais in *Hiroshima Mon Amour* seems to be open to the charge of using the larger pain of atomic war to illuminate his personal center, so that the movement is not that of enlargement but of diminution. Something similar seems to happen in a good many Victorian attempts to enlarge the personal problem, to combine the personal and social pain, and we may well object that the endings of *Bleak House* and *Crime and Punishment* are unsuccessful attempts to solve the large pain by the lesser reconciliation. I have spent what may seem an excessive time on "Nick and the Candlestick" in order to establish not so much a typical feeling, but a form: the particularity and the generalization run together in equal balance, asking questions of each other, eroding each other, unifying in true imaginative modification. I want to suggest that this is the mode of Sylvia Plath's major poetry, and that it succeeds exactly where Resnais failed. But it should be said, perhaps, that this problem of combination or enlargement works in a special way, involving artists working from experience of personal pain, depression, despair. The optimist, like Dickens and Dostoevsky, may well find it easy to join his larger pain and his smaller triumph. For the tragic artist like Sylvia Plath it is more the problem of competitive pains: how to dwell in and on the knives and needles of the personal life without shutting off the knives and needles in Biafra, Vietnam, Dachau, and Hiroshima. It is almost a problem of competing sensibilities, and the tragic artist's temptation in our time is probably to combine indecorously, like Resnais, to make the Hiroshima a metaphor for an adultery, to move from outer to inner and confirm an especially terrible shut box.

Before I move from "Nick and the Candlestick" to the more terrible fusions elsewhere in *Ariel,* I want to look at some of the earlier attempts in *The Colossus* (1960). Many of the poems here show a fairly familiar and conventional tension and control. In some poems there is a narrow sensuous or social image of something painful, something dying: the dryness, unpleasant fruition, hard and yellow starlight, and difficult "borning" of "The Manor Garden" have nothing to say for nature; the inhuman boom and monotony of "Night Shift" show men reduced to tend the machine; "Hardcastle Crags" defeats the walker's energy by massive indifference and hard labor. Such poems accumulate the sense of unreward, ugliness, labor, repulsion, hostility, but each makes only its individual assertion, proffering no generalization.

In another group of poems in this volume, there is an attempt to break up such hardness, though scarcely to redeem or transform. Such poems as "Two Views of a Cadaver Room," "Watercolor of Grantchester Meadows," "The Eye-mote," or "Black Rook in Rainy Weather" show a darkening, rather than a darkened, vision. Affirmation is there, is valued, but is unstable. The destructive eye-

mote is there for good, enlarged and confirmed as more than temporary by the move towards Oedipus, so we know that the sight
cannot return, that the "Horses fluent in the wind" are gone. In
"Black Rook in Rainy Weather" the poem sets out a belief in
meaningful experience, but the belief rocks unsteadily, the experience is erratic and unguaranteed, can only bring "A brief respite
from fear/Of total neutrality." The vigor of the meaningful moment
is certainly there, "hauling up eyelids," but in most of these poems
that weigh gain against loss, there is less vigor, or a final movement
toward the loss. "Black Rook" ends with the naming of the spasmodic trick, the random rare descent, but "The Eye-mote" moves
more characteristically away from the balance between easy fluid
harmony, and the pained, blurred distorted vision, to tip the scales.
We move over into blindness, guilt, loss of more than a small beauty.
"Watercolor of Grantchester Meadows" has a dark landscape, uses
the spring idyll ambiguously, and sharpens one point to drive it hard
against our senses and sense. It creates a swimmy swoony dream of
spring, water, love, in the impressionist blurring and the little nur-
sery-plate brightness, to build a bridge from the world of (superficial) sweetness to destructiveness. In "Two Views of a Cadaver
Room" the movement from death to love is deceptive: the poem
allows only a tiny ambiguous space for "the little country" where
the lovers can be "blind to the carrion army." No redeeming corner,
this, because "Foolish, delicate" and "not for long," stalled only "in
paint," and responding in true Brueghel disproportionateness to the
earlier apparent redemption, in the first half of the poem, where
after the dissection, "He hands her a cut-out heart like a cracked
heirloom." All these poems, with the possible exception of "Black
Rook," fall out of love with the world of love, yearn for it but know
what they are up against. They share a certain static quality: the
pastoral term, for instance, in the Grantchester poem, is decorously
but very carefully planning its own erosion, right from the start, and
the poet's stance seems to be well outside the poem. Even in "The
Eye-mote," where there is an expansion into the Oedipus myth, it
is told rather than enacted: "I dream that I am Oedipus." Though
"the brooch-pin and the salve" effectively revise the splinter and the
eyebath, they do so by a movement of literary reference, very different from the total resonance in "Nick" where the poem is plainly
gathering its strengths and meanings, like all the best art, from
conscious and unconscious assembling. The brilliant stroke of wit
in "Before the brooch-pin and the salve/Fixed me in this parenthe-

sis" is perhaps a limited one: the pun is dazzling in the light of the Oedipal situation, and plainly relates to all those other poems about parent relationships. But after a little reflection one begins to wonder if "parenthesis" is quite the best word, after all, for either the Oedipal blindness or a loss of innocence. A spurt of wit remains on the superficial level. As a pun, it is not quite up to Mercutio's or Lady Macbeth's.

Ted Hughes tells us that the personality of Oedipus and others were important persons in her life, but he is right to say that in this poem, and elsewhere, they may seem literary. It is not a matter of artificiality but of a certain thinness of feeling: the enlargement does not quite come off. Similarly, in the Grantchester poem, which strikes me perhaps as a subdued answer to Dylan Thomas's "Sir John's Hill" (just as "Nick" seems like a subdued answer to Hopkins's "The Starlight Night"), the movement from the human situation to the animal world seems relaxed, cool, insufficiently felt—or rather, felt to be felt in the poem. Her feelings for Greek tragedy and animal life were evidently far from thinly literary, but in some of these poems they were not yet getting sufficiently incorporated and expressed.

There are a number of poems in *The Colossus,* however, where a different stance and structure achieves something much more imaginatively substantial: "Lorelei," "All the Dead Dears," "Suicide off Egg Rock," "Full Fathom Five," "Medallion," "The Burnt-out Spa," and "Mussel Hunter at Rock Harbor" are most impressive poems of a dying fall. Each moves slowly and lucidly into a death or a longing for a death or a blessing of death. They are, if you like, perverse love poems. Instead of working by the usual kind of enlargement, from the personal to the larger world, they attempt an empathetic drama, where a kind of death is explored, imagined, justified. If I list the last lines, a common quality in the conclusions can be my starting point:

> Stone, stone, ferry me down there.
> ("Lorelei")

> Deadlocked with them, taking root as cradles rock.
> ("All the Dead Dears")

> The forgetful surf creaming on those ledges.
> ("Suicide off Egg Rock")

I would breathe water.
("Full Fathom Five")

The yardman's/Flung brick perfected his laugh.
("Medallion")

The stream that hustles us

Neither nourishes nor heals.
("The Burnt-out Spa")

. . . this relic saved/Face, to face the bald-faced sun.
("Mussel Hunter at Rock Harbor")

Each poem is dramatized, individualized. Each constructs a different feeling for death. These conclusions, which all settle for death, are earned in separate and solidly substantial ways, emotionally intense and rationally argued, each working through a distinct human experience which ends by wanting death.

In "Lorelei" it is the peace of death that lures, which is why the sirens' song and their silence are both maddening. The sense of "maddening" is both superficial and profound, for the listener knows that what the sirens offer is illusion, cannot be a solicitation except in nightmare or when "deranged by harmony." The images are fully responsive: "descant from borders/Of hebetude, from the ledge//Also of high windows" and "Drunkenness of the great depths"; and "your ice-hearted calling." It is the earlier "Sisters, your song/Bears a burden too weighty/For the whorled ear's listening" that earns the sense of inevitability in the final weight of "Stone, stone."

The same can be said of all the other poems in this group. Each makes its individual movement to death, each is a dying. In "All the Dead Dears" death is repulsive, but none the less urgent for that. The dead pull us, willy-nilly, into our graves and the three skeletons in the Archaeological Museum are suitably and grotesquely "unmasked" and "dry" witnesses to life's (death's?) eating game. The poem moves step by step from the first instance, from the stranger-in-blood to the sense of ancestral pull, to the father's death, through the family feasts, into a coffin as inevitable as a cradle. The whole poem takes color from the first grotesque image, so that her father's death (of course a recurring image) is seen in the right bizarre fashion: "Where the daft father went down/With orange duckfeet winnowing his hair," and the right, though typically very mild (it strengthens terribly once we see through it, though, this mildness) sense of the animal and human, and the live and dead, overlapping. The final Gulliver image completes the grotesque line and the imagery of a trap.

The image of clarity and cleanness at the end of "Suicide off Egg Rock" finishes off the man who walks away from the debris of the beach and the muck of living—"that landscape/Of imperfections his bowels were part of." Each poem is a separate dying, thoroughly imagined. The apparently stoical image of the crab's face at the end of that very fine poem "Mussel Hunter at Rock Harbor" may look like an emblem proffered to the human world by the animals, but must take on the color of all that goes before. It is only a crab-face saved, a crab death, a scrupulous rejection of symbol made at the end of a poem that has slowly forced the human being to feel itself reduced in and by the seabeast world. The terrible "Full Fathom Five" creates an oceanic image with human features, and the real drowned father colors the terror and makes possible a childlike plea for water rather than thick and murderous air. "The Burnt-out Spa" establishes, rather like "Suicide off Egg Rock," a rubbishy land in contrast to a pure water, and this is reinforced in the final yearning for the purified human reflection: "It is not I, it is not I, it is not I," whose sad wail is explained by all that has gone before.

These are individuated dramas of dying. The obsession is evident: the poetic flexibility, the inventive enlargements, and the self-explanatory structures show the control and the unenclosed sensibility. The actual mythological or literary symbols are part of such enlargement: the Lorelei, the drowned father in Ariel's song, the museum skeletons, Gulliver, the Oriental crab-face are all part of a dense formation of feeling, not tenuous-seeming annexes, like the Oedipus of "The Eye-mote." It is such density that may take them to the verge of allegory, but keeps them substantially on its right side. Like much good poetry, it is tempted to be allegory, but refuses.

Moving to the *Ariel* poems, one recognizes that such inventiveness has become more powerful, and sometimes less lucid. In a poem of pain and delirium, "Fever 103°," the wildness and fast movement of the conceits are excused by the feverishness they dramatize. They cover a wide range. They jerk from Isadora's scarves to Hiroshima ash to lemon water and chicken water; from the bizarre conceit to the simple groping, "whatever these pink things are"; glimpses of horrors to lucidity, self-description, affectionateness, childishness: the range and the confusion establish the state of sickness. There are the other well-known poems of sickness, "Tulips," "In Plaster," and "Paralytic," which dramatize individual, and different, sick states, all of them appropriately formed, in process and style. Each of these four poems is personal (which is not to say that the persona is not imaginary: in "In Plaster" and "Paralytic" it seems to be so, judging from external and internal evidence) but each is a complete and controlled drama of sick mind and body. Because it is sickness that is overtly dramatized, there is no sense of an improperly won competition with the world's ills. They are brought in, by a species of decorous hallucinations. But the plainness of the act of hallucination, the lucid proffering of a febrile, convalescent, enclosed or paralyzed state, allows the larger world to make its presence properly felt. The burning in "Fever 103° " reminds us of atomic ash, while keeping the separation clear. The plaster cast in "In Plaster" reminds us of the other imprisonments and near-successful relationships: "I used to think we might make a go of it together—/After all, it was a kind of marriage, being so close." This is not an allegory about marriage: these poems of sickness allow her to suggest a whole number of identifications which move toward and back from allegory. This is not a sick poem but a poem about being sick. Quite different. Of course it is a sick person who is drawn to poems about sickness, but the physical sickness makes up actual chunks of her existence, and sometimes the poems are about chilblains, cuts, influenza, and appendicitis. She is drawn to sickness, mutilation, attacks, and dying, but each poem is a controlled and dynamic image with windows, not a lining of mirrors. In "Fever 103°" and "In Plaster" the dramatized act of hallucination holds the personal and the social in stable and substantial mutual relationships, neither absorbing the other.

In "Tulips," there is a slow, reluctant acceptance of the tulips, which means a slow, reluctant acceptance of a return to life. The poem dramatizes a sick state, making it clear that it is sickness. The flowers are hateful, as emblems of cruel spring, as presents from the healthy world that wants her back, as suspect, like all presents. They are also emblems of irrational fear: science is brilliantly misused (as indeed in feeble and deranged states of many kinds) and phototro-

pism and photosynthesis are used to argue the fear: the flowers really
do move toward the light, do open out, do take up oxygen. The
tulips are also inhabitants of the bizarre world of private irrational
fantasy, even beyond the bridge of distorted science: they contrast
with the whiteness of nullity and death, are like a baby, an African
cat, are like her wound (a real red physical wound, stitched so as to
heal, not to gape like opened tulips) and, finally, like her heart. The
end of the poem is transforming, opens up the poem. The poem, like
the tulips, has really been opening from the beginning, but all is not
plain until the end, as in "Nick." Moreover, in the end the tulips
win, and that is the point. It is a painful victory for life. We move
from the verge of hallucination, which can hear them as noisy, or
see them as dangerous animals, to a proper rationality, which accepts recovery. The poem hinges on this paradox: while most scientific, it is most deranged; while most surreal, it is most healthy:

> And I am aware of my heart: it opens and closes
> Its bowl of red blooms out of sheer love of me.
> The water I taste is warm and salt, like the sea,
> And comes from a country far away as health.

It is the country she has to return to, reluctant though she is: the
identification of the breathing, opened, red, springlike tulips with
her heart makes this plain. She wanted death, certainly, as one may
want it in illness or, moving back from the poem to the other poems
and to her real death, as she wanted it in life. But the poem enacts
the movement from the peace and purity of anaesthesia and feeble-
ness to the calls of life. Once more, the controlled conceits; and the
movement from one state to another creates expansion. The poem
opens out to our experience of sickness and health, to the overwhelming demands of love, which we sometimes have to meet. The
symbolism of present giving and spring flowers makes a bridge from
a personal death-longing to common experience: something very
similar can be found in the short poem "Poppies in October" which
uses a similar symbolism and situation for a different conclusion and
feeling; and in the magnificent bee poems, where the solid facts and
documentations of beekeeping act as a symbolic base for irrational
and frightening fantasy *and* as a bridge into the everyday and ordinary explanations and existences.

The concept of explicit hallucination seems useful. In the bee
poems we move away from the poetry of sickness to another kind

of rejected allegory. These poems stress technical mysteries. The craft and ritual of beekeeping are described with a Kafkaesque suggestiveness, and can take off into a larger terror and come back after all into the common and solid world. In "The Bee Meeting," her lack of protective clothing, her feeling of being an outsider, then an initiate, the account of the disguised villagers and the final removal of disguise, the queen bee, the spiky gorse, the box—all are literal facts which suggest paranoiac images but remain literal facts. The poem constantly moves between the two poles of actuality and symbolic dimension, right up to and including the end. A related poem, "The Arrival of the Bee Box," works in the same way, but instead of suggesting paranoiac fear and victimization, puts the beekeeper into an unstable allegorical God-position. The casual slangy "but my god" unobtrusively works toward the religious enlargement:

> I am no source of honey
> So why should they turn on me?
> Tomorrow I will be sweet God, I will set them free.
>
> The box is only temporary.

After the suggestiveness comes the last line, belonging more to the literal beekeeping facts, but pulled at least briefly into the symbolic orbit. These are poems of fear, a fear which seems mysterious, too large for its occasion. They allow for a sinister question to raise itself, between the interpretation and the substance. The enlargement which is inseparable from this derangement is morally vital and viable: these poems are about power and fear, killing and living, and the ordinariness and the factual detail work both to reassure us and to establish that most sinister of fears, the fear of the familiar world. Perhaps the most powerful bee poem is "The Swarm." Here the enlargement is total and constant, for the poem equates the destruction of the swarm with a Napoleonic attack, and presents a familiar argument for offensive action: "They would have killed *me.*" It presents two objective correlatives, the bees and Napoleon, in an unfailing grim humor:

> Stings big as drawing pins!
> It seems bees have a notion of honor,
> A black, intractable mind.

Napoleon is pleased, he is pleased with everything.
O Europe! O ton of honey!

The humor comes out of the very act of derangement: imagine comparing this with that, just imagine. It depends on the same kind of rationally alert intelligence that controls "Fever 103°."

It is present in the great *Ariel* poems: "Lady Lazarus," "Daddy," "Death & Co.," "A Birthday Present," and "The Applicant," which are very outgoing, very deranged, very enlarged. In "Lady Lazarus" the persona is split, and deranged. The split allows the poem to peel off the personal, to impersonate suicidal feeling and generalize it. It is a skill, it is a show, something to look at. The poem seems to be admitting the exhibitionism of suicide (and death poetry?) as well as the voyeurism of spectators (and readers?). It is also a foul resurrection, stinking of death. This image allows her to horrify us, to complain of being revived, to attack God and confuse him with a doctor, any doctor (bringing round a suicide) and a Doktor in a concentration camp, experimenting in life and death. It moves from Herr Doktor to Herr Enemy and to miracle makers, scientists, the torturer who may be a scientist, to Christ, Herr God, and Herr Lucifer (the last two after all collaborated in experiments on Adam, Eve, and Job). They poke and nose around in the ashes, and this is the last indignity, forcing the final threat: "I eat men like air." It is a threat that can intelligibly be made by martyred victims (she has red hair, is Jewish), by phoenixes, by fire, by women. The fusion and dispersal, once more rational and irrational, makes the pattern of controlled derangement, creating not one mirror but a hall of mirrors, all differently distorting, and revealing many horrors. Such complexity of reference, such enactment of desperation, hysteria and hate, permits at times the utterly bare cry, like the endearment in "Nick": "I turn and burn." Again, the range of tone is considerable. There is the dry irony, only capable of life in such surroundings of hysteria: "Do not think I underestimate your great concern," and the slangy humor, "I guess you could say I've a call," which, like the communion tablet in "Tulips" is an antireligious joke, not a solemn allusion, though you do not see the joke unless you feel the solemnity. There is the sensuous particularity, extremely unpleasant. It is tactual, visual, and olfactory: "Pick the worms off me like sticky pearls," "full set of teeth" and "sour breath." The sheer active hostility of the poem works through the constant shift from one mode to another, one tone to another, one persona to another. It races violently and spasmodically toward the climax.

This kind of structural derangement of structure, which allows for collision, a complex expansion, and a turn in several directions, sometimes becomes very surrealist in dislocation. It fragments into opaque parts, as in that most baffling poem, "The Couriers," and in "The Applicant." We might be tempted to see the enlargement in "The Applicant" as an allegory of marriage, relationship, dependence, were it not for the violent twist with which the poem shuffles off such suggestion:

> First, are you our sort of a person?
> Do you wear
> A glass eye, false teeth or a crutch,
> A brace or a hook,
> Rubber breasts or a rubber crotch,
>
> Stitches to show something's missing? No, no? Then
> How can we give you a thing?
> Stop crying.
> Open your hand.
> Empty? Empty. Here is a hand
>
> To fill it and willing
> To bring teacups and roll away headaches
> And do whatever you tell it.
> Will you marry it?
> It is guaranteed
>
> To thumb shut your eyes at the end
> And dissolve of sorrow.
> We make new stock from the salt.
> I notice you are stark naked.
> How about this suit—
>
> Black and stiff, but not a bad fit.
> Will you marry it?
> It is waterproof, shatterproof, proof
> Against fire and bombs through the roof.
> Believe me, they'll bury you in it.

The hand to fill the empty hand and shut the eyes, or (later) the naked doll that can sew, cook, talk, move toward this allegory, but the black stiff suit "waterproof, shatterproof" in which "they'll bury you" moves away toward any kind of panacea or protection. What holds the poem together, controlling such opacities of derangement, is the violent statement of deficiency hurled out in the first stanza, and the whole violent imitation of the language of salesmanship, the brisk patter of question, observation, suggestion, and recommendation. The enlargement works not just through the ill-assembled fragments—hand, suit, and in the later stanza, doll—but through the satirized speech, which relates needs, deficiencies, dependence, and stupid panaceas to the larger world. Life (or love) speaks in the cheap-jack voice, as well it may, considering what it may seem to have to offer. This is an applicant not just for relationship, for marriage, for love, for healing, but for life and death.

This brilliant linguistic impersonation works more generally in these poems, as a source of black humor, as satiric enlargement, as a link with ordinariness, as unselfpitying speech. It is present in small doses but with large effect in the massive, rushing, terrible poem, "Getting There." Here the death train is also the painful dying, the dragging life, also wars, machines, labor. The poem questions, and the questions stagger: "How far is it? / How far is it now?" It dwells painfully and slowly in the present tense: "I am dragging my body," "And now detonations," "The train is dragging itself." Its derangements present animals and machines in a mangling confusion: the interior of the wheels is "a gorilla interior," the wheels eat, the machines are brains and muzzles, the train breathes, has teeth, drags and screams like an animal. There is a painful sense of the body's involvement in the machine, the body made to be a wheel. The image creates an entanglement, involves what Sartre calls the "dilapidation" of surrealism. There is the horror of a hybrid monster, a surrealist crossing of animal with machine. The rational arguments and logical connections are frightening in their precision. The wheel and the gorilla's face can be confused into one image, big, round, dark, powerful. Krupp's "brains" is almost literally correct. The train noise can sound like a human scream, the front of a train can look like a face.

The method of combination as well as the content, as in all good poetry, generates the passions. The sense of strain, of hallucination, of doing violence to the human imagery is a consequence of the derangements. The rational excuses simply play into the hands of such sense of strain, by making it work visually, bringing it close, giving it substance and connection with the real European world.

The movement is a double one, it creates a trope and a form for unbearable pain, and intolerable need for release. It enlarges the personal horror and suggests a social context and interpretation, in Krupp, in the train, in Russia, in the marvelously true and fatigued "some war or other," in the nurses, men, hospital, in Adam's side and the woman's body "Mourned by religious figures, by garlanded children." And finally, in Lethe. Its end and climax is as good as that in "Nick":

> And I, stepping from this skin
> Of old bandages, boredoms, old faces
>
> Step to you from the black car of Lethe,
> Pure as a baby.

There is the naked appearance of the myth new made, the feeling that Lethe has had to wait till now to be truly explained, as the Nativity had to wait for "Nick." After such pain of living and dying, after so many bewildered identifications, after such pressure and grotesque confusion, we must step right out of the skin. And when we do, the action reflects back, and the body seems to have been the train. This adds another extension of the derangement of human, animal, and mechanical. After this, only Lethe. The poem then begins to look like a nightmare of dying, the beginning of forgetting, the lurching derangements working as they do in dreams.

Once more, the expansion permits the naked cry. This happens more quietly and sadly in "The Moon and the Yew Tree" where the movement outward is against the Christian myth, but works so as to generalize, to show the active seeking mind in the exercise of knowledge and comparison. This movement explains, permits, and holds up the bare, dreadful admission, "I simply cannot see where there is to get to." The feeling throughout is one of deep and tried depression. The moon is no light, no door:

> It is a face in its own right,
> White as a knuckle and terribly upset.

The oddity and childishness of the funny little analogy and the simple bare statement "terribly upset" all contribute to the tiredness. So does the science of "drags the sea after it like a dark crime" and the conceit "the O-gape of complete despair," which have a slight archness and flickering humor, like someone very tired and wretched who tries to smile. Nature is all too simply interpreted, colored by "the light of the mind," is cold, planetary, black, blue. The moon is quite separate from the consolations of religion, though there are echoes of other myths which emphasize this, of Hecate and witchcraft, as in "The Disquieting Muses." Such sinister suggestions, like the remote and decorative images of the saints, "all blue,/ Floating on their delicate feet over the cold pews,/Their hands and faces stiff with holiness" are made in a matter-of-fact, slightly arch way. These are Stanley Spencer-like visions, made in a childish, tired voice: "The moon is my mother. She is not sweet like Mary./Her blue garments unloose small bats and owls." The very quietness, compared with her more violent poems of fear, has its own stamp of acceptance. The several bald statements in the poem belong to the quiet, tired prevailing tone: "How I would like to believe in tenderness" and "the message of the yew tree is blackness —blackness and silence."

The poem of deep depression still enlarges, still knows about the larger world, still tries a tired but personal humor:

> Eight great tongues affirming the Resurrection.
> At the end, they soberly bong out their names.

The poem's empathy is powerful, but it is perhaps most powerful when it is dropped. The end returns to the explicit act of interpretation—what do the moon and the yew tree mean?—of the beginning. The poem moves heavily into the meditation, then out of it. There has been an attempt at enlargement, but the colors here are the colors of the mind, and the attempts at mythical explanation or extension all fail. It seems like a poem about making the effort to write out of depression, where the act of enlargement is difficult, the distance that can be covered is short.

In "A Birthday Present" the same process shapes a different passion. The enlargement in this poem is again a movement toward Christian myth, this time a perverted annunciation. The poem longs for release, like so many others, but in its individual mood. This time she pleads and reasons carefully, patiently, with humility, is willing to take a long time over it. The pace of her poems varies tremendously, and while "Daddy," "Lady Lazarus," and "Getting There" move with sickening speed, "A Birthday Present" is appallingly slow. Its slowness is right for its patience and its feeling of painful burden. It is created by the pleas, "Let it not . . . Let it not," and the repetitions which here put the brakes on, though in other poems they can act as accelerators. Its questioning slows up, and so does its vagueness, and its unwillingness to argue endlessly—or almost endlessly. The humilities are piteously dramatized: "I would not mind," "I do not want much of a present," "Can you not," "If you only knew," "only you can give it to me," "Let it not." There is the childishness, horrifying in the solemn pleasure of "there would be a birthday." From time to time there is the full, adult, knowing, reasoning voice, that can diagnose: "I know why you will not"; reassure: "Do not be afraid"; and be ironic: "O adding machine—/Is it impossible for you to let something go and have it whole?/ Must you stamp each piece in purple."

It is not surprising that Sylvia Plath felt constrained to speak these late poems: they are dramatized, voiced, often opaque but always personalized. Their enlargements are made within the personal voice: groping for the resemblance to some war, some annunciation, some relationship, some institution, some gothic shape, some prayer, some faith. Even where there is a movement toward the larger world, as in "The Moon and the Yew Tree" or "A Birthday Present," it has a self-consciousness, a deployment of knowledge, a reasoning, a sense of human justice, that keeps it from being sick or private. The woman who measures the flour and cuts off the surplus, adhering "to rules, to rules, to rules," and the mind that sees the shortcomings of adding machines is a persona resisting narcissism and closure, right to the death.

NOTE

1. *The Poet Speaks,* Argo Record Co. No. RG 455, London (recorded October 30, 1962).

Mary Lynn Broe

"Enigmatical, Shifting My Clarities"

> I write only because there
> is a voice within me that
> will not be still.

Twelve years ago, snowbound at an old ski lodge in lower peninsula
Michigan, I listened to tapes of Sylvia Plath reading a handful of late
poems.[1] Poems as varied as "Amnesiac," "Purdah," "Nick and the
Candlestick" and "The Applicant" boomed through the old lodge
with their unexpected and startling tones: a weave of defiance,
cheerful anger, whimper, satire, and sneer. The voice combined
straying Dorothy (a long way from Oz) with vixen Bette Davis
tearing Hellman's tender grapes from the vines. The voice was of
one who gentles the sun, who "intercepts the blue bolts of a cold
moon," but who also begs to be fed "berries of the dark," and who
dares to

> unloose—
> From the small jeweled
> Doll he guards like a heart—
>
> The lioness,
> The shriek in the bath,
> The cloak of holes.
> ("Purdah")

What I heard had nothing to do with previous interpretations of
Sylvia Plath. This was not the Pyrrhic goddess of suicide, no clinically resurrected golden girl with Electra complex, not some Isadora
Duncan reborn into the purer existence of Greek necessity. Here
was no foot-stamping nine-year-old ("the girl who wanted to be
God"), not the tartan-clad coed in love with the "versatility of
sweaters/and men, men, men." Instead I heard the inventive word-
smith, Vulcan of "Fido Littlesoul," "Hagwallow," "Mudsump,"

and "Dogsbody," whose neologisms were tempered by the dramatic impersonations in "Fever 103° " and "The Tour," as well as by the haunting fear of inadequacy and failure: "If I am little, I can do no harm."

We lack a critical vocabulary for these rich tones. We lack a critical vocabulary precisely because our society lacks any definition of power which *transforms* rather than *coerces*. Adrienne Rich describes this kind of power as, in fact, "ourselves as we are/in these painful motions of staying cognizant": power as pain, accuracy, and complexity. And Sylvia Plath's voice is powerful because it succeeds in encompassing—not negating—vital contradictions: no polarities, no classifications, merely "a direct perception of contraries that disposes of argument." Paradoxes that coalesce include the mother who, in the last four months of her life, counseled mere dailiness to her children, a "life no higher than the grasstops or/The hearts of sheep," yet who, at the same time, worshiped a force of pure motion which destabilized her rhetoric:

> Now I break up in pieces that fly about like clubs.
> A wind of such violence
> Will tolerate no bystanding: I must shriek.
>
> ("Elm")

Or

> Is there no still place
> Turning and turning in the middle air,
> Untouched and untouchable.
>
> ("Getting There")

Mock assumptions recklessly mingle with carnival, psychological, and holocaustal imagery in what Plath insisted was a matter of "wresting the wasteful accident of life" into a meaningful pattern.[2] If we are to reconcile these counsels of minimalism with the astringently defiant self-spectacles, we must braid them together in that feminine weave of gabardine and flannel, khakhi and cotton voile of handloomed rag rug—the tangible, textured thing made by hand that Plath infinitely preferred over mere crochet or embroidery (*J*, 295).

I knew when I heard those poems that we had not been asking the right questions. Even now, it is hard to ask questions with any expectation of an answer. Sylvia Plath's own weirdly futuristic warning of "Lady Lazarus" echoes against this posthumous use, this fashioning her into a *mythos ex machina:*

> Do I terrify?—
>
> The nose, the eyepits, the full set of teeth?
> . . . .
> The peanut-crunching crowd
> Shoves in to see
>
> Them unwrap me hand and foot—
> The big strip tease.
> Gentlemen, ladies
>
> These are my hands
> My knees.
> I may be skin and bone,
>
> Nevertheless, I am the same, identical woman.
> . . . .
> For the eyeing of my scars, there is a charge
> For the hearing of my heart—
> It really goes.
>
> And there is a charge, a very large charge
> For a word or a touch
> Or a bit of blood
> . . . .
> I am your opus,
> I am your valuable,
> The pure gold baby
>
> That melts to a shriek.

There has been, as Plath herself feared, what might be called a "sleight of fact." For the real Plath myth is not the poet herself— not "Plath as her own prosthesis," as one recent reviewer claimed[3] —but the Plath chronology of the past twenty years. Diagnostic critics continue to prescribe in glib partisanship polarities for the warring selves: "imminent volcano" versus the "prickly defense," the homeostatic versus the lithic impulse, ingenue versus bitch goddess, and at last, writer versus mother.

. . . Give me back my shape

In a rather ironic display of "psychic osmosis" Plath, at a certain point in her career, recycled her intellectual and creative heritage as official Muse. The *Letters Home* verify that while she may have begun and ended her career as Pygmalion, Plath spent a great part of it as Galatea, inextricably confusing her poetic identity with the stimulation of romantic involvement. In one letter to her mother, for example, Plath talks of "becoming one with myself, growing toward the best in me." At the same time she brags that Hughes "will work with me and make me a woman poet like the world will gape at." Acting as Hughes's U.S. literary agent, Plath typed and kept circulating at all times at least thirty of his manuscripts. She scouted the Amherst job scene for him, cooked, kept house, arranged several moves, prepared for her own Newnham honors exams, ambitiously calculated her own stories for "the big money slicks," while she held a grueling "composition" job at Smith. "I am using every fiber of my being to love him," she bluntly announced. And then: "he is always just that many steps ahead of me intellectually and creatively, so that I feel very feminine and admiring".[4]

It is in Plath's *Journals,* however, that she and Hughes's "impregnable togetherness" reaches epic proportions, marking creative resources in the service of the romantic imagination. At Cambridge, in the first year of their marriage, Plath says: "my whole being has grown and interwound so completely with Ted's that if anything were to happen to him, I do not see how I could live. I would either go mad, or kill myself. I cannot conceive of life without him" (*J,* 156). And a few months later on Cape Cod: "We will work. And he sets the sea of life steady, flooding it with the deep rich color of his mind and his love and constant amaze at his perfect being: as if I had conjured, at last, a god from the slack tides" (*J,* 165). Or early in 1958 at Smith College, Plath boasts: "But I got rid of my gloom and sulking sorrows by spending the day typing sheafs of Ted's new poems. I live in him until I live on my own" (*J,* 185). At times Plath waxes purely sacramental: "I need Ted . . . as I need bread and wine" (*J,* 200). Or, "Strange what vicarious pleasure I get from Ted's acceptances: pure sheer joy; almost as if he were holding the field open, keeping a foot in the door to the golden world, and thus keeping a place for me" (*J,* 202). "My savior," "the god creator risen," she spoke of him. "This is the man the unsatisfied ladies scan the stories in *The Ladies' Home Journal* for . . ." (*J*, 221). "He is a genius. I his wife" (*J*, 259). And back in Boston in 1958: "Whatever Ted does, I'd like to submit myself to it . . . a long discipleship" (*J*, 283). Only late in 1959 does she dare to suggest, "Dangerous to be so close to Ted day in and day out. I have no life separate from his, am likely to become a mere accessory . . . I am inclined to go passive, let Ted be my social self" (*J*, 328).

While the heritage of Aurelia Plath's adoring handmaidenhood seems appropriate here (much of Aurelia Plath's marriage was spent aiding Otto Plath in his career; in the last years of his life she served as his "nurse" as he suffered from diabetes), other factors limit its complete success. Plath the daughter searches for a healthier matrilineal bond *both* as a point of identification *and* abrasion. She runs through a virtual litany of women: Olive Prouty, Dr. Ruth Beuscher, Mary Ellen Chase, Dorothea Krook, Joan, Jaycee, and an inexhaustible battery of roommates. Louise Bernikow has charged Plath with being the perpetual daughter,[5] but the important point is that Plath enlarges the definition of motherhood from one of passivity to an active transforming power.

Plath searches for maternal recognition temporarily in lieu of naming her own sensibility. The comic women performers of the early Smith poems (who, by the way, have learned a bitter lesson about harboring too lively an imagination) become the ultimate mother-sponsors of tangible realities in the late volumes, *Ariel* and *Winter Trees.* Knowing a mother's feeling of powerful love for, yet vulnerable separateness from, her children's lives, they uphold simple, factual existence—things with "little particular lusters," the sun blooming like a geranium, a brass paperweight, salt-stiffened sails, the "haloey glow of a single candle's power," or "whatever green stars can make it to our gate." In between, Plath explores in *Crossing the Water* woman's myth heritage ("Witch-burning," "Stillborn," "Magi," and others) at the same time she searches for a poetic form appropriate *to*—and a literary version *of*—her emotional growth.

The poet's impulse to transform the mother-daughter bond is a model for the transforming protean impulse behind all of Plath's poetry. As Helen Vendler says, she longs to capture the contours of the mind's own specificity, the "truth of the mental quirk of the moment, the individual feeling over the habitual one, the spontaneous over the rehearsed response, the fluctuations of consciousness rather than its rigidities."[6] With true imaginative modification, Plath transforms her pleas to the various mothers with the same energy she transforms herself: while she may be tiny and inert as a rice grain, she may also be the "mother of white Nike and several bald-eyed Apollos." While she can announce, "Empty, I echo to the last footfall," she can also boast: "I shone mica-scaled, and unfolded/To pour myself out like a fluid."

Frequently the daughter recognizes the intrusion of—even catalysis by—another force apart from the mother, some impersonal male one: "Hairtusk," "bullman," "happy sty-face," "Fido Littlesoul," the "Bowel's familiar," "Mumblepaws," or "Dogsbody." In "Maenad," the banal realm of the father, collapsed in its own unnatural fictions ("The birds made milk"), functions as an unlikely catalyst for the young girl's changes which will prove her anything *but* an ordinary poet. The boast of the willfully naïve persona only prompts, by the poem's end, a greater dramatic awareness of her reluctant progress toward a more complex identity:

> Once I was ordinary:
> Sat by my father's bean tree
> Eating the fingers of wisdom.
> The birds made milk.
> When it thundered I hid under a flat stone.
>
> The mother of mouths didn't love me.
> The old man shrank to a doll.

As the poet stops dissembling, the framework of a fairy-tale narrative is abandoned. She shifts her power to a new linearity ("the lids won't shut"), uttering direct imperatives, stark statements of fact, and a pointed warning: "Mother, keep out of my barnyard,/I am becoming another." She knows something momentous is happening to her, feels its complications, but has no words for it yet: "Time/Unwinds from the great umbilicus of the sun/Its endless glitter.//I must swallow it all." So, foundering in *process*—the fluid state we know is representative of female personality formation—and at times misguided by childish fear, the daughter ends the poem with the only role she knows. She pleads for a mother-assigned identity for her enlarged dramatic awareness:

> Lady, who are these others in the moon's vat—
> Sleepdrunk, their limbs at odds?
> In this light the blood is black.
> *Tell me my name.* [Italics mine]

But just as her search in *The Colossus* for intersections between the worlds of poetic and visual art met with ambiguous silence, Plath meets with silence in her attempt to name her forceful changing, to describe her dramatic energy. The question asked, rather than the fact of no response, becomes the power: "What am I to make of these contradictions?"

For the world of the father fails her by obscuring reality:

> O I am too big to go backward:
> Birdmilk is feathers,
> The bean leaves are dumb as hands.

Power gained in the poet's kind of revision may free her to make a stark, linear plea, but she still shows a complex reaction to that woman who represents to us "the unfree, the victim, the martyr." She is the one with whom "our personalities seem dangerously to blur and overlap," according to Adrienne Rich. The poet blurts out: "Mother, stay out of my barnyard/I am becoming another," or:

> Give me back my shape. I am ready to construe the days
> I coupled with dust in the shadow of a stone.
> My ankles brighten. Brightness ascends my thighs.
> I am lost, I am lost in the robes of all this light.
>
> ("Witch Burning")

That complex process of interplay between the history a woman inherits and the clear articulation of her developing consciousness is no more able to be disentangled than the saintly white plaster cast ("In Plaster") can be severed from the hairy, shrunken body within: "Without me, she wouldn't exist . . . I wasn't in any position to get rid of her." Interdependent, each is inextricably bound to the other for versions of *sameness* as well as *difference*. ("Two, of course, there are two./It seems perfectly natural now—" Plath claims in "Death & Co.") For unlike the *male* identity formation, a single-shot initiatory rite of either triumph or failure, Plath's search for identity, for the "contours of the mind's own specificity," is a tribute to the flexible, protean nature of *female* identity formation. If for a moment we imagine received history as the saintly white plaster cast around the hairy yellow, developing consciousness in the poem "In Plaster," the dialogue becomes more revealing. While "without me" the "she" of received history "wouldn't exist," the developing "I" isn't "in any position to get rid of her." The dialogue between the cast and the body, the substance of the poem, suggests an interrelationship that is close to Rich's description of the power of mother-bond: it "cracks consciousness, threatens at times to lead the daughter back into those secret chambers . . . becoming like waters poured in one jar, inextricably the same, one with the object adored."

One poem in particular explores the intricate legacy existing between mother and daughter. In "The Disquieting Muses" the mother's world and the function of the female inheritance prompt the daughter to accept her distinct mission as a woman artist. Again what is suggested is the powerful but often contradictory "osmotic bond" between mother and daughter: "I learned, I learned elsewhere/From muses unhired by you, dear mother." The poem rehearses the painful but requisite stages in the daughter's becoming a fully conscious woman. But as she moves *physically* from naïveté to a powerful acceptance of the female tradition, the *physical* dynamics of the poem tell a different story. The dismal, bald-headed muses, borrowed from the world of art (de Chirico's *Les Muses Inquiétantes*), gradually overwhelm her. In the course of the poem, the awesome silence of these woman figures—*the sheer weight and volume of it*—contrasts with the credulous daughter's narration of childhood and adolescent anecdotes. As the heaps of childhood words and images fill space—gingerbread witches, twinkle dresses, the "glowworm song" on the piano, the mother's soap-bubble unreality—they exhaust and deplete the daughter's real world. In contrast, those "dismal-headed" godmothers grow in volume, intensity, their shadows physically lengthening, stretching, and finally altogether enveloping the poet:

> Day now, night now, at head, side, feet,
> They stand their vigil in gowns of stone . . .

Curiously, it is in the *daughter's perception* that these muses change from vengeful wedding Furies (slighted, according to fairy-tale protocol because they were not invited to a christening) to unwitting mentors, insistent guides, and finally—reluctantly—to the daughter's "traveling companions." Their animated weight contrasts to the ephemeral world of the mother which does, quite literally, bob away "like a soap bubble." The poet cannot locate with a name, or shape to the contours of her imagination, the mother's sentimental fictions. For the daughter, only continual and forceful changing—a process undetermined by a name—is her reality, one for which she alone must find expressive form in art.

The force of "The Disquieting Muses" seems to be this: while the daughter has no use for adopting the mother's "soap-bubble" world, she is, nevertheless, catalyzed by it. But, tragically, the daughter has not yet formed a substitute reality of her own. Inarticulate as the nodding muses, she can only measure how far her own emotional imaginative transformations are from the mother's. The final three lines of the poem are a consummate achievement in tone, surely one of the clearest tributes to Plath's sophisticated emotional range. The lines express her willingness to risk nonresolution and ambivalence, her reluctance toward—yet absolute necessity for— allegiance to the other realm, the Muses' kingdom of the creative imagination:

> And this is the kingdom you bore me to,
> Mother, mother. But no frown of mine
> Will betray the company I keep.

How different are the poems of *Crossing the Water* from the sound-clotted, turgid early poems of, say, the Cambridge Manuscript, poems which show a peculiar womanly silence in their linguistic compression.[7] They are not nimble works. They strive after grand effects in an overzealous, student way. "Lucky strike jungle verse," Plath called it. The poet's credo in these early poems—"I imagine, therefore I am"—is repeatedly corrected in little pat narratives in which women are disciplined for excesses of imagination. And the imagination seems awkward, ready to break out of those contrived forms: terza rima, villanelle, varieties of sonnet. In a number of such verses, Hughes is praised for his catalytic role—"Wreath for a Bridal," "Epitaph for Fire and Flower"—but these so-called "great paeans to creativity and love" are virtually *unreadable*. Linguistic survival in many such early poems is, as one Plath poem describes, a matter of our doing "verbal calisthenics" with themes!

How different, too, are *The Colossus* poems, where the search for maternal connections in the realm of visual arts and graphic landscapes results in discovery of ambiguous silence. The too-ideal deranging harmony of those sirens, the Lorelei, lead the poet to beg:

"Stone, stone, ferry me down there." The search for such a voice, however, lacks empathic identification: "It is not I, it is not I." In "Point Shirley," clearly one of the finest poems in *The Colossus*, the emotional power of identification with the grandmother—prover-bial, unspoken—threatens to break out of rigid formal structure in its "collusion of mulish elements":

> And I come by
> Bones, bones only, pawed and tossed,
> . . . .
> I would get from these dry-papped stones
> The milk your love instilled in them.
> The black ducks dive.
> And though your graciousness might stream,
> And I contrive,
> Grandmother, stones are nothing of home
> To that spumiest dove.
> Against both bar and tower the black sea runs.

. . . but I have a self to recover

Among the late poems, Plath's six poems on the art of beekeeping[8] redefine a kind of power: that which transforms and is located in the queen mother here. As the poems in the sequence describe a young girl's movement from youthful naïveté to historical disillusionment, they look *backward* in their anatomy of the process of maturation to *Crossing the Water*, *forward* to the cultural revision of power inherent in the simple factual reality counseled by the mother of *Winter Trees:* "Meaning leaks from the molecules. . . .//The heart has not stopped" ("Mystic").

Now the microcosm of the bee world becomes the poet's vehicle to redefine power in its many shapes—seller, worker-drudge, keeper, even queen. However, the poet *revises* the highly organized and scientifically regulated world of her father: it is important to note that his theoretical world of *bumblebees* becomes *her* real world of *honeybees*. And as we watch the poetic employed in the six poems change from dramatic enactment of growing consciousness to the spare imagism, the poems physically, metrically, replicate the power of the minimal, for the queen displays a capacity of the imagination over the mere physical will-to-power of the father, the beekeeper,

maestro, "Hieratical in your frock coat." As overt physical power
begins to suffer in the sequence, the form of the verse becomes more
and more cryptic and compressed. Finally in "Wintering," the
drone-workers' power of minimal survival and self-determination is
praised: "It is *they* who own *me,*" the keeper of the bees announces.
And he echoes the safe, minimal reality praised by the mother in
poems as widely separated in the Plath canon as "Resolve" (1956)
and "Sheep in Fog," revised as late as January 28, 1963:

> The hills step off into whiteness.
> People or stars
> Regard me sadly, I disappoint them.
>
> The train leaves a line of breath.
> O slow
> Horse the color of rust,
>
> Hooves, dolorous bells—
> . . . .
> My bones hold a stillness, the far
> Fields melt my heart.

Central to Plath's developing consciousness, and visually central
in the sequence, is "Stings." It seems that in the queen bee's double-
bind situation, Plath identifies with the complexities of her institu-
tional position as queen versus her experiences as mother. The
young girl makes this stark discovery of kinship as early as the first
poem, "Beekeeper's Daughter":

> Here is a queenship no mother can contest—
> A fruit that's death to taste: dark flesh, dark parings.
> . . . .
> I set my eye to a hole-mouth and meet an eye
> Round, green, disconsolate as a tear.

(We must remember that the apiary is a world of curiously inverted
sexual principles. The queen, parthenogenic, can only produce idle
male drones—"the blunt clumsy stumblers, the boors"—who will
ruin the hive. Only the drone mate can contribute the female principle to the union.) One law, however, is central to the apiary. The
queen, old and plushless, neither directs nor participates in any of
her subjects' riches of cross-pollination, never sees daylight, has no
bodily provisions for work. To her the virgin worker's world of

activity is "death to the taste." She remains ill-fated, hidden, and otherwise useless in her singular mission of motherhood.

The paradoxical nature of the queen extends to other levels as well. The queen lives for one moment—a brief nuptial flight, blend of ecstasy and tragedy, life and death. Apiarists tell us that the mate of the queen—chosen from thousands of suitors who pursue her high-spiraling nuptial flight—lives for a single moment of delight. But in this instant of "dark pa(i)ring" as he impregnates the queen, his abdomen slits open, loosing the entrails which the queen then totes behind her as a kind of triumphal banner. Dispensable (his death required for propagation of the hive), the mate falls to earth as a carcass. The queen sports her murderous trophy, proof she has guaranteed the future of the hive.

Yet when required, the queen can be mistress of evasion, proving her cleverness by refusing to show herself in the smoking-out ritual (when the virgins are moved so they do not kill the old queen bee). "She is very clever./She is old, old, old, she must live another year, and she knows it." Her power is in *absence:* refusing to show herself in duel with younger virgins or to escape some random fate from villagers. To her—and this is what Plath learns about *power* in a sequence where physical power is at least undermined, if not continually mocked—power is an attitude, a matter of perceiving life and death, the familiar and the terrible comprehensively, wholly. She manipulates the visible from the vantage point of isolation. Though physically her fate is in others' hands, imaginatively she remains untouched, "sealed in wax." Likewise the young girl speaker at the bee induction—exhausted from the tedium of ignorance, fear, and hosts of unanswered questions—chooses *immobility*. Despite outward conformity, she remains a "gullible head untouched by their [the bees'] animosity."

In "Stings" the speaker successively dons the roles of beekeeper, honey-drudge, and queen in a dramatic exploration of their various functions. "It is almost over./I am in control," she announces midway through the process of adopting and rejecting various forms of power. And indeed Plath *is* in control. She conducts us from the literal level of "sweet bargaining" for honey, through the mechanical collection of it by drudges, finally to the queen bee's controlling *inactivity* which is her last triumph.

In the final stanza, despite the imagined ritual deaths throughout

the sequence, the elusive queen, at last visible, is a triumph of contradictions. She comprises images of illness, vulnerability (red scar,
wings of glass) as well as those of vital resilience. Here—in fact, in
the whole sequence—*the authoritative mode is abandoned.*

The last two poems in the sequence—"Wintering" and "The
Swarm"—praise the self-determining minimal survival of the work-
ers in winter. Here we find an application of the power-in-evasive-
ness suggested by the queen's existence. In "The Swarm," the physical self-defensive will is mocked, indicating the historical plight of
imaginative and emotional versus physical power. History is collapsed into 1) the man with "asbestos receptacles" for hands, the
victim of self-delusion with his Napoleonic master plan; and 2) the
swarm, with its collective delusions of grandeur. In this poem,
the most facile sort of power-mongering functions as a defunct
comic backdrop, much as the "lamp-headed Platos" and the "gray
Magi" do in later poems. Bearing "the star, the old story" as they
gobble the "pill of the Communion tablet," they contrast to the
matrilineal world of "sheep and wagons,/Red earth, motherly
blood," for throughout the late poems, Plath, "having one too many
dimensions to enter," begs repeatedly for a remedy for seeing and
feeling too much:

> Once one has seen God, what is the remedy?
> Once one has been seized up
>
> Without a part left over,
> Not a toe, not a finger, and used,
> Used utterly, in the sun's conflagrations, the stains
> That lengthen from ancient cathedrals
> What is the remedy?
> . . . .
> Is there no great love, only tenderness?
>
>   ("Mystic")

Likewise, in the last poem of the bee sequence, history defers to the
illusionless reality of "The woman, still at her knitting,/At the
cradle of Spanish walnut,/Her body a bulb in the cold. . . ."

In her bee poems, Plath repeats the process of discovering a new
tonal authority that she has enacted in many earlier poems. But now
she does so within the cultural-historical context of the apiary, and
within the revised context of a personal, patriarchal legacy. (Her
father was a Boston biologist, author of *Bumblebees and Their Ways.*

Otto Plath actually became the real prototype of self-destruction for her; he willed his own death by refusing life-saving medical care. He eventually died from advanced effects of diabetes mellitus.) This bee sequence in particular signals the measure of Plath's poetic strength, for here she convincingly articulates a revision of personal as well as historical forms of power. Plath proves that she has found both a critical and an emotional vocabulary for *encompassing*—not pejoratively canceling out—the vital contradictions of her last poems. With their pure clean lyrical rhythms that, like spirit voices, swell up from under, the last poems counsel adherence to the ordinary anonymous life. In addition, the frenetic wit and bodily gusto of other self-spectacles move theatrically through time and history as if to deny the limitations of each—"the pure acetylene virgin" who rises, beads of hot metal flying, selves dissolving.

NOTES

1. Sylvia Plath taped thirteen poems and an interview with Peter Orr for the BBC on October 30, 1962.

2. *The Journals of Sylvia Plath* (New York: The Dial Press, 1982), p. 131. Future references to the *Journals* will be abbreviated by *J* and included in the text.

3. Irvin Ehrenpreis, "The Other Sylvia Plath," *New York Review of Books* (February 4, 1982), p. 24.

4. *Letters Home* by Sylvia Plath. Correspondence, 1950–1963, selected and edited with commentary by Aurelia Schober Plath (New York: Harper & Row, 1975), page 270. Future references to *Letters Home* will be abbreviated *LH* and included in the text.

5. Louise Bernikow, *Among Women* (New York: Harper & Row, 1980), p. 63. Additional mother-daughter references are from Adrienne Rich's *Of Woman Born: Motherhood as Experience and Institution* (New York: W.W. Norton and Co., 1976).

6. Helen Vendler, "The Poetry of Sylvia Plath," Ziskind Lecture Series, Part I (December 13, 1971), p. 7, a lecture on file in the Sophia Smith Women's Archives, Smith College.

7. Jeanne Kammer, "The Art of Silence and the Forms of Women's Poetry," p. 156. The essay is included in *Shakespeare's Sisters*, edited by Sandra Gilbert and Susan Gubar (London and Bloomington: Indiana University Press, 1979).

8. General source information on bee culture is given in my book, *Protean Poetic* or, more specifically, in my article, "Recovering the Complex Self: Sylvia Plath's Beeline," *Centennial Review* 24 (Winter 1980), pp. 1–24.

Katha Pollitt

A Note of Triumph

ON THE COLLECTED POEMS

Literary evaluations of Sylvia Plath have a way of turning into sermons, in which critics forsake close reading in favor of moral pronouncements on whatever issues strike them as pertinent to her case. Is life worth living? Most critics think it is. Is madness admirable? Most agree it is not. Are men the enemy? A chorus of cheers from feminists. Can one justifiably connect one's small, private, middle-class life with fascism, war, and the Holocaust? Yes, claims A. Alvarez, for whom Plath is the ultimate literary risk-taker. No, argues Irving Howe, who is not only outraged by Plath's appropriation of the death camps to her personal situation but does not understand what, exactly, she was so upset about, anyway. The very fact that Plath was a woman has dazed many a strong mind. For Stephen Spender she is "a priestess cultivating her hysteria"; for Robert Lowell she is "hardly a person at all, or a woman," but Dido, Phaedra, Medea. George Steiner sees her poems as propelled by "the need of a superbly intelligent, highly literate young woman to cry out about her especial being, about the tyrannies of blood and gland, of nervous spasm and sweating skin, the rankness of sex and childbirth in which a woman is still compelled to be wholly of her organic condition." And you thought men sweated too.

What lies behind these responses is Plath's suicide—she killed herself, as all the world knows, in the winter of 1963 while separated from her husband, the British poet Ted Hughes. She was not, as many feminists like to think, completely unknown at the time of her death. Hughes's reputation was much more established, but Plath had won grants and prizes, had been published in magazines and had received favorable, although not very insightful, reviews of her first book of poems, *The Colossus,* which came out in 1960. It was the

94

posthumous publication of *Ariel* in 1965, though, that made her fame—the wrong kind of fame, for it was based on the notion that her poems could be read as if they were a suicide note that "explained" her death. The possibility that her poems made a literary shape of their own has only recently been considered.

Probably nothing could have prevented the sensationalizing of Plath's work. Her voice, once she found it, was too strong, too strange, not to have struck a note of challenge, her life too brief and intense not to have been packaged as that of yet another doomed female genius. It must be said, though, that the way in which her work was presented to the public did little to bring about a better understanding of it. There was the chronologically jumbled release of her poems in the two post-*Ariel* volumes, *Winter Trees* and *Crossing the Water* (both 1971). There was the publication of still more poems in tiny limited editions and the failure to publish others at all. Most important, though, was the fact that *Ariel* itself, as printed, was not the manuscript of that name completed by Plath three months before her death but a selection put together by her executors in an order of their choosing.

The published book contained poems written after Plath's manuscript had been completed, an addition for which we must be grateful. But it omitted poems Plath herself had chosen for the book: "Mystic," "Purdah," "Brasilia," "The Jailer," and others. This editorial decision meant that late poems of great distinction were out of circulation while Plath's literary place was being debated; those that did belatedly appear, in *Winter Trees*, were mingled with poems Plath had put aside, and were discounted along with them.

Worse, the published *Ariel* destroyed the artistic pattern of Plath's manuscript. The *Ariel* we know ends on a note of absolute despair, and virtually invites the reader to luxuriate in the *frisson* of knowing that a week after writing "Edge" ("The woman is perfected./Her dead//Body wears the smile of accomplishment"), Plath would herself be dead. The actual manuscript ended quite differently, on the note of triumph sounded by the magnificent cycle of bee poems, whose subject is the reclaiming of an autonomous womanly self. Its final word, as Plath noted, was "spring." Would it have made a difference to her reputation, I wonder, if Plath's pattern had been preserved, with the last poems added as a separate section? Or even if a complete edition of her poems had appeared, say, ten years ago, when interest in Plath was still high?

Well, who knows. Plath's image may be too firmly established by now for any information short of news that she is alive and living in Brazil to alter it, but those who care can at long last have her work entire, in a handsome edition chronologically arranged, introduced and annotated by Ted Hughes. *The Collected Poems* is a beautiful book, prepared with seriousness and love. Every poet should be so well served—although I do think most would prefer to forgo the hefty appendix of high school and college verse included in the volume.

Complete collections often have an unintended effect: instead of displaying a poet's accomplishment, they subtly diminish it. Swamped by their pale, sluggish brothers and sisters, the special poems seem less and less unusual. We put the book away with the thought that the poet was, after all, quite right to have left half his work in the drawer.

That is not what happens with Plath's *Collected Poems*. One reason is that Plath was a superb craftsman who never, Hughes tells us, abandoned a poem until it had "exhausted her ingenuity." She wrote recalcitrant poems and failed poems, but none that were idle or blathering or tentative. With very few exceptions, every poem has a shape of its own. Another reason is that she was dazzlingly inventive. Even poems that fail to come off frequently contain lines of extraordinary loveliness. "Ouija" may bog down in Stevensish rhetoric, but it opens with eerie splendor: "It is a chilly god, a god of shades,/Rises to the glass from his black fathoms." The dreadful "Leaving Early," a savage account of a visit to an elderly woman who has somehow incurred the poet's hatred, offers the startling image of the poet "bored as a leopard" in her hostess's fuggy living room.

But the most important source of the pleasure to be found in these pages is the fact that Plath's was one of those rare poetic careers —Keats's was another—that moved consistently and with gathering rapidity and assurance to an ever greater daring and individuality. She was always becoming more distinctly herself, and by the time she came to write her last seventy or eighty poems, there was no other voice like hers on earth. Her end may have been tragic, her character not what we would choose in our friends, but her work records a triumph.

It was not an easy process. *The Collected Poems* shows just how hard Plath worked to transform herself from a subdued, well-man- nered student of Auden, Eliot, Ransom, and Lowell into the effortlessly associative poet of the late work. Discards vastly outnumber "book poems" in the entries for 1956–1959, the years Plath was working on *The Colossus,* and it's hard to disagree with her verdicts. For all their skill, the rejects strike me as devitalized, strangled by the very technical proficiency that was later to be so liberating:

> Loam-humps, he says, moles shunt
> up from delved worm-haunt;
> blue fur, moles have; hefting chalk-hulled flint
> he with rock splits open
> knobbed quartz; flayed colors ripen
> rich, brown, sudden in sunglint.
>
> ("Ode for Ted")

The Colossus is a book of considerable interest quite apart from the fact that it was written by the author of *Ariel.* "Black Rook in Rainy Weather," "The Disquieting Muses," "Full Fathom Five," "All the Dead Dears," and many others have a controlled, melancholy beauty and a redeeming wit. Yet all but a handful—the musical, dreamlike "Lorelei," the playful "Mushrooms," and "The Thin People"—have about them a quality of having been willed into existence, of having fought for breath against an anxiety or depression that threatened to engulf them:

> Leaning over, I encounter one
> Blue and improbable person
>
> Framed in a basketwork of cat-tails.
> O she is gracious and austere,
> Seated beneath the toneless water!
> It is not I, it is not I.
>
> No animal spoils on her green doorstep.
> And we shall never enter there
> Where the durable ones keep house.
> The stream that hustles us
>
> Neither nourishes nor heals.
>
> ("The Burnt-out Spa")

"A fury of frustration," she wrote after completing the elegant pastoral "Watercolor of Grantchester Meadows." "Some inhibition keeping me from writing what I really feel."

It is certainly cause for wonder that this same poet should a mere three years later be turning out poems like "Daddy," "Lady Lazarus," and "Elm" with the speed, in Hughes's phrase, of urgent letters. Nonetheless, critics who deny a continuity between the early and late Plaths—usually to dismiss one in favor of the other —will want to rethink their positions in light of the wealth of evidence provided in *The Collected Poems* for a broadly continuous development. As the chronological arrangement makes clear, Plath found and lost her voice many times. "The Stones," the first poem that hints at the new manner, was followed by a raft of poems in the old. The old bobs up long after the new has established itself: the Lowellian exercise "The Babysitters" postdates "The Rival" and "Tulips."

On the deeper level of themes and images, there was not so much a rift as a reformulation. Throughout her career, Plath worked with a tightly connected cluster of concerns—metamorphosis, rebirth, the self as threatened by death, the otherness of the natural world, fertility and sterility—and applied them all to what she saw as the central situation of her life, the death of her worshiped father when she was eight years old and the complex emotions of loss, guilt, and resentment it aroused in her even as an adult. But where the early Plath is autobiographical, Freudian ("Electra on Azalea Path," "The Colossus"), the later Plath is working in another mode entirely—of fixed symbols, drama, and myth.

Jon Rosenblatt has argued that the late poems are governed by a vision of "negative vitalism," a conviction that all life is at the mercy of a cosmic, merciless principle of death, of which the dead father—along with God, male-dominated marriage, fascism, war and mass society—is only an aspect. Judith Kroll, who has traced the profound influence on Plath of Robert Graves's *The White Goddess*, makes a similar point, and shows how Plath cast her life in the form of a ritual drama of death and rebirth which the poems enact. "Tulips," "Ariel," "Daddy," and "A Birthday Present" are thus not confessional poems in which the poet displays her wounds, but dramatic monologues in which the speaker moves from a state of psychological bondage to freedom, from spiritual death to life, with suicide, paradoxically, standing as a metaphor for this transformation. In the late poems, Plath enters the world of death—the hospital room in "Tulips," the death train in "Getting There," the fever-induced fantasy of Hades in "Fever 103° "—suffers a ritual death and emerges reborn. This explains why Plath described Lady Lazarus, who is a kind of professional suicide ("One year in every ten

I manage it"), as having "the great and terrible gift of being reborn
. . . . She is the Phoenix, the libertarian spirit, what you will":

> Herr God, Herr Lucifer
> Beware
> Beware.
>
> Out of the ash
> I rise with my red hair
> and I eat men like air.
> ("Lady Lazarus")

The impact of "Ariel" has been so great that other late poems,
as well as the "transitional" ones of the early 1960s, have been
overshadowed. One of the accomplishments of *The Collected Poems*
is, I hope, to remind us of the strength of much of this work. Any
poet less rapidly evolving than Plath would have been tempted to
rest on such laurels as "I am Vertical," "Wuthering Heights," and
"Parliament Hill Fields." It is a great thing, too, to see late poems
like "Stopped Dead," "Purdah," and "The Jailer" placed, finally, at
the culmination of Plath's career, where they belong.

All these poems, but especially the late ones, fill out and qualify
our sense of Plath's vision. To give but one instance: the critics who
see her work as a rejection of life, and the feminists, too, will have
to come to terms with the tenderness and purity of Plath's maternal
feelings, as displayed in "Brasilia," "Child," "For a Fatherless Son,"
and her radio verse play *Three Women*.

If Sylvia Plath were alive now, she would be younger than
Adrienne Rich, John Ashbery, Philip Levine, and W. S. Merwin—
younger, incredibly, than Allen Ginsberg. It is often said that when
she died, she had gone as far as poetry could take her, and indeed,
the very last poems do seem to leave no way out. I cannot believe,
though, that a poet as fertile and energetic and fearless as Plath could
ever be reduced to silence by her own imagination. Had she lived,
like Lady Lazarus, she would surely have transformed herself yet
again, as she had done before.

Elizabeth Hardwick

On Sylvia Plath

In Sylvia Plath's work and in her life the elements of pathology are so deeply rooted and so little resisted that one is disinclined to hope for general principles, sure origins, applications, or lessons. Her fate and her themes are hardly separate and both are singularly terrible. Her work is brutal, like the smash of a fist; and sometimes it is also mean in its feeling. Literary comparisons are possible, echoes vibrate occasionally, but to whom can she be compared in spirit, in content, in temperament?

Certain frames for her destructiveness have been suggested by critics. Perhaps being born a woman is part of the exceptional rasp of her nature, a woman whose stack of duties was laid over the ground of genius, ambition, and grave mental instability. Or is it the 1950s, when she was going to college, growing up—is there something of that here? Perhaps; but I feel in her a special lack of national and local roots, feel it particularly in her poetry, and this I would trace to her foreign ancestors on both sides. They were given and she accepted them as a burden, not as a gift; but there they were, somehow cutting her off from what they weren't. Her father died when she was eight years old and this was serious, central. Yet this most interesting part of her history is so scorched by resentment and bitterness that it's only the special high burn of the bitterness that allows us to imagine it as a cutoff love.

For all the drama of her biography, there is a peculiar remoteness about Sylvia Plath. A destiny of such violent self-definition does not always bring the real person nearer; it tends, rather, to invite iconography, to freeze our assumptions and responses. She is spoken of as a "legend" or a "myth"—but what does that mean? Sylvia Plath was a luminous talent, self-destroyed at the age of thirty, likely to remain, it seems, one of the most interesting poets in American literature. As an *event* she stands with Hart Crane, Scott Fitzgerald, and Edgar Allen Poe rather than with Emily Dickinson, Marianne Moore, or Elizabeth Bishop.

The outlines of her nature are odd, especially in her defiant and extensive capabilities, her sense of mastery, the craft and preparation she almost humbly and certainly industriously acquired as the foundation for an overwhelming ambition. She was born in Jamaica Plain, Massachusetts. Her mother's parents were Austrian; her father was a German, born in Poland. He was a professor of biology, a specialist, among other interests, in bee-raising. (The ambiguous danger and sweetness of the beehive—totemic, emblematic for the daughter.) Her father died and the family moved to Wellesley, Massachusetts, to live with her grandparents. The mother became a teacher and the daughter went to public schools and later to Smith College. Sylvia Plath was a thorough success as a student and apparently was driven to try to master everything life offered—study, cooking, horseback riding, writing, being a mother, housekeeping. There seemed to have been in her character no empty patch or seam left for the slump, the incapacity, the refusal.

An early dramatic death gives one, in a literary sense, a real life, a throbbing biography. People discovered they had known a vehement, disturbing genius in their school days; mere propinquity became a challenge, and the brief life has been the subject for memories of no special usefulness. Sylvia Plath does not come closer, shine more clearly. Poems have followed her poems, making their statements and to most of these her own harsh eloquence is the proper rebuke. We do not by any means have all of her letters, and the ones she must have written during the last year haunt the mind—that is, if she had the dependent, needy relationship that can make a letter an action, a true telling of feeling. The letters—at least the excerpts we have seen thus far—tend to be minimal, flat, suppressed, impersonal, rather more an instance of her lack of genuine closeness to the recipient than of any wish to reveal herself. A. Alvarez in *The Savage God* has done the greatest credit to the live person as he knew her. He is restrained, deeply knowledgeable about Sylvia Plath's poetry, and moved by the sufferings of her last days and the moment of suicide.

Sylvia Plath went on a Fulbright to Cambridge University. She met and later married the distinguished poet Ted Hughes, and after a year or so back in America they returned to live in England. Her first book of poems, *The Colossus,* was published in 1960, the same year her daughter Frieda was born. In 1962 her son Nicholas was born—and then life began to be hard and disturbing, except that she was able to write the poems later issued under the title *Crossing the Water.* She was separated from her husband, came back to London with two small children, tried to live and work and survive alone in a bare flat during one of the coldest years in over a century. *The Bell Jar* was published under a pseudonym just before she died, in January 1963.

In the last freezing months of her life she was visited, like some waiting stigmatist, by an almost hallucinating creativity—the astonishing poems in *Ariel* and in a later volume called *Winter Trees.*

The creative visitation was not from heaven, but from the hell of rage. Yet so powerful is the art that one feels an unsettling elation as one reads the lacerating lines. The poems are about death, rage, hatred, blood, wounds, cuts, deformities, suicide attempts, stings, fevers, operations—there is no question of coming to terms with them. There is no consolation in our experience of the poems but they are alive, filled with hurt, excitement; a grinding, grating joy in the perfection of the descriptive language overcomes hesitations of the spirit.

There are also poems about children, her own, who were intensely loved. And yet "child" and "baby" as mere words are often attached to images of pain and death. Many of the poems are *tirades,* voiced at such a pitch of eloquence and passion they take your breath away. She, the poet, is frighteningly there all the time. Orestes rages, but Aeschylus lives to be almost seventy. Sylvia Plath, however, is both heroine and author; when the curtain goes down, it is her own dead body there on the stage, sacrificed to her plot.

She has the rarity of being, in her work at least, never a "nice person." There is nothing of mystical and schizophrenic vagueness about her. No dreamy loss of connection, no manic slackness, impatience, and lack of poetic judgment. She is, instead, all strength, ego, drive, endurance—and yet madly concentrated somehow, perplexing. Disgust is very strong in her nature, but she faces things with a classical fierceness and never loses dignity. That is why her vision is more powerful and more pure than the loose abandon of other poets of her period.

She is capable of anything—that we know. Alvarez reminds us how typical of her nature is the scene in *The Bell Jar* in which she dashes down a ski slope without knowing how to ski; he remembers her reckless way with horses, and tells of a deliberate smashing of her own car in a suicidal burst before the final one.

It is not recklessness that makes Sylvia Plath so forbidding, but destructiveness toward herself and others. Her mother thought *The Bell Jar* represented "the basest ingratitude" and we can only wonder at her innocence in expecting anything else. For the girl in the novel, a true account of events so far as we know, the ego is disintegrating and the stifling self-enclosure is so extreme that only death —and after that fails, shock treatment—can bring any kind of relief. Persons suffering in this way simply do not have room in their heads for the anguish of others—and later many seem to survive their own torments only by an erasing detachment. But even in recollection —and *The Bell Jar* was written a decade after the happenings— Sylvia Plath does not ask the cost.

There is a taint of paranoia in her novel and also in her poetry. The person who comes through is merciless and threatening, locked in violent images. If she does not, as so many have noticed, seem to feel pity for herself, neither is she moved to self-criticism or even self-analysis. It is a sour world, a drifting, humid air of vengeance. *The Bell Jar* seems to be a realistic account of her suicide attempt during the summer before her senior year at Smith. But the novel is about madness as well, and that separates it from the poems. Death, in the poetry, is an action, a possibility, a gesture, complete in itself, unmotivated, unexamined.

The Bell Jar opens with the line, "It was a queer, sultry summer, the summer they electrocuted the Rosenbergs." The Rosenbergs are in no way a part of the story and their mention is the work of an intelligence, wondering if the sufferings of a solitary self can have general significance. Also with her uncanny recognition of connections of all kinds—sound, sensation—and her poetic ordering of material, the electrocution of the Rosenbergs and the shock treatment at the end of the book have a metaphorical if not a realistic kinship. In the end the Rosenbergs just mean death to Sylvia Plath. "I couldn't help wondering what it would be like, being burned alive, all along your nerves."

After a summer in New York, the girl goes back to Massachusetts and madness begins to close in on her. "I hadn't slept for twenty-one nights. I thought the most beautiful thing in the world must be shadow, the million moving shapes and cul-de-sacs of shadow. There was shadow in bureau drawers and closets and suit-cases, and shadows under houses and trees and stones, and shadow at the back of people's eyes and smiles, and shadow, miles and miles of it, on the night side of the earth."

Commiting suicide is desperation, demand for relief, but I don't see how we can ignore the way in which it is edged with pleasure and triumph in Sylvia Plath's work. In *The Bell Jar* she thinks of slashing her wrists in the tub and imagines the water "gaudy as poppies"—an image like those in her late poems. When she is unable to do the act, she still wants to "spill a little blood" for practice. "Then I felt a small, deep thrill, and a bright seam of red welled up at the lip of the slash. The blood gathered darkly, like fruit, and rolled down my ankle into the cup of my black patent leather shoe." These passages, and others much more brilliant in her poems, show a mind in a state of sensual distortion, seeking pain as much as death, contemplating with grisly lucidity the mutilation of the soul and the flesh. In "Daddy,"

> Every woman adores a Fascist,
> The boot in the face, the brute
> Brute heart of a brute like you.

With Sylvia Plath the submission to, the pursuit of pain are active, violent, *serious,* not at all in a Swinburnian mood of spank-ings and teasing degradation. Always, behind every mood, there is rage—for what reason we do not know, not even in the novel where the scene is open and explicit. In some poems the rage is directed blankly at her father, in others more obliquely, but with intensity, at her husband.

The actual suicide she attempted, and from which she was res-cued only by great luck and accident, is very distressing in its details. The girl goes down into a cold, damp, cob-webbed corner of a cellar. There she hides herself behind an old log and takes fifty sleeping pills. The sense of downness, darkness, dankness, of un-bearable rot and chill is savored for its ugliness and hurt. "They had to call and call/And pick the worms off me like sticky pearls" ("Lady Lazarus").

In real life there was a police search, newspaper headlines, an empty pill bottle discovered; it was dramatic, unforgettable. Sylvia Plath was found, sent to the hospital, had shock treatment, and "the bell jar" in which she had been suffocating was finally lifted. The novel is not equal to the poems, but it is free of gross defects and embarrassments. The ultimate effort was not made, perhaps, but it is limited more in its intentions than in the rendering. The book has an interestingly cold, unfriendly humor. We sympathize with the heroine because of her drudging facing of it all and because of her suffering. The suffering is described more or less empirically, as if it were a natural thing, and the pity flows over you partly because she herself is so hard and glassy about her life.

This autobiographical work is written in a bare, rather collegiate 1950s style, and yet the attitude, the distance, and bitter carelessness are colored by a deep mood of affectlessness. The pleasures and sentiments of youth—wanting to be invited to the Yale prom, losing your virginity—are rather unreal in a scenario of disintegration, anger, and a perverse love of the horrible. The seduction of Esther Greenwood, as the heroine is called, is memorably grotesque and somehow bleakly suitable. The act led to a dangerous, lengthy, very unusual hemorrhaging. The blood—an obsession with the author—flows so plentifully that the girl is forced to seek medical help. She rather grimly pursues the young man with demands that he pay the doctor's bill, as if in some measure to get revenge for an action she herself cooperated with in the interest of experience.

The atrocious themes, the self-enclosure, the pain, blood, fury, infatuation with the hideous—all of that is in *The Bell Jar*. But, in a sense, softly, hesitantly. The poems in *Ariel* are much more violent. Indeed, the celebrated poem "Daddy" is as mean a portrait as one can find in literature.

Suicides are frequent enough, but the love of death, the teasing joy of it are rarely felt. Hart Crane, Virginia Woolf, many others, committed suicide. Some believe even Sappho threw herself from a rock into the sea. We think of these self-destructive actions as more or less sudden or as the culmination of an unbearable depression, one that brings with it a feeling of unworthiness and hopelessness, a despair that cannot imagine recovery.

Some of the journals Virginia Woolf wrote during the days before her death have in them the glittering contempt of a Sylvia Plath poem such as "Lesbos."

> Viciousness in the kitchen!
> The potatoes hiss.
> It is all Hollywood, windowless.

It goes on:

> You have stuck her kittens outside your window
> In a sort of cement well
> Where they crap and puke and cry and she can't hear.

This poem was written in the last months of Sylvia Plath's life and I have no clue as to whether or not it was an actual scene. The excessive violence of the language, remarkable as it is, seems to come from a mind speeding along madly and yet commanding an uncanny control of language, sound, rhythm, and metaphor that is the very opposite of madness.

In the entry of Virginia Woolf's diary there is a similar impatience. "They were powdering and painting, these common little tarts. . . . Then at Fuller's. A fat, smart woman in red hunting cap, pearls, check skirt, consuming rich cakes. Her shabby dependant also stuffing. . . . Where does the money come from to feed these fat white slugs?"

Anger and contempt. And yet, when the day comes for Virginia Woolf, the pain of the illness bears down on her and she feels only apology, gratitude, and depression. Her letter to her husband reads, "Dearest, I feel certain that I am going mad again. I feel we can't go through another of those terrible times. . . . I can't fight any longer. I know I am spoiling your life, that without me you could work." She weighted her skirts and managed to drown in the river.

With Sylvia Plath suicide is a performance. "Lady Lazarus" describes it with a raging, confident pride. There is no apology or fearfulness. Suicide is an assertion of power, of the strength—not the weakness—of the personality. She is no poor animal sneaking away, giving up; instead she is strong, threatening, dangerous.

> I have done it again.
> One year in every ten
> I manage it—
> ("Lady Lazarus")

Sometimes the performance is a reposeful one, as in "Edge":

> The woman is perfected.
> Her dead
>
> Body wears the smile of accomplishment,
> The illusion of a Greek necessity.

Occasionally, as in the ending of "Last Words," domesticity and annihilation are mixed together:

> When the soles of my feet grow cold,
> The blue eye of my turquoise will comfort me.
> Let me have my copper cooking pots, let my rouge pots
> Bloom about me like night flowers, with a good smell.
> They will roll me up in bandages, they will store my heart
> Under my feet in a neat parcel.

Sylvia Plath's preoccupation with the body at the moment of death reminds me of Mishima, although her concern is not to be "fit" as his apparently was, but simply to have the sensation of the corpse. With both of these suicides, the action is asserted as a value, a definition, a pure leap. It is even sometimes thought of as beautiful, "pure and clean as the cry of a baby."

The circumstances of her suicide in London, the expectation that a girl would be coming in early to help with the children, the knowledge that the man in the flat below awakened early, the note with the doctor's name and phone number: these facts lead Alvarez to speculate that Sylvia Plath didn't *entirely* want to kill herself. She *risked* death—and lost.

Suicide, in that view, is thought of as a cry for help, one that cannot be uttered in the usual ways. The sheer fact of it was a tragic culmination, and yet it is not the death but the obsessions with it that are her inexplicable subject matter. Torture, mutilation, destruction are offered as interesting in themselves, without any suggestions that they are a "problem." Mishima tried to decorate his death with ideas of national policy which were, of course, ridiculous fantasies. Sylvia Plath always seems to be describing her self-destruction as an exhilarating act of contempt.

Perhaps it is important to remember that the poems are about suicide rather than about death as the waiting denouement of every life. The oddity of this is almost inexhaustible and the poems break with the universal theme of the passage of time, decay of the body, union with God, whatever death in the English poetic tradition has attached itself to. The idea of killing oneself, the sensuality of it, the drama of it, the precision, based on other attempts, cannot fail to be a distortion, a decadence. The death wish, that limping, hanging-back companion to life, is, if it exists, an instinctual complement to the vast and intricate efforts to survive. It is not one with a steady compulsion to jump, slit one's throat, swallow pills, turn on the gas.

The suicides are, then, a group apart, technicians, planners, plotters. Anne Sexton shared the wish, and her prose and poem about Sylvia Plath's death are strange, jaunty, casual, and rather rapid, as if one were telling an anecdote in fear of interruption. She speaks of the two of them as "death-mongers," and tells with great excitement of the way they talked "their deaths in the Ritz Bar in Boston." Feel the air, imagine the scene, she says, "We talked about death with a burned-up intensity, both of us drawn to it like moths to an electric light bulb. Sucking on it!" The gaiety is profoundly saddening, the glittering eye frightens us. Anne Sexton tries, in a poem, to explain the peculiar concern for craft that dominates the suicide's imagination:

> Like carpenters they want to know *which tools.*
> They never ask *why build.*

Suicide is only one of the distressing themes in Sylvia Plath's work. There is fascination with hurt and damage and fury; she is a bluntly acute and rather heartless observer. There is a blind man at the table on a ship, feeling for his food. "His fingers had the noses of weasels. I couldn't stop looking." The bright reds of poppies and tulips become bloody and threatening. Gifts are not easily accepted. Slashing a finger in the kitchen is the occasion for "Cut," with its transfixed accuracy.

> What a thrill—
> My thumb instead of an onion.
> The top quite gone
> Except for a sort of hinge
>
> Of skin,
> A flap like a hat,
> Dead white.
> Then that red plush.

A bruise is, in like manner, painted in "Contusion."

> Color floods to the spot, dull purple.
> The rest of the body is all washed out,
> The color of pearl.

Is the poem "Daddy" to be accepted as a kind of exorcism, a wild dramatic monologue of abuse screamed at a lost love?

> You do not do, you do not do
> Any more, black shoe
> In which I have lived like a foot
> For thirty years, poor and white,
> Barely daring to breathe or Achoo.

Her father died of a long illness, but there is no pity for *his* lost life. Instead he is not the dead one; he is the murderer:

> An engine, an engine
> Chuffing me off like a Jew.
> A Jew to Dachau, Auschwitz, Belsen.
> I began to talk like a Jew.
> I think I may well be a Jew.

The association of her own pain with that of the Jews in Europe has been named very well by George Steiner, "a subtle larceny." The father did not kill anyone and "the fat black heart" is really her own. How is it possible to grieve for more than twenty years for one as evil and brutal as she asserts her father to have been? On the grounds of psychology every opposite can be made to fall neatly into place —that jagged, oddly shaped piece is truly part of a natural landscape if only you can find the spot where its cutting corners slip into the blue sky. The acrimonious family—yes, any contrary can turn up there, logically as it were. But even strangers, the town, are brought into the punishment of her father and this is somehow the most biting and ungenerous thought of all:

> There's a stake in your fat black heart
> And the villagers never liked you.
> They are dancing and stamping on you.
> They always *knew* it was you.
> Daddy, daddy, you bastard, I'm through.

She insists that she is the victim—poor and white, a Jew, with a pretty red heart. But she is a dangerous and vindictive casualty: "Herr God, Herr Lucifer / Beware / Beware." "Daddy," with its hypnotic rhythms, its shameful harshness, is one of Sylvia Plath's most popular and known works. You cannot read it without shivering. It is done, completed, perfected. All the hatred in our own hearts finds its evil unforgiving music there—the Queen of the Night.

Love for her children, what about that? There is warmth and

even joy. The boy and girl are "two roses," a child's smile is "found money," children are "the one solid the spaces lean on," the baby is a "high-rises, my little loaf." But children also appear in the images of destruction. In "Edge" the woman who is perfected by death has her dead children with her.

> She has folded
>
> Them back into her body as petals
> Of a rose close when the garden
>
> Stiffens and odors bleed
> From the sweet, deep throats of the night flower.

A child's smile is a "hook." There is a poem about the deformities occasioned by thalidomide. In "Death & Co.":

> He tells me how sweet
> The babies look in their hospital
> Icebox, a simple
>
> Frill at the neck,
> Then the flutings of their Ionian
> Death-gowns,
> Then two little feet.

What can we make of a poet so ambitious and vengeful, so brilliant and yet so willfully vulnerable? How can we judge such a sense of personal betrayal, such rage, and such deformed passions? Her work is overwhelming; it is quite literally irresistible. The daring, the skill, the severity. It shocks and thrills. She called—in a typically awful phrase—her last burst of poetry "the blood jet."

When the time came she had earned it by all those earlier poems, slowly, carefully written, by that long ambition, burning, waiting, learning, by her A's, her Phi Beta Kappa, her driven perfectionism, her arrogance, her madness controlled to just the right degree. The loneliness which Alvarez so compellingly preserves for us, the freezing flat—without curtains—the icy early mornings, furiously writing before the children cried and before the "glassy music" of the milkman, her husband off with someone else—there we have a "modern instance" if there ever was one.

It is not a question in these last weeks of the conflict in a woman's life between the claims of the feminine and the agonized work of art. Every artist is either a man or a woman and the struggle is pretty much the same for both. All art that is not communal is, so to speak, made at home. Sylvia Plath was furious. Alvarez writes, "I suspect that finding herself alone again now, however temporarily and voluntarily, all the anguish she had experienced at her father's death was reactivated: despite herself, she felt abandoned, injured, enraged and bereaved as purely and defenselessly as she had as a child twenty years before."

The sense of betrayal, even of hatred, did not leave her weak and complaining so much as determined and ambitious. Ambitious rage is all over *Ariel* and in the poems written at the same time and published in *Winter Trees.* "The Applicant" is a very bitter poem about the woman's part in marriage. In "For a Fatherless Son" she speaks to the child about the absence of the father that will gradually grow in the child's consciousness like a tree:

> A death tree, color gone, an Australian gum tree—
> Balding, gelded by lightning—an illusion,
> And a sky like a pig's backside, an utter lack of attention.

And that is what her own life was like at the end—the husband and father's "utter lack of attention."

In the explosive energy of her last months I see a determination to "win." Indeed I feel, from the evidence of her work, that it is sentimental to keep insisting that the birth of her children unlocked her poetic powers. Why should that be? The birth of children opens up the energy for taking care of them and for loving them. The common observation that one must be prepared to put off other work for a few years is strongly founded. Of course, it is foolish to generalize and it is the work itself, its hard competitiveness that glare out at every turn. When she died she was alone, exhausted from writing, miserable—but triumphant too, achieved, defined and defiant.

The suicide of a young woman with the highest gifts is inevitably a circumstance of the most moving and dramatic sort. We cannot truly separate the work from the fascination and horror of the death. It is a fact that the poems in *Ariel* were read, while Sylvia Plath was alive, with full self-control and detachment by editors, who then rejected many that have since become important additions to our literature. In the end this does not strike me as more than an astonishment and it is certain the poems would have been published. Everything, everything is published, and no matter that the claim upon our attention is more often than not unfathomable. What is more teasing to the mind and the imagination is how the poems of a dramatic suicide would read to us if the poet had held on to life, given interviews, public readings, finished a second novel, more poems.

It is interesting to make the effort to read Sylvia Plath's poems as if she were still alive. They are just as brilliant, just as much creations of genius, but they are obscured and altered. Blood, reds, the threats do not impress themselves so painfully upon us. "Cold blanks approach us:/They move in a hurry." What is that? we wonder. Unhappiness, agitation, fear? "Edge" seems to be a Greek heroine, Medea perhaps, once more. "Last Words," a profoundly well-written poem:

> I do not want a plain box, I want a sarcophagus
> With tigery stripes, and a face on it
> Round as the moon, to stare up.

A beautiful poem in which, as the textbooks might say, the poet imagines her own death and is buried in a tomb, like an ancient Babylonian goddess of love. "The Detective," a prophetic poem about a death (or is it a murder?) that imagines us as we have become —detectives, putting the pieces together, working on the case. "Make notes," it says at the end.

Her poems have, read differently, the overcharged preoccupation with death and release found in religious poetry. For indeed she saw eternity the other night, also; she cries out "no end?" as Herbert does. But she was not religious; instead she is violently secular in her eternities, realistic about the life that slides from her side. Suicide was not a necessity to the passion and brilliance of the poems; nevertheless the act is a key, central to the overwhelming burst of achievement. She lived on her poetry during the last months of her life. Great she knew it to be; we feel that. It had to be *serious*, final. To imagine anyone's taking his life as a way of completing, fulfilling, explaining the highest work of that life may appear impudent, insulting to death. And yet is it more thoughtful to believe that love, debts, ill health, revenge are greater values to the human soul than creative, artistic powers? Artists have often been cruel to others for what they imagined to be advantages to their work. Cruelty to oneself, as the completion of creation, is far from unimaginable, especially to a spirit tempted throughout life to self-destruction.

If anything could have saved Sylvia Plath it would have been that she, in life, might have had the good fortune to know her own fulfillment, her hard, glittering achievement. In *The Review*, Douglas Dunn wrote about her: "Sylvia Plath was one of the most remarkable talents in any art of the decade, if not of the century." She has won the green cloth—no writer ever wanted it more. Or it would be more careful to say that she *earned* the green cloth and along with the first determination to be preeminent as a poet there came money and power, all by her own efforts. But it came too late, of course, and lesser spirits usurped the ground, began the sentimentalization of her own ungenerous nature and unrelenting anger.

Beyond the mesmerizing rhythms and sounds, the flow of brilliant, unforgettable images, the intensity—what does she say to her readers? Is it simple admiration for the daring, for going the whole way? To her fascination with death and pain she brings a sense of combat and brute force new in women writers. She is vulnerable, yes, to father and husband, but that is not the end of it at all. I myself do not think her work comes out of the cold war, the extermination camps, or the anxious doldrums of the Eisenhower years. If anything, she seems to have jumped ahead of her dates and to have more in common with the late 1960s. Her lack of conventional sentiment, her destructive contempt for her family, the failings in her marriage, the drifting, rootless rage, the peculiar homelessness, the fascination with sensation and the drug of death, the determination to try everything, knowing it would not really stop the suffering—no one went as far as she did in this.

There is nothing of the social revolutionary in her, but she is whirling about in the center of an overcharged, splitting air and she especially understands everything destructive and negative. What she did not share with the youth of the 1960s is her intense and perfect artistry, her belief in it. That religion she seemed to have gotten from some old Prussian root memory of hard work, rigor, self-command. She is a stranger, an alien. In spite of her sea imagery —and it is not particularly local but rather psychological—she is hard to connect with Massachusetts and New England. There is nothing Yankee in her. So "crossing the water" was easy—she was as alien to nostalgia and sentiment as she was to the country itself. A basic and fundamental displacement played its part.

Sylvia Plath has extraordinary descriptive powers; it is a correctness and accuracy that combine the look of things with their fearsome powers of menace. It is not close to the magnifying-glass descriptions in Marianne Moore and Elizabeth Bishop, that sense these two writers have of undertaking a sort of decoding, startling in the newness of what is seen. When Elizabeth Bishop writes that the "donkey brays like a pump gone dry," this is a perfectly recognizable and immensely gratifying gift of the sort we often get also in Sylvia Plath. But the detail in Elizabeth Bishop's "The Fish" is of another kind:

> I looked into his eyes
> which were far larger than mine
> but shallower, and yellowed,
> the irises backed and packed
> with tarnished tinfoil
> seen through the lenses
> of old scratched isinglass.

Marianne Moore's abstruse, peering investigations, her shining, gleaming mirror reflect—more than anything else—words. For instance, "Smooth Gnarled Crepe Myrtle" and its flowing compounds:

> A brass-green bird with grass-
> green throat smooth as a nut springs from
> twig to twig askew, copying the
> Chinese flower piece—business-like atom
> in the stiff-leafed tree's blue-
> pink dregs—of wine pyramids
> of mathematic
> circularity; one of a
> pair.

In Marianne Moore and Elizabeth Bishop we are never far away from the comic spirit, from tolerance and wisdom—qualities alien to the angry illuminations of *Ariel*. But the tradition is also strong in Sylvia Plath—and taste, too, in the sense of craft utterly conquered and absorbed. Precision interests her, and she is immensely learned like the other two poets, never wishing to be a "natural" in any sense. She has also the power of the visual, part of the preference for precision over rhetoric. Perhaps this greed for particulars is the true mark of the poetry of women in our time. In the end, what is overwhelming, new, original in Sylvia Plath is the burning singularity of temperament, the exigent spirit clothed but not calmed by the purest understanding of the English poetic tradition.

Long after I had been reading her work I came across the recording of some of her poems she made in England not long before she died. I have never before learned anything from a poetry reading, unless the clothes, the beard, the girls, the poor or good condition of the poet can be considered a kind of knowledge. But I was taken aback by Sylvia Plath's reading. It was not anything like I could have imagined. Not a trace of the modest, retreating, humorous Worchester, Massachusetts, of Elizabeth Bishop; nothing of the swallowed plain Pennsylvania of Marianne Moore. Instead these bitter poems—"Daddy," "Lady Lazarus," "The Applicant," "Fever 103°"—were "beautifully" read, projected in full-throated, plump, diction-perfect, Englishy, mesmerizing cadences, all round and rapid, and paced and spaced. Poor recessive Massachusetts had been erased. "I have done it again!" Clearly, perfectly, staring you down. She seemed to be standing at a banquet like Timon, crying, "Uncover, dogs, and lap!"

It is a tragic story, completely original and unexpected in its scenes and its themes. Ted Hughes, her husband, has a poem about wives:

> Their brief
> Goes straight up to heaven and nothing more is heard of it.

That was not true of Sylvia Plath, and since we now have no choice perhaps there is no need to weigh and to wonder whether her awful black brief was worth it.

Rosellen Brown

Keeping the Self at Bay

Sylvia Plath wrote a great deal more fiction than most of her readers imagine if they have encountered only *The Bell Jar.* In fact she said in her journal, "For me poetry is an evasion from the real job of writing prose." It is clear from those journals that she began early with the truest mark of the natural writer, an unspecific love of words, verbal argument, and elaboration; as a teenager she wrote both. Yet her impulse to be a fiction writer produced little more than ordinary stories, struck again and again by the pure light of her verbal gifts and her psychological cunning. At the last, what elevated the poems beyond the ordinary and kept her stories from success had to do with extra-literary factors: for Plath, most of the time, fiction served the world's purposes and poetry served the self's; and just as she was never clear about who or what that self ought to be, so her choice of form was arbitrary and tuned to needs other than those of the work.

For the rare writer who is at ease with fiction and poetry, the relation of form to character and subject is free until the specifics of the case—and each is *sui generis*—begin to assert themselves. The details to be accommodated are exhaustive or meager, the confrontation with character intimate or distant, and the writer searches for his and for his reader's perfect placement in narrative space, just as the visual artist chooses his vanishing point. Furthermore, the fiction writer tends to make up or to find stories which create the occasion for emotion; the poet more often than not begins with the relative "truth" of a real occasion and brings up out of it the emotion it embodies. Most of the time, however, Plath appeared to have been preoccupied with being an obedient girl in her prose: the woman who ate men like air emerged elsewhere.

Sylvia Plath had sent forty-five stories to *Seventeen* by the time she was eighteen years old. In 1950 the magazine finally accepted "And Summer Will Not Come Again." In 1951, "Sunday at the Mintons" appeared in *Mademoiselle* and the following summer she won a competition to become a guest editor at the magazine, a member of its "College Board." At a time when there were significantly fewer "alternative" models for clever young women than there are now, and certainly very little access to a serious literary scene (I will testify, having hung on every college issue of *Mademoiselle* myself), such honors loomed large. Plath had no *Ms.*, let alone a dozen other serious, supportive cultural institutions, to validate her misgivings about the idols a fashion magazine served. This was the experience, this summer in New York writing sappy descriptions of models in their furs, smiling artificially for the cameras (and, undoubtedly in the same boosterish spirit, meeting a few writers), to which, much later, she was to devote *The Bell Jar*. Whether in spite of her contempt for the ideals of the magazine and most of the people who worked there, or perversely because of it, publication in such places remained one of her most potent dreams; her experience with the shallowness and the pandering of the women's magazine world seemed to have formed her ambition even as it repulsed her.

For her poetry Plath dreamed only of *The New Yorker*—her journals are awash with the tears she shed, the actual nightmares she endured before and after every rejection by this single arbiter of her talent, her value, the valence of her soul. It is hard to imagine a more rigorous split, but then anyone who has read the journals can see that her life in every aspect was driven by that old dichotomy, evenly divided between values that were called at that time "inner directed" and "outer directed."

The only stories that hold any interest, and parts of *The Bell Jar*, Plath's earnest attempt to render the events leading up to and away from one of her breakdowns, are the nasty ones that do not try to ingratiate themselves with the "women's magazine" audience which was preoccupied, as she saw it, with conventions of form and language and, below that flat surface, with conventions of politeness and feminine subservience. Everywhere in the stories there are flashes of intensity, and almost everywhere they are suppressed by contrivance like sparks that might ignite the landscape. Only the title story of the collection of short pieces assembled posthumously, *Johnny Panic and the Bible of Dreams*, dares to acknowledge the horror to which *The Bell Jar* is given over, that wild and irrational part of herself which had to be humbled by shock treatments: "I am shaken like a leaf in the teeth of glory. . . . His [Johnny Panic's] love is the twenty-story leap, the rope at the throat, the knife at the heart." But this confrontation with darkness did not repeat itself until the novel.

Far more typical is "Day of Success," in which a young wife and mother undergoes a crisis in self-confidence and trust in her husband's loyalty when his writing success threatens to put him in proximity to the evil seductresses of the big city, the beautiful professionals (editors and such), movie stereotypes all, who will surely ensnare him. But as it happens, the lucky little woman has a husband who really *wants* a country wife in braids who (literally) keeps the home fires burning. Whatever irony a less conflicted or more worldly writer might have introduced beneath the surface of this desperately patronizing exemplum, Plath has expunged or has not allowed herself to discover. She is, I think, writing out of the sunny side of her own daydream of simple domesticity, the one her own life consistently denied her.

In a far more harsh and honest story, "Sweetie Pie and the Gutter Men," written a year earlier, before Plath had her own children, a young woman who represents herself (as does one protagonist after another) visits an old college friend who is complacently mired in suburban motherhood. There she watches her friend's two little daughters have a good rivalrous go at each other and, filled with inchoate fury, discovers a kind of juvenile soulmate in the one child who delights in secretly tormenting her doll: "What do you do to Sweetie Pie when she is *very* bad?" she asks, and is told "I hit her." The woman urges her on and the child continues almost manically, "I throw her up in the sky. I knock her down. I spank her and spank her. I bang her eyes in." "Good," replies the woman, whom we see at the story's end standing with her hands "listless and empty at her sides, like hands of wax, 'Good. You keep on doing that.'" What the story lacks in subtlety it makes up for in intensity and in the shock of that ending, which should not really, as it happens, be such a surprise: a death charge of frustrated anger has been building as the visitor watches her friend good-naturedly submitting to stupefaction by mother- and wifehood, "morning, noon and night." Tolstoy spoke of the necessity of a focus in a work of art which "must not be able to be completely explained in words."

In "Sweetie Pie and the Gutter Men" sufficient mystery, or at least complexity, is embodied in the woman who is as of now "something of a maiden aunt" among the children of her relatives and friends, but who appears to be on the brink of a commitment to her own family. Although this is an ill-calculated metaphor which put me in mind of a giraffe, the feeling is unmistakable when, after her description as a maiden aunt she acknowledges that "Lately . . . she had taken to tearing off low-hanging leaves or tall grass heads with a kind of wanton energy. . . ." Typical of every one of Plath's stories that rises above the ordinary is the compressed rage and ambivalence at its center. And equally typical is the stunned passivity with which the woman is last seen, standing with those empty waxen hands which do not wave good-bye. "Stone Boy with Dolphin," which began with fewer details as a journal entry from her time at Cambridge, "Johnny Panic," a few bits of other more contrived stories —all the work that succeeds, even in part, has anger as its spur, or at least allows it to puddle dangerously on the surface. The others struggle to make their author ordinary and acceptable and, just as such impulses in her own daily life failed, these do as fiction.[1]

Many, perhaps most, of the poems which came before her final months of self-immolating fury are verbally but not emotionally compelling. If the poetry of *Ariel* is what makes Plath's work more than routinely interesting, then it might be argued that, since we do not have her prose from the same period (with exceptions like the essay discussed in note 1), we are not comparing the work of the same woman: the Plath of 1957, say, was very unlike the Plath of 1963. But even the earlier work, when it appears in both forms, is a good deal more intense as poetry: the narrowing of focus that characterizes the poem, that element of tight control, seemed to have made the necessary conduit to her deepest feelings. It is very hard to write conventional stories that are all passionate scrutiny and magnified disquieting detail. She had called her "Johnny Panic" story a "breakthrough," but she never repeated its tone or its fantastic plotless surge of dream material, and if, in fact, she wanted to write for *The Ladies' Home Journal*, she was right to have abandoned it.

There is in her notebooks, reproduced in *Johnny Panic*, a section called "Rose and Percy B," a series of vignettes concerning the Hughes's middle-aged neighbors, a gabby, friendly, rather "common" woman named Rose and her husband Percy, an ex-pubkeeper who declines and dies in the course of her note-taking. Plath was in her Flaubertian period, practicing an intense scrutiny as a sort of exercise for suppleness of style, and to increase the acuity of her vision. She was trying to learn to observe exhaustively; the casual note would not do. Nowhere in the piece does Plath evince much personal sympathy for Percy, whom she chillingly calls "a marginal man," marveling that even for such, the end is "a horror." (By which she appears to mean that she, as witness to the spectacle of his death, is repulsed. Death assaults her, but not any loss more specific.) After they'd left the open grave she notes "an unfinished feeling. Is he to be left up there uncovered, all alone? Walked home over the back hill, gathering immense stalks of fuchsia foxgloves and swinging our jackets in the heat." There is skill in her prose rhythm when it isn't being forced; again and again the journal shows her to be a naturally elegant writer, when she is not bending herself out of shape to keep the story moving along. The poem she makes of the funeral, though, "Berck-Plage," is effective precisely because she uses that same element of coldness—here in the notebook merely a neutrality—as a kind of emotional organizing principle. Although it isn't anger, it's a related emotion: awe, fear, a kind of respect for the integrity of the man's state:

> A wedding-cake face in a paper frill.
> How superior he is now.
> . . . .
> This is what it is to be complete. It is horrible.
> . . . .
> They propped his jaw with a book until it stiffened
> And folded his hands, that were shaking: goodbye, goodbye.
> . . . .
> It is a blessing, it is a blessing:
> The long coffin of soap-colored oak,
>
> The curious bearers and the raw date
> Engraving itself in silver with marvelous calm.

The poem concludes:

> Six round black hats in the grass and a lozenge of wood,
> And a naked mouth, red and awkward.
>
> For a minute the sky pours into the hole like plasma.
> There is no hope, it is given up.

Every detail which appears in the poem has been committed first to the journal: the propped face and wired jaw, the soapy wood of the coffin, the black hats. But the poem demands a tone where, justifiably, the journal needs none, having the automatic authority of the recorder's straightforward voice, and that stiffening of the substance of her observation acts as an armature. The details are shaped around it and the emotion, and it holds.

Another astonishing instance in which the candid, rather anonymously charming narrator/self of the notebooks is transformed, in a series of poems, into a vivid and terrifying presence begins with a section called "Charlie Pollard and the Beekeepers"—titles, of course, have been given the excerpts—and culminates in "The Bee Meeting," "The Arrival of the Bee Box," "The Swarm," "Stings," and "Wintering," poems written in October 1962. Fear, exhaustion, death—Plath's late obsessions that give the 1962–63 poems their frightening energy—hardly make a ripple in the casual surface of the notebook prose. But the poems move from lethal image to lethal image, and the poet is a victim in a succession of nightmares spun of the specifics she has so cheerfully put in her notes. Granted notebooks are not intended to be art, still it is instructive to see— she is not the only poet of whom this is true—how the formal work intensifies, even creates, emotions that are entirely invisible in its chatty surface. It is only when she approaches them through the mediation of the poem's compression that the details cease to be objects and become provocations.

Earlier, Plath had castigated herself for the "bland ladylike archness or slightness" of some of her poetry. She was similarly harsh about her stories: this one was "slick (but one I consider good)" and that one "artificial and not worth reading." (But she had sent that one to the *Saturday Evening Post* and worried that it would come back without a word. And rejection by magazines about whose needs she was cynical of course hurt doubly—she couldn't even dirty her skirt hem successfully to gain their approval: "It is safer from rejection not to—then I haven't the opportunity to be in jeopardy. . . . Oh, to break out into prose.")

"I write a sort of imagey, static prose," Plath contended, and she admired stories with "plot, people changing, learning something. . . . My one salvation is to enter into other characters in stories. . . . The thing is, to develop other first persons. . . . Slangy language is one way of breaking my drawing room inhibitions." Yet, in fact, this was the very place where her ideals for herself demonstrated how little Plath understood the nature of her own (still potential) genius which, in fact, was for just that—"imagey, static prose," prose heightened, like the best of her poetry, by the urgency of its emotional charge. "I just can't get outside myself," she lamented and yet had she realized that she could instead get *into* herself—had she abandoned the objectivity she was too preoccupied to investigate well—she might have discovered a totally different kind of prose to serve her obsessions. (Ted Hughes puts it perfectly in his introduction to *Johnny Panic:* "She had an instant special pass to the center and no choice but to use it.")

As it was, the closest she came to that center was in her attempt to use her most hideous memories in *The Bell Jar,* which she thought of as "an autobiographical apprentice work," according to a friend, "which I had to write in order to free myself from the past." Peculiarly, again she distanced herself from her work's seriousness. She told her mother, "It's a pot boiler, really, but I think it will show how isolated a person feels when he [sic] is suffering a breakdown."

The book *is,* in its way, a potboiler: somehow it manages to trivialize, by its uncertainty of tone, its heavy freight of pain. Yet again, one has to ask why she chose, if it was within her control, to make it something whose artlessness she could repudiate. Probably she was safer from her own ultimate self-contempt that way. Furthermore, it was bad enough to incur the fury of the real actors in her life, her mother among many others, for a book she could pretend to shrug off; how much more serious a breach of propriety to be caught taking seriously the work that contained them. Plath wrote in her journal:

> What to do with anger, ask her [her psychiatrist]. One thing to say: Yes, I want the world's praise, money & love, and am furious with anyone . . . getting ahead of me. Well, what to do when this surges up and over & over? Last night I knew that Mother didn't matter— she is all for me, but I have dissipated her image and she becomes all editors and publishers and critics and the World, and I want acceptance there, and to feel my work good and well-taken. Which ironically freezes me at my work, corrupts my nunnish labor of work-for-itself-as-its-own-reward.

No one could analyze her failures better than Plath herself—how hard she fought to change what she so well understood! No wonder she despised her stories, on an honest day, she who quotes Stevie Smith in her essay called "Context": "Art is wild as a cat and quite separate from civilization."

And so the prose represents both sides of that argument with herself. On the one hand there are the lightning-bolt images: "People swam past, undulant, with no feet, no faces"; "A knock beat on the blank white door"; "he [was] doing a slow wide brand of British jive with a girl in sweater and skirt of hunter's green close-cloven as frog skin"; "I'm a wormy hermit in a country of prize pigs so corn-happy they can't see the slaughterhouse at the end of the track. I'm Jeremiah vision-bitten in the Land of Cockaigne." Put against these snatches the commodity-hungry purveyor of easy and condescending prose: "I shall call myself *Sylvan Hughes*—pleasantly woodsy, colorful—yet sexless and close to my own name: a perfectly euphonious magazine name."

When by the end of her life she was writing at full force, Sylvia Plath's skill was to swallow the things of her world and extrude them as if through her own pores: "The blood jet is poetry./There is no stopping it." It is impossible to imagine anything she'd have called fiction (using her all-too-conventional definition) emerging when she had turned herself into her own flaming words. She was all self by then, and her idea of fiction was that it be about other (and ordinary) people. Kafka never let his obsessive concentration on himself inhibit him: instead of cutting his characters into dainty morsels the world would recognize and swallow without a ripple of discomfort, he made non-people to represent his non-personhood. This Plath failed to do, failed even to consider. She was, sadly for her own hopes, versatile only when it came to inventing variations of self-inflicted pain. Her fictions, the presentable daughter's orderly gallery of decent acquaintances, was only one of the skins she shed along the way to her final victorious intensity whose only true character was "I."

NOTE

1. Parenthetically, the *Johnny Panic* volume contains a little essay that combines irritation and cheerfulness as it details Plath's encounters with the weather

and the breakdown of London services during her last winter. What is horribly compelling about this breezy piece is that it would appear to undermine the contention of some of her friends and biographers that the snow and its wet seepage into her house seemed to rot her composure as well as her walls in its slow encroachment. If that is so, then the buoyant woman who ends her essay by predicting that her children will grow up "resolute, independent and tough, fighting through queues for candles for me in my aguey old age. While I brew waterless tea . . . on a gas ring in the corner. If the gas, too, is not kaput" was in a manic period awesomely dissociated from the depression which was to drive her to suicide a few months later. This is not in itself terribly surprising, perhaps, but it is interesting to note that her poetry at this time—this is 1963—was already in its final phase of ice-hot rage, at war with the physical world. Whatever hidden part of her contained the impulse to write prose was not so tightly in the grip of pain that she couldn't summon this amiable, amused "company face."

Howard Moss

Dying: An Introduction

The story of a poet who tries to end her life written by a poet who did, Sylvia Plath's *The Bell Jar* was first published under a pseudonym in England in 1963, the month before she committed suicide. We had to wait almost a decade for its publication in the United States, but it was reissued in England in 1966 under its author's real name. A biographical note in the present edition makes it plain that the events in the novel closely parallel Sylvia Plath's twentieth year. For reasons for which we are not wholly to blame, our approach to the novel is impure; *The Bell Jar* is fiction that cannot escape being read in part as autobiography. It begins in New York with an ominous lightness, grows darker as it moves to Massachusetts, then slips slowly into madness. Esther Greenwood, one of a dozen girls in and on the town for a month as "guest editors" of a teenage fashion magazine, is the product of a German immigrant family and a New England suburb. With "fifteen years of straight A's" behind her, a depressing attachment to a dreary but handsome medical student, Buddy Willard, still unresolved, and a yearning to be a poet, she is the kind of girl who doesn't know what drink to order or how much to tip a taxi driver but is doing her thesis on the "twin images" in *Finnegans Wake,* a book she has never managed to finish. Her imagination is at war with the small-town tenets of New England and the big-time sham of New York. She finds it impossible to be one of the army of college girls whose education is a forced stop on the short march to marriage. The crises of identity, sexuality, and survival are grim, and often funny. Wit, irony, and intelligence, as well as an inexplicable, withdrawn sadness, separate Esther from her companions. Being an involuntary truth-seeker, she uses irony as a weapon of judgment, and she is its chief victim. Unable to experience or mime emotions, she feels defective as a person. The gap between her and the world widens: "I couldn't get myself to react. I felt very still and very empty." "The silence depressed me. It wasn't the silence of silence. It was my own silence." "That morning I had tried to hang myself."

Camouflage and illness go together in *The Bell Jar;* moreover, illness is often used to lift or tear down a façade. Doreen, a golden girl of certainty admired by Esther, begins the process by getting drunk. The glimpse of her lying with her head in a pool of her own vomit in a hotel hallway is repellant but crucial. Her illness is followed by a mass ptomaine poisoning at a "fashion" lunch. Buddy gets tuberculosis and goes off to a sanatorium. Esther, visiting him, breaks her leg skiing. When she has her first sexual experience, with a young math professor she has picked up, she hemorrhages. Taken in by a lesbian friend, she winds up in a hospital. Later, she learns that the friend has hanged herself. A plain recital of the events in *The Bell Jar* would be ludicrous if they were not balanced by genuine desperation at one side of the scale and a sure sense of black comedy at the other. Sickness and disclosure are the keys to *The Bell Jar.* On her last night in New York, Esther climbs to the roof of her hotel and throws her city wardrobe over the parapet, piece by piece. By the end of the novel, she has tried to get rid of her very life, which is given back to her by another process of divestment—psychiatry. Pain and gore are endemic to *The Bell Jar,* and they are described objectively, self-mockingly, almost humorously to begin with. Taken in by the tone (the first third of *The Bell Jar* might be a mordant, sick-joke version of *Breakfast at Tiffany's*), the reader is being lured into the lion's den—that sterile cement room in the basement of a mental hospital where the electric-shock-therapy machine waits for its frightened clients.

The casualness with which physical suffering is treated suggests that Esther is cut off from the instinct for sympathy right from the beginning—for herself as well as for others. Though she is enormously aware of the impingements of sensation, her sensations remain impingements. She lives close to the nerve but the nerve has become detached from the general network. A thin layer of glass separates her from everyone, and the novel's title, itself made of glass, is evolved from the notion of disconnection: the head of each mentally ill person is enclosed in a bell jar, choking on its own foul air.

Torn between conflicting roles—the sweetheart-*Hausfrau*-mother and the "life of the poet," neither very real to her—Esther finds life itself inimical. Afraid of distorting the person she is yet to become, she becomes the ultimate distortion—nothing. As she descends into the pit of depression, the world is a series of wrong reverberations: her mother's face is a perpetual accusation; the wheeling of a baby carriage underneath her window, a grinding irritation. She becomes obsessed by the idea of suicide, and one of the great achievements of *The Bell Jar* is that it makes real the subtle distinctions between a distorted viewpoint and the distortions inherent in what it sees. Convention may contribute to Esther's insanity, but she never loses her awareness of the irrationality of convention. Moved to Belsize, a part of the mental hospital reserved for patients about to go back to the world, she makes the connection explicit: "What was there about us, in Belsize, so different from the girls playing bridge and gossiping and studying in the college to which I would return? Those girls, too, sat under bell jars of a sort."

Terms like "mad" and "sane" grow increasingly inadequate as the action develops. Esther is "psychotic" by definition, but the definition is merely a descriptive tag: by the time we learn how she got to be "psychotic" the word has ceased to be relevant. (As a work of fiction, *The Bell Jar* seems to complement the clinical theories of the Scottish analyst R. D. Laing.) Because it is written from the distraught observer's point of view rather than from the viewpoint of someone observing her, there is continuity to her madness; it is not one state suddenly supplanting another, but the most gradual of processes.

Suicide, a grimly compulsive game of fear and guilt, as addictive as alcohol or drugs, is experimental at first—a little blood here, a bit of choking there, just to see what it will be like. It quickly grows into an overwhelming desire for annihilation. By the time Esther climbs into the crawlspace of a cellar and swallows a bottle of sleeping pills—by the time we are faced by the real thing—the event, instead of seeming grotesque, seems like a natural consequence. When she is about to leave the hospital, after a long series of treatments, her psychiatrist tells her to consider the breakdown "a bad dream." Esther, "patched, retreaded, and approved for the road," thinks, "To the person in the bell jar, blank and stopped as a dead baby, the world itself is the bad dream."

That baby is only one of many in *The Bell Jar*. They smile up from the pages of magazines, they sit like little freaks pickled in glass jars on display in the pediatric ward of Buddy's hospital. A "sweet baby cradled in its mother's belly" seems to wait for Esther at the end of the ski run when she has her accident. And in the course of the novel she witnesses a birth. In place of her never-to-be-finished thesis on the "twin images" in *Finnegans Wake,* one might be written on the number and kinds of babies that crop up in *The Bell Jar.* In a gynecologist's office, watching a mother fondling her baby, Esther wonders why she is so separated from this easy happiness, this carrying out of the prescribed biological and social roles. She does not want a baby; she is a baby herself. But she is also a potential writer. She wants to fulfill herself, not to *be* fulfilled. To her, babies are The Trap, and sex is the bait. But she is too intelligent not to realize that babies don't represent life—they *are* life, though not necessarily the kind Esther wants to live; that is, if she wants to live at all. She is caught between the monstrous fetuses on display in Buddy's ward and the monstrous slavery of the seemingly permanent pregnancy of her neighbor Dodo Conway, who constantly wheels a baby carriage under Esther's window, like a demented figure in a Greek chorus. Babies lure Esther toward suicide by luring her toward a life she cannot—literally—bear. There seem to be only two solutions, and both involve the invisible: to pledge faith to the unborn or fealty to the dead. Life, so painfully visible and present, defeats her, and she takes it, finally, into her own hands. With the exception of the psychiatrist's disinterested affection for her, love is either missing or unrecognized in *The Bell Jar.* Its overwhelming emotion is disgust—disgust that has not yet become contempt and is therefore more damaging.

Between the original and the second publications of *The Bell Jar* in England, Sylvia Plath's second, and posthumous, volume of poems, *Ariel,* was printed. Some of the poems had appeared in magazines, but no one was prepared for their cumulative effect. Murderous experiences of the mind and the body, stripped of all protection, they were total exposures, and chilling. They made clear almost instantly that someone who had been taken for a gifted writer might well be one of genius, whose work—intense, luxurious, barbarous, and worldly—was unlike anything ever seen before. Although the extraordinary quality of the poems made her death the more lamentable, that death gave her work certain immediate values it might not otherwise have had. Death cannot change a single word written down on paper, but in this case who the poet was and what had been lost became apparent almost at the same time, as if the poems had been given and the poet taken away in one breath. An instantaneous immortality followed. Sylvia Plath also became an extra-literary figure to many people, a heroine of contradictions—someone who had faced horror and made something of it as well as someone who had been destroyed by it. I don't think morbid fascination accounts for her special position. The energy and violence of the late poems were acted out. What their author threatened she performed, and her work gained an extra status of truth. The connection between art and life, so often merely rhetorical, became all too visible. The tragic irony is that in a world of public-relations liars Sylvia Plath seemed a truth-dealer in life by the very act of taking it.

The Bell Jar lacks the coruscating magnificence of the late poems. Something girlish in its manner betrays the hand of the amateur novelist. Its material, after all, is what has been transcended. It is a frightening book, and if it ends on too optimistic a note as both fiction and postdated fact, its real terror lies elsewhere. Though we share every shade of feeling that leads to Esther's attempts at suicide, there is not the slightest insight in *The Bell Jar* into suicide itself. That may be why it bears the stamp of authority. Reading it, we are up against the raw experience of nightmare, not the analysis or understanding of it.

Robert Scholes

Esther Came Back Like
a Retreaded Tire

On the surface *The Bell Jar* is about the events of Sylvia Plath's twentieth year: about how she tried to die, and how they stuck her back together with glue. It is a fine novel, as bitter and remorseless as her last poems—the kind of book Salinger's Franny might have written about herself ten years later, if she had spent those ten years in Hell. It is very much a story of the Fifties, but written in the early Sixties, and, after being effectively suppressed in this country for eight years, was published in the Seventies.

F. Scott Fitzgerald used to claim that he wrote with "the authority of failure," and he did. It was a source of power in his later work. But the authority of failure is but a pale shadow of the authority of suicide, as we feel it in *Ariel* and in *The Bell Jar*. This is not so much because Sylvia Plath, in taking her own life, gave her readers a certain ghoulish interest they could not bring to most poems and novels, though this is no doubt partly true. It is because she knew that she was "Lady Lazarus." Her works did not only come to us posthumously. They were written posthumously: between suicides. She wrote her novel and her *Ariel* poems feverishly, like a person "stuck together with glue" and aware that the glue was melting. Should we be grateful for such things? Can we accept the price she paid for what she has given us? Is dying really an art?

There are no easy answers for such questions, maybe no answers at all. We are all dying, of course, banker and bum alike, spending our limited allotment of days, hours, and minutes at the same rate. But we don't like to think about it. And those men and women who take the matter into their own hands, and spend all at once with prodigal disdain, seem frighteningly different from you and me.

130

Sylvia Plath is one of those others, and to them our gratitude and our dismay are equally impertinent. When an oracle speaks it is not for us to say thanks but to attend to the message.

The Bell Jar is about the way this country was in the Fifties and about the way it is to lose one's grip on sanity and recover it again. It is easy to say (and it is said too often) that insanity is the only sane reaction to the America of recent years. And it is also said frequently (especially by R. D. Laing and his followers) that the only thing to do about madness is relax and enjoy it. But neither of these "clever" responses to her situation occur to Esther Greenwood, who is the narrator and central character in *The Bell Jar*.

To Esther, madness is the descent of a stifling bell jar over her head. In this state, she says, "wherever I sat . . . I would be sitting under the same glass bell jar, stewing in my sour air." And she adds, "To the person in the bell jar, blank and stopped as a dead baby, the world itself is the bad dream." Which is not to say that Esther believes the world outside the asylum is full of people living an authentic existence. She asks, "What was there about us, in Belsize, so different from the girls playing bridge and gossiping and studying in the college to which I would return? Those girls, too, sat under bell jars of a sort."

The world in which the events of this novel take place is a world bounded by the cold war on one side and the sexual war on the other. We follow Esther Greenwood's personal life from her summer job in New York with *Ladies' Day* magazine, back through her days at New England's largest school for women, and forward through her attempted suicide, her bad treatment at one asylum and her good treatment at another, to her final reentry into the world like a used tire: "patched, retreaded, and approved for the road."

But this personal life is delicately related to larger events— especially the execution of the Rosenbergs, whose impending death by electrocution is introduced in the stunning first paragraph of the book. Ironically, that same electrical power which destroys the Rosenbergs restores Esther to life. It is shock therapy which finally lifts the bell jar and enables Esther to breathe freely once again. Passing through death she is reborn. This novel is not political or historical in any narrow sense; but in looking at the madness of the world and the world of madness, it forces us to consider the great questions posed by all truly realistic fiction: what is reality and how can it be confronted?

In *The Bell Jar*, Sylvia Plath has used superbly the most important technical device of realism—what the Russian critic Viktor Shklovsky called "defamiliarization." True realism defamiliarizes our world so that it emerges from the dust of habitual acceptance and becomes visible once again. This is quite the opposite of that comforting false realism that presents the world in terms of clichés that we are all too ready to accept.

Sylvia Plath's technique of defamiliarization ranges from tiny verbal witticisms that bite, to images that are deeply troubling. When she calls the hotel for women that Esther inhabits in New York the "Amazon," she is not merely enjoying the closeness of the sound of that word to "Barbizon," she is forcing us to rethink the entire concept of a hotel for women: "mostly girls of my age with wealthy parents who wanted to be sure that their daughters would be living where men couldn't get at them and deceive them." And she is announcing a major theme in her work, the hostility between men and women.

With Esther Greenwood this hostility takes the form of obsessive attempts to get herself liberated from a virginity she finds oppressive, by a masculinity she finds hideous. When her medical-student boyfriend suggests that they play a round of the traditional children's game—I'll show you mine if you show me yours—she looks at his naked maleness and reacts this way: "The only thing I could think of was turkey neck and turkey gizzards and I felt very depressed." This is defamiliarization with a vengeance. The image catches up all cocky masculine pride of flesh and reduces it to the level of giblets. It sees the inexorable link between generation and death and makes us see it too, because the image is so fitting. All flesh comes from this—and comes to this.

In the face of such cosmic disgust, psychological explanations like "penis envy" seem pitifully inadequate. Esther Greenwood is not a woman who wants to be a man but a human being who cannot avoid seeing that the price we pay for life is death. Sexual differentiation itself is only a metaphor for human incompletion. The battle of the sexes is, after all, a civil war.

Esther Greenwood's account of her year in the bell jar is as clear and readable as it is witty and disturbing. It makes for a novel such as Dorothy Parker might have written if she had not belonged to a generation infected with the relentless frivolity of the college-humor magazine. The brittle humor of that earlier generation is reincarnated in *The Bell Jar,* but raised to a more serious level because it is recognized as a resource of hysteria.

In the back of the Harper & Row edition of the *The Bell Jar* eight pen-and-ink drawings by Sylvia Plath have been added. These drawings are landscapes and still lifes, caught by a meticulous draftsman who understands almost too well what it means to work in a medium where black is the only color.

Vance Bourjaily

Victoria Lucas and Elly Higginbottom

1.

What happens to the way we read and estimate *The Bell Jar* if we really go along with Sylvia Plath, taking it as the first novel of the young American writer, Victoria Lucas, then living in England, otherwise unknown? Under the Lucas pseudonym it was published, in January 1963, the month before the poet's death, by Heinemann of London—published, locally reviewed, modestly promoted, and briefly sold. With which, as most books do, it disappeared. It was pretty much unheard of, at least in this country, until eight years later, in February 1971, when it was ready to become a major item in a tragic legend, and Harper & Row had the business-wit to bring it out.

I am beginning in this way not to be tough but to be fair. *The Bell Jar* is obviously relevant to the life and death of Sylvia Plath, but the life and death need not be held relevant to *The Bell Jar*. A book is what the author puts between its covers, not what the publisher writes to wrap it in, nor critics and psychologists cull out to analyze, nor elegists to improvise upon. It isn't that I feel like shutting anybody up, out, or away—publisher with books to sell, wan reader wanting fellow-sufferance, ghost seeker, keen case hunter, or grinding biographer in need of grist. The book is here now, one way or another, for all of us, and what shrewd Peter sees in it to talk about may not at all be what young Paul wishes to discuss.

What interests me first is *The Bell Jar*, all by itself—the story, the social report, the view of life, the characters, the organization, the prose, the images and the working out—and what is achieved and with what intrinsic value. Then I'll return (if it's all right with you and Peter and Paul) to the autobiographical problem.

2.

The Bell Jar, by Victoria Lucas, though not so-divided by its author, is nevertheless a novel in three parts. In the first, Esther Greenwood is an academically brilliant, socially insecure, and constantly introspective college junior. She has won, along with eleven others, a fashion magazine contest "by writing essays and stories and poems and fashion blurbs and as prizes they gave us jobs in New York for a month, expenses paid" (p. 2).[1]

In New York, Esther is especially attracted by two of the other winners, both blondes—a decadent, flamboyant platinum number called Doreen, and a sweet, wholesome daisy of a girl named Betsy. Esther can't decide which she'd rather be like. When she attaches herself to Doreen, they are picked up by a disc jockey named Lenny, with eyes for Doreen. Esther invents for herself a drab, protective identity as Elly Higginbottom. When Esther/Elly leaves the pair in Lenny's apartment, to walk back alone to her hotel through the New York night, Doreen and Lenny have been jitterbugging, kissing, and biting, and Doreen is being whirled on the disc jockey's shoulder, belly-down and breasts out.

Late that night, Esther is waked up by Doreen's voice at her door saying "Elly, Elly, Elly," while a hotel maid calls " 'Miss Greenwood, Miss Greenwood, Miss Greenwood,' as if I had a split personality or something" (p. 17). Opening the door, she finds Doreen slumped against the jamb, drunk and grown dark and heavy. Doreen collapses in her own vomit at Esther's door.

When Esther attaches herself to Betsy, they do what is expected of them. They behave with girlish propriety—though Esther is covertly gobbling Betsy's caviar—at an elaborate luncheon. This, too, ends in vomit as the whole crew of nice young editors is struck down by ptomaine. Doreen has stayed away.

Recovering, Esther detaches herself, and operates next on her own. She offers her burdensome virginity, one evening, to a United Nations simultaneous interpreter named Constantin. Though they lie down together, he will do no more than squeeze her hand, touch her hair, and go to sleep. Consequently, she fails to catch up in sexual experience with Buddy Willard, the Yale medical student whom it was assumed Esther would marry. Buddy's courtship, told in interspersed flashbacks, has been agreeably gruesome, featuring her attendance at the dissection of cadavers; a tour of the exhibit of pickled, premature babies; a lecture during which sickle-cell anemia victims were wheeled onto the platform; and a bloody childbirth. There was also a ski trip during which Esther broke her leg, an evening when Buddy exhibited himself—and the boy is now tubercular. But Esther's reason for rejecting him, as she does, is Buddy's confessional boasting of a consummated summer affair with a waitress.

At the opening of the book, and recurring as a prelude to Esther's final New York indignity, are passages about the real horror she feels at the impending electrocution of Julius and Ethel Rosenberg. When the indignity occurs, Esther is Doreen's satellite once more. Doreen has arranged a date for her reticent friend.

" 'Honestly,' " Doreen promises, " 'This one'll be different' " (p. 84). He sure is.

Marco is an immaculate Peruvian who tangos masterfully with Esther, escorts her outdoors, knocks her down in the mud and tries to rape her. When she bloodies his nose, he marks her cheeks with his blood.

The first part, and the New York adventure, end with Esther on the hotel roof, just before dawn, throwing out into the darkness, item by item, the expensive, not-quite-sophisticated wardrobe bought with scholarship money for the trip.

She goes home by train to Route 28, outside of Boston, wearing a silly dirndl skirt and frilled white blouse. Marco's blood is still on Esther's face.

Though the tone of much of this is wry, reminiscently detached, even amusing, it shows us Esther on her way down into melancholia, with little spurts toward recovery after each of which the psychotic despair deepens. There is evidence enough to justify using some harsh, psychiatrist's jargon about her—words like narcissistic and infantile—but if each quality is there, it is so only in such measure as seems normal for a vulnerable, imaginative, mostly appealing young woman, at odds with society. What is not normal is the growing split we are shown into the two selves, Esther and the very-much lesser, unappealing self she has named Elly Higginbottom.

In the second part of *The Bell Jar*, returned to a depressing Boston suburban home with her widowed mother, Esther is neither a Doreen nor a Betsy, but only Elly now. And while poor, dull Elly tells a young sailor, whom she allows to pick her up on the Boston Common, that she comes from Chicago, her real home is underneath a bell jar, an archaic laboratory fixture for displaying specimens. The specimen, on its dark base, is kept airtight, dust-free and out of contact, by a cylindrical glass cover. We can see it well enough, but if we imagine the specimen itself having life inside, the sights and sounds which reach it through the suffocating glass are distorted, muffled, and meaningless.

Our specimen, Elly Higginbottom, doesn't want to be alive. In this second part of the book, she tries, with razor blades, by drowning, and by hanging, to kill herself. At last, using sleeping pills, she so nearly succeeds that the search for and discovery of her drugged body are the subject of tabloid news stories.

During this section she has been seen by a disastrously unprofessional psychiatrist named Gordon with "eyelashes so long and thick they looked almost artificial" and features "so perfect he was almost pretty" (p. 105). When she has finished telling him that she cannot sleep or eat or read, Dr. Gordon asks (p. 107):

> "Where did you say you went to college?"
> Baffled, I told him. I didn't see where college fitted in.
> "Ah!" Dr. Gordon leaned back in his chair, staring . . . over my shoulder with a reminiscent smile. . . .
> "I remember your college well. I was up there during the war. They had a WAC station, didn't they? Or was it WAVES? . . . Yes, a WAC station. I remember now . . . my, they were a pretty bunch of girls."
> Dr. Gordon laughed.

He decides to try electroshock therapy, and bungles it. The sleeping pills are only a few days off, now, for Esther/Elly. She takes fifty of them.

In part three, institutionalized, given increasingly better psychiatric care, and finally successful shock treatments, Elly sees the cover of the bell jar start to rise, and begins to emerge as Esther once again.

In the hospital with her is someone she knew at college named

Joan Gilling. Joan has also been a near-fiancée to Buddy Willard, and also a campus achiever. Joan, reading in the papers of Esther/ Elly's suicide attempt, a few weeks back, was actually led to emulate it, going off to New York to try to kill herself.

As Esther improves, Joan declines. Near the end of the book, Esther, on parole, finally manages to get rid of her virginity in a painful, rather impersonal way, and is satisfied with herself if not by the instrumental stranger she has chosen, whom she only sees once. Joan's new experience is homosexual, with another inmate. As Esther is ready to face the committee of doctors who will release her to return to college, news comes that Joan has slipped away in the night, to the woods, by the frozen ponds, has hanged herself and is dead.

3.

Death and its agents are epicene in *The Bell Jar*. The sexual outcome is important because movement toward it is the positive movement in the novel. Through emotionally neutral defloration, Esther has become her own woman in a world of inadequate, repressive men. She says, "I hate the feeling of being under a man's thumb" (p. 189). It is in this regard that *The Bell Jar* is a feminist novel, repudiating the double-dealing by means of which society is stacked against talented, independent women.

Negative movement in the book is toward sexlessness—and death, whose woman Joan becomes. There are others, the living dead: Valerie, the snow-maiden whose lobotomy has taken away her anger, and Joan's lesbian partner Dee Dee, rejected by her husband. But it is Joan who is Esther's double in the book. This is a pretty easy point to make, since the author makes it for us. At first, when it is Joan who seems to be recovering faster, Esther is bitterly jealous: "Joan was the beaming double of my own best self, specifically designed to follow and torment me" (p. 167). Later, as Joan relapses, as indicated by the lesbian involvement, "Joan fascinated me. Her thoughts were not my thoughts, nor her feelings my feelings, but we were close enough so that her thoughts and feelings seemed a wry, black image of my own" (p. 179).

Negative and positive again.

"I like you better than Buddy," Joan has said suggestively (p.

179), and Esther replies: "That's tough, Joan . . . because I don't like you. You make me puke, if you want to know" (p. 180).

Vomit again—but there can be no break this side of the grave between doubles. It is, necessarily, Joan whose help Esther needs when hemorrhaging, after the session with Irwin, the instrumental stranger.

4.

Others have seen *The Bell Jar* as a book full of Esther-doubles, but in my reading only Joan is truly one (and I admire the restraint with which, though it's prepared for early, Joan's effective entrance into the book is delayed). Other characters do not double Esther but double one another, in the positive-negative way I've been discussing. This seems to me true, for example, of Betsy and Doreen—the latter's platinum hair has dark roots. Only Betsy is wholesome, with the emphasis on *whole*.

There are two mother-figures, similarly related: Jay Cee, the magazine editor, whose no-nonsense handling of Esther seems to straighten the heroine out briefly, and the biological mother, Mrs. Greenwood, who nearly drowns in nonsense, and whose well-meaning pushes Esther toward disaster.

There is Buddy Willard's father, trusting, henpecked, and alive. And there is Esther's father, also a professor, a bitter atheist who never gave his wife a moment's peace, and long since dead.

Constantin and Marco are negative-positive, in the sense of harmless and harmful. Irwin the instrument and Dee Dee the lesbian have something of polarity about them. And certainly there are negative and positive psychiatrists—the detestable Dr. Gordon, and Dr. Nolan, who is a warm and capable woman.

5.

It is interesting that polarity and its reversal are characteristic of electricity as well as photography. I am about to quote quite a lot, to show how electricity moves from fearful to benign in Esther Greenwood's life. Let me give the page numbers all at once, with the explanation that I'm using five incidents chronologically, rather than in the order in which they are placed in the book. The pages are 118, 1, 117–118, 175, and 176.

Sometime or other, long before the New York trip, Esther decided to move an old floor lamp in her father's former study at home.

I closed both hands around the lamp and the fuzzy cord, and gripped them tight.

Then something leapt out of the lamp in a blue flash and shook me till my teeth rattled, and I tried to pull my hands off, but they were stuck and I screamed, or a scream was torn from my throat, for I didn't recognize it, but heard it soar and quaver in the air like a violently disembodied spirit.

Then my hands jerked free, and I fell back onto my mother's bed. A small hole, blackened as if with pencil lead, pitted the center of my right palm.

This remembered terror must be part of what is in Esther's mind when, at the opening of the novel, in New York, brooding about the Rosenbergs, she says,

The idea of being electrocuted makes me sick. . . . I couldn't help wondering what it would be like, being burned alive, all along your nerves.

I thought it must be the worst thing in the world.

This is nearly confirmed at Dr. Gordon's private hospital, when the electrodes are in place on Esther/Elly's temples, and the inept man gives his patient a wire to bite.

There was a deep silence, like an indrawn breath.

Then something bent down and took hold of me like the end of the world. Whee-ee-ee-ee-ee, it shrilled, through an air crackling with blue light, and with each flash a great jolt drubbed me till I thought my bones would break and the sap fly out of me like a split plant.

I wondered what terrible thing I had done.

Shock treatment itself finally has its own, positive double. Wise Dr. Nolan has promised that, when done right, it only puts people to sleep, that some even like it. Themes come together here:

I saw the high bed, with its white, drumtight sheet, and the machine behind the bed and the masked person—I couldn't tell whether it was a man or a woman—behind the machine, and the other masked people flanking the bed on both sides. . . .

[Miss Huey, "a tall, cadaverous woman,"] set something on my tongue and in panic I bit down, and darkness wiped me out like chalk on a blackboard. . . .

I woke out of a deep, drenched sleep. . . . All the heat and fear had purged itself. I felt surprisingly at peace. The bell jar hung, suspended, a few feet above my head. I was open to the circulating air.

6.

The vision in *The Bell Jar* seems to be that human life is a shifty affair, of doubled people and doubled experience, reflecting and reversing, of many betrayals and rare, unexpected redemptions. One may be taught to find help in oneself, but if this happens it's sheer luck, because self-appraisal is always a distortion and truth what Snow White's mother saw in the mirror.

An early title for the novel was *The Girl in the Mirror.* Here are some of the girls Esther sees when she looks at herself. (Again the page numbers from which I quote: 15, 16, 83, 92, 104, 121, 150.)

In the hotel mirror, after the walk back from Lenny's: "a big, smudgy-eyed Chinese woman staring idiotically into my face . . . I was appalled to see how wrinkled and used-up I looked."

A few minutes later, in her room: "the reflection in a dentist's ball of mercury."

After she has cried, when directed to smile, for a photograph, and using her compact mirror: a "face peering from the grating of a prison cell after a prolonged beating. It looked bruised and puffy and all the wrong colors. It was a face that needed soap and water and Christian tolerance."

On the train, after Marco: "The face in the mirror looked like a sick Indian."

Then, in Dr. Gordon's waiting room: "there were no mirrors."

When she is unable to cut herself deeply enough with a razor blade, though the tub is full of hot water awaiting: "If I looked in the mirror while I did it, it would be like watching someone else, in a book or a play." But the mirror knows: "the person in the mirror was paralyzed, and too stupid to do a thing."

Finally, waking in the hospital, after the sleeping pills. This will be the ultimate mirror and, once again, a place where some themes come together. Against orders, a young nurse has left Esther with the looking glass.

At first I didn't see what the trouble was. It wasn't a mirror but a picture.

You couldn't tell whether the person in the picture was a man or a woman, because their hair was shaved off and sprouted in bristly chicken-feather tufts all over their head. One side of the person's face was purple, and bulged out in a shapeless way, shading to green along the edges, and then to a sallow yellow. The person's mouth was pale brown, with a rose-colored sore at either corner.

The most startling thing about the face was its supernatural conglomeration of bright colors.

I smiled.

The mouth in the mirror cracked into a grin.

A minute after the crash another nurse ran in. She took one look at the broken mirror, and at me, standing over the blind, white pieces. . . .

After this, there are no more mirrors in *The Bell Jar*. After this, in place of them, enter the double, doomed Joan Gilling. I don't think the replacement unintentional.

7.

Whatever the abstract roles we decide to assign the characters in *The Bell Jar*, they are never abstractions. It is one of the strengths of the book that each is brought to brief, vivid, and particular life, even the most minor. It's done with snapshot physical description, a quick ear, and a little irony.

For example, Esther is naïve about tipping (p. 43):

A dwarfish, bald man in a bellhop's uniform carried my suitcase up in the elevator and unlocked my room for me. . . . After a while I was aware of this bellhop turning on the hot and cold taps in the washbowl and saying "This is the hot and this is the cold" and switching on the radio and telling me all the names of all the New York stations and I began to get uneasy, so I kept my back to him and said firmly, "Thank you for bringing up my suitcase."

"Thank you thank you thank you. Ha!" he said, in a very nasty, insinuating tone, and before I could wheel around to see what had come over him he was gone, shutting the door behind him with a rude slam.

In the case of an important character, when Joan Gilling is first mentioned as the girl Buddy Willard has come to see at college, the irony is in unacknowledged jealousy (p. 48):

She was a big wheel—president of her class and a physics major and the college hockey champion. She always made me feel squirmy with her starey pebble-colored eyes and her gleaming tombstone teeth and her breathy voice. She was big as a horse, too. I began to think Buddy had pretty poor taste.

If the author is adept at quick-stroke characterization, she is equally so at quick-drawn scenes. I've made occasion to quote some of these, at least partially, and will be quoting others. For now I'll simply do some casual arithmetic, and report that there are seventy-five or eighty distinct scenes in the two hundred pages of *The Bell Jar,* most of them completed in fewer than a thousand words. The effect is movielike, and the movie smartly paced. It is fast, absorbing stuff, except in two stretches. Some of the first-section flashbacks seem uncontrolled and repetitious, and we are not always perfectly oriented in time. Some of the second-section, Elly material is a little tedious, because Elly, obsessed with the how-to of suicide and insensitive to others, is a tedious girl, with whom we lose patience; I do, anyway. But these are partly faults of inexperience in the writer— and there are some vastly experienced novelists around who still have trouble managing time, making dullness interesting and obsession sympathetic; likely we all do.

Much of the prose in *The Bell Jar* is direct, lucid and in no need of ornament—the description I quoted of Esther's face in the hospital mirror, for example, or the little scene with the bellhop. In the passage about Dr. Gordon's awful shock treatment the writing is more intense and more figured, as we will see again when I quote a passage concerning Esther's preoccupation with the Rosenberg execution. Admittedly, there is careless prose here and there too, as in the lamp-gripping recollection with its tooth-rattling, and its scream torn from the throat, quavering in the air like a disembodied spirit. It isn't like Victoria Lucas to be that Victorian.

Examples like that are rare. Mostly the language and image combination in *The Bell Jar* is of an easy, colloquial voice in which the thing to be visualized can grow as if in a culture. Take this, from the very first page:

> It was like the first time I saw a cadaver. For weeks afterwards, the cadaver's head floated up behind my bacon and eggs at breakfast and behind the face of Buddy Willard . . . and pretty soon I felt as though I were carrying that cadaver's head around with me on a string, like some black, noseless balloon stinking of vinegar.

When Buddy wants Esther to have a look at him with his pants down: "I kept staring at him. The only thing I could think of was turkey neck and turkey gizzards and I felt very depressed" (p. 55). Surrealist filmmakers do things like these to us, but the transformations in *The Bell Jar* are never too arbitrary to make sense, the language they're reported in never dense. Occasionally, it is labored or imitative as, for example, in a passage (bottom of p. 16) about the virtues of a hot bath, or another (p. 134) about Catholicism. The imitation seems to be of Salinger, and while I won't claim there are many vastly experienced novelists around exhibiting that particular influence, there are still certainly plenty of young ones.

8.

The flaws of execution in *The Bell Jar* are not many and not serious. They are outnumbered by examples of felicity by a margin of, say, fifty to one. There is, however, a flaw of intention to consider, though the effects of it are hard to measure. We must leave the text, for now, but not for good, and deal with Victoria Lucas as a mask.

Victoria Lucas was not supposed to be a totally serious writer. She was to write best-sellers. There is plenty of evidence for this in memoirs like Lois Ames's (*The Bell Jar*, p. 203), and in the entry for Monday, March 4, 1957, on page 156 of *The Journals of Sylvia Plath*.

Victoria Lucas, as I've tried to show, was pretty good. She had her limits. Sometimes she fell below them, more often she exceeded them. In general, she was a necessary fiction through which Sylvia Plath could hold back a really reckless commitment of talent, thought, and feeling at the depths where they are too nearly inexpressible to make for easy reading. I'll need to return to this at the end of my piece, but for now I hope you'll accept it as one of my reasons for not wanting to treat *The Bell Jar* as an autobiographical effort, in which Sylvia Plath demeans herself as Esther Greenwood. The book is something better than a document. It is a work of fiction in which, to sum up, an unhappy, intelligent schizoid, Esther Greenwood, sinks into the lesser of her two selves, becomes Elly Higginbottom—in which Elly must die so that Esther may be reborn.

If I may so describe it, then, *The Bell Jar* is a brave try at a minor work of art, rarely undercut by the inexperience and light intention permitted Victoria Lucas, instead of a nervously clever piece of confession and catharsis. It stands, supported by the poet's reputation but not really in need of it, as a small, rather haunting, American youth-book. Exit Victoria. She has served, and disserved, but not so much. Leave her to Heinemann.

9.

Now, to try to make my view persuasive, let me try to find some of the ways in which Esther, though she shares experiences with Sylvia Plath, is actually a created character.

We can begin, but not get very far, with the only physical trait Esther gives about herself, other than that she was tall, as Sylvia Plath was, too: "This dress was cut so queerly that I couldn't wear any sort of bra under it, but that didn't matter much as I was skinny as a boy and barely rippled" (p. 6). Please turn to any grown-up photograph of Sylvia Plath, including one taken in 1953, *The Bell Jar* year. You will see a buxom enough young woman.

More tellingly, as a college junior, Esther is not a poet. She isn't even much of a writer: "The only thing I was good at was winning scholarships and prizes" (p. 62). Esther is an academic overkiller, with low-key inclinations toward graduate school, or a professorship, or writing poetry, or getting into publishing, or something. There are thousands like her. There are hardly any like Sylvia Plath, who had been dedicated to writing poetry since childhood, who had begun sending out her work in high school, who had, by junior year in college at nineteen, started to accumulate publications.

Listen once more to Esther in New York: "I wasn't steering anything, not even myself. I just bumped from my hotel to work and to parties and from parties to my hotel and back to work like a numb trolleybus. . . . I couldn't get myself to react. I felt very still and very empty" (p. 2). She tags along, camp-follower of women, victim of men, listless, secretive, gluttonous, mostly depressed, and always introverted.

The Sylvia Plath we read about in the biographies could get depressed—horribly, insanely depressed—but she was still no Esther. Even when hellbent, she had energy and discipline. She sparkled, was intense, came on strong to men, women, and situations. She could dominate, entertain, flirt, impress, tease, dissimulate, and win. She was introspective often, at times introverted; we see it in the journals. But we also see in the journals a lively, attractive, passionate, and gifted young woman, probably a genius. Nobody would call Esther Greenwood a genius. I just cannot take her as a portrait of the artist as a young woman.

10.

Let me try to demonstrate this now in a way closer to my writer's heart. I am contending, still, that Sylvia Plath was creating a character, not just spilling her guts. There are five paragraphs surviving in the journals which were written during the actual New York whirl, and one of them turns on a light, for we can find it again, transmuted, in the book.

In *The Journals*, it is June 19, 1953. The Rosenbergs are to be electrocuted late that night. Sylvia Plath, in New York, helping to edit an issue of *Mademoiselle*, feels as if only she is disturbed about the execution (*Journals*, p. 82):

> The tall, beautiful, catlike girl who wore an original hat to work every day rose to one elbow from where she had been napping on the divan in the conference room, yawned, and said with beautiful, bored nastiness: "I'm so glad they're going to die." She gazed vaguely and very smugly around the room, closed her enormous green eyes, and went back to sleep.

Now watch Sylvia (or Sylvia/Victoria, if you wish) make fiction out of that, and make it thematic (p. 80):

> The night before I'd seen a play where the heroine was possessed by a dybbuk, and when the dybbuk spoke from her mouth its voice sounded so cavernous and deep you couldn't tell whether it was a man or a woman.

On page 81:

> So I said, "Isn't it awful about the Rosenbergs?" . . .
> "Yes!" Hilda said, and at last I felt I had touched a human string in the cat's cradle of her heart. It was only as the two of us waited for the others in the tomblike morning gloom of the conference room that Hilda amplified that Yes of hers.
> "It's awful such people should be alive."
> She yawned then, and her pale mouth opened on a large darkness. Fascinated, I stared at the blind cave behind her face until the two lips

met and moved and the dybbuk spoke from its hiding place, "I'm so glad they're going to die."

Isn't it the character Esther who sees tomblike gloom and large darkness, and a blind cave from which she hears the dybbuk speak, frightful and sad?

11.

My third kind of demonstration comes from the text, and will look for further irony. An author has put ironic distance between self and character when author and reader share an understanding which eludes the character. Okay. From page 10:

> "Hey, Lenny, you owe me something. Remember, Lenny, you owe me something, don't you Lenny?"
> I thought it odd Frankie should be reminding Lenny he owed him something in front of us, and we being perfect strangers, but Frankie kept saying the same thing over and over, until Lenny dug into his pocket.

Oh, come on, Esther, don't you see what's going on? Lenny was lounging about under a restaurant awning with some of the guys, when they spotted you and Doreen in the stalled cab. The others watched, laughing about it, while Lenny strolled over and persuaded the two of you to leave your cab and have a drink with him. As the three of you went by the group, Lenny said, "Come on, Frankie." And short, scrunty Frankie came along into the restaurant. Lenny went in first with Doreen. You tried to pretend you didn't see Frankie at your elbow. You sat away from him, close to Doreen. You made awkward conversation. You decided to call yourself Elly Higginbottom. You laughed at and looked down on Frankie when he asked you to dance. You said coldly that you weren't in the mood. Now Lenny and Doreen are giggling together, and Frankie has said he'd better go, stood up, and is asking for a ten-dollar payoff. You don't know what it's for? Sylvia Plath does.

Next example. On page 4, about Doreen, Esther thinks "she really was wonderfully funny."

I've looked at all the dialogue given Doreen on occasions which might produce wit. Here is what I've found (on pages 4, 6, 12–13, 39, 84).

"The only thing Doreen ever bawled me out about was bothering to get my assignments in by a deadline.

" 'What are you sweating over that for?' "

And: "You know old Jay Cee won't give a damn if that story's in tomorrow or Monday . . . Jay Cee's ugly as sin . . . I bet that old husband of hers turns out all the lights before he gets near her or he'd puke otherwise."

And: "I fitted the lid on my typewriter. . . .

"Doreen grinned. 'Smart girl.' "

And: "In private Doreen called her [Betsy] Pollyanna Cowgirl."

And, in Lenny's apartment, when Lenny is cutting up: " 'What a card. Isn't he a card?' "

And: " 'Stick around, will you? I wouldn't have a chance if he tried anything funny. Did you see that muscle?' "

After the banquet luncheon, given by *Ladies' Day*, when Esther is recovering from food poisoning (Doreen's is the first speech):

> "Well, you almost died."
>
> "I guess it was all that caviar."
>
> "Caviar nothing! It was the crabmeat. They did tests on it and it was chockfull of ptomaine."
>
> I had visions of the celestially white kitchens of *Ladies' Day* stretching into infinity. I saw avocado pear after avocado pear being stuffed with crabmeat and mayonnaise and photographed under brilliant lights. I saw the delicate, pink-mottled claw meat poking seductively through its blanket of mayonnaise. . . . Poison.
>
> "Who did tests?"
>
> "Those dodos on *Ladies' Day*. As soon as you all started keeling over like ninepins, somebody called into the office . . . and they did tests on everything left over from the big lunch. Ha!"

Finally, before the blind date with Marco:

> "Honestly . . . this one'll be different."
>
> "Tell me about him," I said stonily.
>
> "He's from Peru."
>
> "They're squat," I said. "They're ugly as Aztecs."
>
> "No, no, no, sweetie. I've already met him."

If either of this pair has been given a touch of comic vision or a glint of verbal wit, surely it's Esther, not Doreen.

Shall we believe it's unintentional?

The last example is Constantin, the simultaneous interpreter, who will squeeze no more than a girl's hand. Subtly, Sylvia Plath makes him gay—by association, when he and Esther sit by his colleague, "a stern muscular Russian girl with no makeup . . . in her double-breasted grey suit" (pp. 60–61). To have been more open than this at the outset would, of course, have taken the tension out of the failure of Esther's plan of submission. Constantin's nature never becomes clear to Esther, and the author reveals it to the reader only gradually. In his apartment after dinner (pp. 67, 68, 69, and 70), "I asked him if he was engaged or had any special girlfriend, thinking maybe that was what was the matter, but he said no, he made a point of keeping clear of such attachments."

Esther goes into his bedroom, takes off her shoes and lies down.

> Then I heard Constantin sigh and come in from the balcony. One by one his shoes clonked on the floor, and he lay down by my side. . . .
>
> I thought he must be the most beautiful man I'd ever seen . . . I thought if only I had a keen, shapely bone-structure . . . Constantin might find me interesting enough to sleep with.
>
> I woke to the sound of rain. . . .
>
> Constantin . . . was lying in his shirt and trousers and stocking feet just as I had left him when he dropped asleep . . . as I stared down, his eyelids lifted and he looked at me, and his eyes were full of love. I watched dumbly as a shutter of recognition clicked across the blur of tenderness and the wide pupils went glossy and depthless as patent leather.
>
> Constantin sat up, yawning. "What time is it?" . . .
>
> As we sat back to back on our separate sides of the bed fumbling with our shoes . . . I sensed Constantin turn around. "Is your hair always like that?"
>
> "Like what?"
>
> He didn't answer but put his hand at the root of my hair and ran his fingers out slowly to the tip ends like a comb. A little electric shock flared through me and I sat quite still. . . .
>
> "Ah, I know what it is," Constantin said. "You've just washed it."
>
> And he bent down to lace up his tennis shoes.

12.

Now, at the end of all this, I need to speculate, in a way you may feel I have no business doing. I half agree, for I have no proof outside myself that what I'm going to talk about exists, and only intuition to tell me Sylvia Plath contended with it. Yet if I were talking with Peter and Paul, I would insist on this. Shall I fear the coldness of print at my age?

I believe there is a psychic region, corresponding to the unspeakable in general human experience, which is, for writers, the unwritable. In it is that emotional experience which can never be recollected in tranquility, because to recollect it is to become disturbed again.

There is an area of feeling in myself. I feel pretty sure (but this begins to attenuate) that I've seen hints of it, now and then, in others, during thirty years of close association with younger writers —some of them not so young anymore, a few whose names you'd recognize; this has been in my second profession, which is teaching.

One of the ways of recognizing the unwritable is that you do keep trying to deal with it, to make something of it, and can, finally if at all, only in one of three ways.

The first, with awe and admiration, I shall set aside, since what comes of it is neither fiction nor poetry, but that direct confession in prose for which the term "agonized" is often used. Writing it must be like walking through the sharp streets barefoot and naked, with your head and body hair shaved off, your hands raised, everyone else in fur and the cold wind blowing. Saints can do it, I guess.

The second is more commonly available. It is to fictionalize the unwritable thoroughly enough, by wishing it off on an invented character, so that it's no longer autobiographical. This is what I feel Sylvia Plath was able to do successfully in parts one and three of *The Bell Jar*. In the third, for a final pair of instances, I'm relying on biographical information from which I learned that there was no Joan Gilling failing in the asylum while Esther Greenwood was recovering, and that Irwin the Instrument wasn't one, but another sort of man, met with after the time of maidenhood, and in a less significant way.

It was in part two, about Elly and her attempted suicide, which I've called sometimes tedious, almost antipathetic, that my intuition says the unwritable could not be written in the second way, of making fiction.

This left the third way, which is to reveal the unwritable in a system of symbols, language, allusions, and images so nearly private that only perfect, perfectly dedicated readers, to whom the reading is as serious as writing to the writer, will deserve to make them out.

While Victoria Lucas was working with Esther Greenwood and Elly Higginbottom, Sylvia Plath was writing *Ariel.*

NOTE

1. All quotes refer to the Bantam Windstone edition of *The Bell Jar* (1975).

Ted Hughes

Sylvia Plath and Her Journals

Sylvia Plath's journals exist as an assortment of notebooks and bunches of loose sheets, and the selection just published here contains about a third of the whole bulk. Two other notebooks survived for a while after her death. They continued from where the surviving record breaks off in late 1959 and covered the last three years of her life. The second of these two books her husband destroyed, because he did not want her children to have to read it (in those days he regarded forgetfulness as an essential part of survival). The earlier one disappeared more recently (and may, presumably, still turn up).

The motive in publishing these journals will be questioned. The argument against is still strong. A decisive factor has been certain evident confusions, provoked in the minds of many of her readers by her later poetry. *Ariel* is dramatic speech of a kind. But to what persona and to what drama is it to be fitted? The poems don't seem to supply enough evidence of the definitive sort. This might have been no bad thing, if a riddle fertile in hypotheses is a good one. But the circumstances of her death, it seems, multiplied every one of her statements by a wild, unknown quantity. The results, among her interpreters, have hardly been steadied by the account she gave of herself in her letters to her mother, or by the errant versions supplied by her biographers. So the question grows: how do we find

---

NOTE: "Sylvia Plath and Her Journals" was written originally as the prologue to *The Journals of Sylvia Plath*; however, an earlier, substantially shorter draft of the essay was run instead. The essay, in its present form, was then published in *Grand Street*. When I asked Ted Hughes to contribute an essay to this anthology, his decision was to include an unedited version of his proposed prologue. Grace Schulman's essay which follows, "Sylvia Plath and Yaddo," can be read as a companion piece since the appearance of Hughes's essay in *Grand Street* proved to be a seminal influence.—PA

our way through this accompaniment, which has now become almost a part of the opus? Would we be helped if we had more firsthand testimony, a more intimately assured image, of what she was really like? In answer to this, these papers, which contain the nearest thing to a living portrait of her, are offered in the hope of providing some ballast for our idea of the reality behind the poems. Maybe they will do more.

Looking over this curtailed journal, we cannot help wondering whether the lost entries for her last three years were not the more important section of it. Those years, after all, produced the work that made her name. And we certainly have lost a valuable appendix to all that later writing. Yet these surviving diaries contain something that cannot be less valuable. If we read them with understanding, they can give us the key to the most intriguing mystery about her, the key to our biggest difficulty in our approach to her poetry.

That difficulty is the extreme peculiarity in kind of her poetic gift. And the difficulty is not lessened by the fact that she left behind two completely different kinds of poetry.

Few poets have disclosed in any way the birth circumstances of their poetic gift, or the necessary purpose these serve in their psychic economy. It is not easy to name one. As if the first concern of poetry were to cover its own tracks. When a deliberate attempt to reveal all has been made, by a Pasternak or a Wordsworth, the result is discursive autobiography—illuminating enough, but not an X ray. Otherwise poets are very properly bent on exploring subject matter, themes, intellectual possibilities and modifications, evolving the foliage and blossoms and fruit of a natural cultural organism whose roots are hidden, and whose birth and private purpose are no part of the crop. Sylvia Plath's poetry, like a species on its own, exists in little else but the revelation of that birth and purpose. Though her whole considerable ambition was fixed on becoming the normal flowering and fruiting kind of writer, her work was roots only. Almost as if her entire oeuvre were enclosed within those processes and transformations that happen in other poets before they can even begin, before the muse can hold out a leaf. Or as if all poetry were made up of the feats and shows performed by the poetic spirit Ariel. Whereas her poetry is the biology of Ariel, the ontology of Ariel —the story of Ariel's imprisonment in the pine, before Prospero opened it. And it continued to be so even after the end of *The Colossus,* which fell, as it happens, in the last entries of this surviving bulk of her journal, where the opening of the pine took place and was recorded.

This singularity of hers is a mystery—an enigma in itself. It may be that she was simply an extreme case, that many other poets' works nurse and analyze their roots as doggedly as hers do, but that she is distinguished by an unusually clear root system and an abnormally clear and clinically exact system of attending to it. It may have something to do with the fact that she was a woman. Maybe her singularity derives from a feminine beeline instinct for the real priority, for what truly matters—an instinct for nursing and repairing the damaged and threatened nucleus of the self and for starving every other aspect of her life in order to feed and strengthen that, and bring that to a safe delivery.

The root system of her talent was a deep and inclusive inner crisis which seems to have been quite distinctly formulated in its chief symbols (presumably going back at least as far as the death of her father, when she was eight) by the time of her first attempted suicide, in 1953, when she was twenty-one.

After 1953, it became a much more serious business, a continuous hermetically sealed process that changed only very slowly, so that for years it looked like deadlock. Though its preoccupation dominated her life, it remained largely outside her ordinary consciousness, but in her poems we see the inner working of it. It seems to have been scarcely disturbed at all by the outer upheavals she passed through, by her energetic involvement in her studies, in her love affairs and her marriage, and in her jobs, though she used details from them as a matter of course for images to develop her X rays.

The importance of these diaries lies in the rich account they give of her attempts to understand this obscure process, to follow it, and (in vain) to hasten it. As time went on, she interpreted what was happening to her inwardly, more and more consciously, as a "drama" of some sort. After its introductory overture (everything up to 1953), the drama proper began with a "death," which was followed by a long "gestation" or "regeneration," which in turn would ultimately require a "birth" or a "rebirth," as in Dostoevsky and Lawrence and those other prophets of rebirth whose works were her sacred books.

The "death," so important in all that she wrote after it, was that almost successful suicide attempt in the summer of 1953. The mythical dimensions of the experience seem to have been deepened, and made absolute, and illuminated, by two accidents: she lay undiscovered, in darkness, only intermittently half-conscious, for "three days"; and the electric shock treatment which followed went wrong, and she was all but electrocuted—at least so she always claimed. Whether it did and she was, or not, there seems little doubt that her "three day" death, and that thunderbolt awakening, fused her dangerous inheritance into a matrix from which everything later seemed to develop—as from a radical change in the structure of her brain.

She would describe her suicide attempt as a bid to get back to her father, and one can imagine that in her case this was a routine reconstruction from a psychoanalytical point of view. But she made much of it, and it played an increasingly dominant role in her recovery and in what her poetry was able to become. Some of the implications might be divined from her occasional dealings with the Ouija board, during the late Fifties. Her father's name was Otto, and "spirits" would regularly arrive with instructions for her from one Prince Otto, who was said to be a great power in the underworld. When she pressed for a more personal communication, she would be told that Prince Otto could not speak to her directly, because he was under orders from The Colossus. And when she pressed for an audience with The Colossus, they would say he was inaccessible. It is easy to see how her effort to come to terms with the meaning this Colossus held for her, in her poetry, became more and more central as the years passed.

The strange limbo of "gestation/regeneration," which followed her "death," lasted throughout the period of this journal, and she drew from the latter part of it all the poems of *The Colossus,* her first collection. We have spoken of this process as a "nursing" of the "nucleus of the self," as a hermetically sealed, slow transformation of her inner crisis; and the evidence surely supports these descriptions of it as a deeply secluded mythic and symbolic inner theater (sometimes a hospital theater), accessible to her only in her poetry. One would like to emphasize even more strongly the weird autonomy of what was going on in there. It gave the impression of being a secret crucible, or rather a womb, an almost biological process—and just as much beyond her manipulative interference. And like a pregnancy, selfish with her resources.

We can hardly make too much of this special condition, both in our understanding of her journal and in our reading of the poems of her first book. A reader of the journal might wonder why she did not make more of day-to-day events. She had several outlandish adventures during these years, and interesting things were always happening to her. But her diary entries habitually ignore them. When she came to talk to herself in these pages, that magnetic inner process seemed to engross all her attention, one way or another. And in her poems and stories, throughout this period, she felt her creative dependence on that same process as subjection to a tyrant. It commandeered every proposal. Many passages in this present book show the deliberate—almost frantic—effort with which she tried to extend her writing, to turn it toward the world and other people, to stretch it over more of outer reality, to forget herself in some exploration of outer reality—in which she took, after all, such constant, intense delight. But the hidden workshop, the tangle of roots, the crucible, controlled everything. Everything became another image of itself, another lens into itself. And whatever it could not use in this way, to objectify some disclosure of itself, did not get onto the page at all.

Unless we take account of this we shall almost certainly misread the moods of her journal—her nightmare sense of claustrophobia and suspended life, her sense of being only the flimsy, brittle husk of what was going heavily and fierily on, somewhere out of reach inside her. And we shall probably find ourselves looking into her poems for things and qualities which could only be there if that process had been less fiercely concentrated on its own purposeful chemistry. We shall misconstrue the tone and content of the poetry that did manage to transmit from the center, and the psychological exactness and immediacy of its mournful, stressful confinement.

A Jungian might call the whole phase a classic case of the alchemical individuation of the self. This interpretation would not tie up every loose end, but it would make positive meaning of the details of the poetic imagery—those silent horrors going on inside a glass crucible, a crucible that reappears in many forms, but always glassy and always closed. Above all, perhaps, it would help to confirm a truth—that the process was, in fact, a natural and positive process, if not the most positive and healing of all involuntary responses to the damage of life: a process of self-salvation—a resurrection of her deepest spiritual vitality against the odds of her fate. And the Jungian interpretation would fit the extraordinary outcome too: the birth of her new creative self.

The significant thing, even so, in the progress she made, was surely the way she applied herself to the task. Her battered and so-often-exhausted determination, the relentless way she renewed the assault without ever really knowing what she was up against. The seriousness, finally, of her will to face what was wrong in herself, and to drag it out into examination, and to remake it—that is what is so impressive. Her refusal to rest in any halfway consolation or evasive delusion. And it produced some exemplary pieces of writing, here and there, in her diaries. It would not be so impressive if she were not so manifestly terrified of doing what she nevertheless did. At times, she seems almost invalid in her lack of inner protections. Her writing here (as in her poems) simplifies itself in baring itself to what hurts her. It is unusually devoid of intellectual superstructures—of provisional ideas, theorizings, developed fantasies, which are all protective clothing as well as tools. What she did have, clearly, was character—and passionate character at that. One sees where the language of *Ariel* got its temper—that unique blend of courage and vulnerability. The notion of her forcing herself, in her "Japanese silks, desperate butterflies," deeper into some internal furnace, strengthens throughout these pages, and remains.

But she was getting somewhere. Late in 1959 (toward the end of the surviving diaries) she had a dream, which at the time made a visionary impact on her, in which she was trying to reassemble a giant, shattered, stone Colossus. In the light of her private mythology, we can see this dream was momentous, and she versified it, addressing the ruins as "Father," in a poem which she regarded, at the time, as a breakthrough. But the real significance of the dream emerges, perhaps, a few days later, when the quarry of anthropomorphic ruins reappears, in a poem titled "The Stones." In this second poem, the ruins are none other than her hospital city, the factory where men are remade, and where, among the fragments, a new self has been put together. Or rather an old shattered self, reduced by violence to its essential core, has been repaired and renovated and born again, and—most significant of all—speaks with a new voice.

This "birth" is the culmination of her prolonged six-year "drama." It is doubtful whether we would be reading this journal at all if the "birth" recorded in that poem, "The Stones," had not happened in a very real sense, in November 1959.

The poem is the last of a sequence titled "Poem for a Birthday."

Her diary is quite informative about her plans for this piece, which began as little more than an experimental poetic idea that offered scope for her to play at imitating Roethke. But evidently there were hidden prompters. As a piece of practical magic, "Poem for a Birthday" came just at the right moment. Afterward, she knew something had happened, but it is only in retrospect that we can see what it was. During the next three years she herself came to view this time as the turning point in her writing career, the point where her real writing began.

Looking back further, maybe we can see signs and portents before then. Maybe her story "Johnny Panic and the Bible of Dreams" was the John the Baptist. And in her own recognition of the change, at the time, she spread the honors over several other poems as well—"The Manor Garden" (which is an apprehensive welcome to the approaching unborn), "The Colossus" (which is the poem describing the visionary dream of the ruined Colossus), and "Medallion" (which describes a snake as an undead, unliving elemental beauty, a crystalline essence of stone). But this poem, "The Stones," is the thing itself.

It is unlike anything that had gone before in her work. The system of association, from image to image and within the images, is quite new, and—as we can now see—it is that of *Ariel*. And throughout the poem what we hear coming clear is the now-familiar voice of *Ariel*.

In its double focus, "The Stones" is both a "birth" and a "rebirth." It is the birth of her real poetic voice, but it is the rebirth of herself. That poem encapsulates, with literal details, her "death," her treatment, and her slow, buried recovery. And this is where we can see the peculiarity of her imagination at work, where we can see how the substance of her poetry and the very substance of her survival are the same. In another poet, "The Stones" might have been an artistic assemblage of fantasy images. But she was incapable of free fantasy, in the ordinary sense. If an image of hers had its source in sleeping or waking "dream," it was inevitably the image of some meaning she had paid for or would have to pay for, in some way—that she had lived or would have to live. It had the *necessity* of a physical symptom. This is the objectivity of her subjective mode. Her internal crystal ball was helplessly truthful, in this sense. (And truthfulness of that sort has inescapable inner consequences.) It determined her lack of freedom, sure enough, as we have already seen. But it secured her loyalty to what was, for her, the most important duty of all. And for this reason the succession of images in "The Stones," in which we see her raising a new self out of the ruins of her mythical father, has to be given the status of fact. The "drama," in which she redeemed and balanced the earlier "death" with this "birth/rebirth," and from which she drew so much confidence later on, was a great simplification, but we cannot easily doubt that it epitomizes, in ritual form, the main inner labor of her life up to the age of twenty-seven.

And this is the story her diaries have to tell: how a poetic talent was forced into full expressive being, by internal need, for a purpose vital to the whole organism.

"Birth," of the sort we have been talking about, is usually found in the context of a religion, or at least of some mystical discipline. It is rare in secular literature. If "The Stones" does indeed record such a birth, we should now look for some notable effects, some exceptional flowering of energy. It is just this second phase of her career that has proved so difficult to judge in conventional literary terms. But whatever followed November 1959, in Sylvia Plath's writing, has a bearing on our assessment of what is happening in this journal.

Shortly after the date of the last poems of *The Colossus,* and the last date of her diary proper, a big change did come over her life. It took a few weeks to get into its stride.

When she sailed for England in December with her husband, though she had her new, full-formed confidence about her writing to cheer her, her life still seemed suspended, and all her ambitions as far off as ever. In a poem she wrote soon after, "On Deck," she mentions that one of her fellow passengers on the S.S. *United States,* an American astrologer—he was physically a double for James Joyce—had picked that most propitious date for launching his astrological conquest of the British public. His optimism did not rub off on her. With her last college days well behind her, and only writing and maternity ahead, the December London of 1959 gave her a bad shock—the cars seemed smaller and blacker and dingier than ever, sizzling through black wet streets. The clothes on the people seemed even grubbier than she remembered. And when she lay on a bed in a basement room in a scruffy hotel near Victoria, a week or two later with *The Rack,* by A. E. Ellis, propped open on her pregnant stomach, it seemed to her she had touched a new nadir.

Yet within the next three years she achieved one after another almost all the ambitions she had been brooding over in frustration for the last decade. In that first month her collection of poems, *The Colossus,* was taken for publication in England by Heinemann. With that out of the way, in April she produced a daughter. In early 1961, at high speed, and in great exhilaration, she wrote her autobiographical novel *The Bell Jar,* and though both Harper and Knopf rejected it in the States, Heinemann took it at once for publication in England. One important part of her life-plan was to acquire a "base," as she called it, somewhere in England, from which she hoped to make her raids on the four corners of the earth, devouring the delights and excitements. And accordingly, later in 1961, she acquired a house in the west of England. In January of 1962, she produced a son. In May of that year *The Colossus* was published in the States by Knopf.

Meanwhile, she went on steadily writing her new poems. After the promise of "The Stones," we look at these with fresh attention. And they *are* different from what had gone before. But superficially not very different. For one thing, there is little sign of *Ariel.* And she herself seemed to feel that these pieces were an interlude. She published them in magazines, but otherwise let them lie—not exactly rejected by her, but certainly not coaxed anxiously toward a next collection, as this journal shows her worrying over her earlier poems. The demands of her baby occupied her time, but this does not entirely explain the lull in her poetry. The poems themselves, as before, reveal what was going on.

Everything about her writing at this time suggests that after 1959, after she had brought her "death-rebirth" drama to a successful issue, she found herself confronted, on that inner stage, by a whole new dramatic situation—one that made her first drama seem no more than the preliminaries, before the lifting of the curtain.

And in fact that birth, which had seemed so complete in "The Stones," was dragging on. And it went on dragging on. We can follow the problematic accouchement in the poems. They swing from the apprehensions of a woman or women of sterility and death at one extreme, to joyful maternal celebration of the living and almost-born fetus at the other—with one or two encouraging pronouncements from the oracular fetus itself in between. But evidently much had still to be done. Perhaps something like the writing of *The Bell Jar* had still to be faced and got through. It is not until we come to the poems of September, October, and November of 1961—a full two years after "The Stones"—that the newborn seems to feel the draft of the outer world. And even now the voice of *Ariel*, still swaddled in the old mannerisms, is hardly more than a whimper. But at least we can see what the new situation is. We see her new self confronting—to begin with—the sea, not just the sea off Finisterre and off Hartland, but the Bay of the Dead, and "nothing, nothing but a great space"—which becomes the surgeon's 2 A.M. ward of mutilations (reminiscent of the hospital city in "The Stones"). She confronts her own moon-faced sarcophagus, her mirror clouding over, the moon in its most sinister aspect, and the yews —"blackness and silence." In this group of poems—the most chilling pieces she had written up to this time—what she confronts is all that she had freed herself from.

Throughout the *Colossus* poems, as we have seen, the fateful part of her being, the part—a large, inclusive complex—that had formerly been too much for her, had held her, as a matrix, and nursed her back to new life. Death, in this matrix (and in one sense the whole complex, which had tried to kill her and had all but succeeded, came under the sign of death), had a homeopathic effect on the nucleus that survived.

But now that she was resurrected, as a self that she could think of as an Eve (as she tried so hard to do in her radio play *Three Women*), a lover of life and of her children, she still had to deal with everything in her that remained otherwise, everything that had held her in the grave for "three days," The Other. And, it was only now, for the first time, at her first step into independent life, that she could see it clearly for what it was—confronting her, separated from her at last, to be contemplated and, if possible, overcome.

It is not hard to understand her despondency at this juncture. Her new Ariel self had evolved for the very purpose of winning this battle, and much as she would have preferred, most likely, to back off and live in some sort of truce, her next step was just as surely inescapable.

From her new position of strength, she came to grips quite quickly. After *Three Women* (which has to be heard, as naïve speech, rather than read as a literary artifact) quite suddenly the ghost of her father reappears, for the first time in two and a half years, and meets a daunting, point-blank, demythologized assessment. This is followed by the most precise description she ever gave of The Other —the deathly woman at the heart of everything she now closed in on. After this, her poems arrived at a marvelous brief poise. Three of them together, titled "Crossing the Water," "Among the Narcissi," and "Pheasant," all written within three or four days of one another in early April 1962, are unique in her work. And maybe it was this achievement, inwardly, this cool, light, very beautiful moment of mastery, that enabled her to take the next step.

Within a day or two of writing "Pheasant," she started a poem about a giant wych elm that overshadowed the yard of her home. The manuscript of this piece reveals how she began it in her usual fashion, as another poem of the interlude, maybe a successor to "Pheasant" (the actual pheasant of the poem had flown up into the actual elm), and the customary features began to assemble. But then we see a struggle break out, which continues over several pages, as the lines try to take the law into their own hands. She forced the poem back into order, and even got a stranglehold on it, and seemed to have won, when suddenly it burst all her restraints and she let it go.

And at once the *Ariel* voice emerged in full. From that day on, it never really faltered again. During the next five months she produced ten more poems. The subject matter didn't alarm her. Why should it, when Ariel was doing the very thing it had been created and liberated to do? In each poem, the terror is encountered head on, and the angel is mastered and brought to terms. The energy released by these victories was noticeable. According to the appointed coincidence of such things, after July her outer circumstances intensified her inner battle to the limits. In October, when she and her husband began to live apart, every detail of the antagonist seemed to come into focus, and she started writing at top speed, producing twenty-six quite lengthy poems in that month. In November she produced twelve, with another on December 1, and one more on December 2, before the flow stopped abruptly.

She now began to look for a flat in London. In December she found a maisonette, in a house adorned with a plaque commemorating the fact that Yeats had lived there, near Primrose Hill. She decorated this place, furnished it prettily, moved in with her children before Christmas, and set about establishing a circle of friends.

By this time she knew quite well what she had brought off in October and November. She knew she had written beyond her wildest dreams. And she had overcome, by a stunning display of power, the bogies of her life. Yet her attitude to the poems was detached. "They saved me," she said, and spoke of them as an episode that was past. And indeed it was blazingly clear that she had come through, in Lawrence's sense, and that she was triumphant. The impression of growth and new large strength in her personality was striking. The book lay completed, the poems carefully ordered. And she seemed to be under no compulsion to start writing again. On December 31 she tinkered with a poem that she had drafted in October but had not included in the *Ariel* canon, and even now she did not bother to finish it—one of the few poems (only two or three in her mature career) that she did not carry through to a finished copy.

In January 1963 what was called the coldest freeze-up in fifteen years affected her health and took toll of her energy. She was in resilient form, however, for the English publication of *The Bell Jar* on January 23. If she felt any qualms at the public release of this supercharged piece of her autobiography, she made no mention of it at the time, either in conversation or in her diary. Reading them now, the reviews seem benign enough, but at the time, like all reviews, they brought exasperation and dismay. But they did not visibly deflate her.

Then on January 28 she began to write again. She considered these poems a fresh start. She liked the different, cooler inspiration (as she described it) and the denser pattern, of the first of these, as they took shape. With afterknowledge, one certainly looks at something else—though the premonitory note, except maybe in her very last poem, is hardly more insistent than it had seemed in many an earlier piece.

But in that first week of February a number—a perverse number —of varied crises coincided. Some of these have been recounted elsewhere. No doubt all of them combined to give that unknowable element its chance, in her final act, on the early morning of Monday, February 11.

All her poems are in a sense by-products. Her real creation was that inner gestation and eventual birth of a new self-conquering self, to which her journal bears witness, and which proved itself so overwhelmingly in the *Ariel* poems of 1962. If this is the most important task a human being can undertake (and it must surely be one of the most difficult), then this is the importance of her poems, that they provide such an intimate, accurate embodiment of the whole process from beginning to end—or almost to the end.

That her new self, who could do so much, could not ultimately save her, is perhaps only to say what has often been learned on this particular field of conflict—that the moment of turning one's back on an enemy who seems safely defeated, and is defeated, is the most dangerous moment of all. And that there can be no guarantees.

Grace Schulman

Sylvia Plath and Yaddo

Sylvia Plath and Ted Hughes spent some two months at Yaddo, an artists' colony in Saratoga Springs, New York, in the autumn of 1959. There they lived and worked from September 10 until just before Thanksgiving, when they returned to her Wellesley home, soon to begin their long residence in England. It was at Yaddo that Sylvia Plath wrote the last poems in *The Colossus,* poems that marked a decisive change in her development as a woman and as a writer.

In his essay "Sylvia Plath and Her Journals," Ted Hughes recalls that these Yaddo poems brought her from the first to the second phase of her work, from "death" to "birth": "the birth of her new creative self." He writes in that essay: "During the next three years she came to view this time as the turning point in her writing career, the point where her real writing began."

The "death" he recounts was her first failed suicide attempt in 1953, when she lay undiscovered in darkness for three days, and subsequently was subjected to unsuccessful electric shock therapy. The long process of rebuilding the self took place over the following years and, in the autumn of 1959, she perceived a new measure of her own being and moved into herself.

In terms of external events of her life that autumn, we know from her letters, from her mother's comments, and from Ted Hughes's recollections, that she learned she was pregnant (with her first child, Frieda, the girl she was to deliver in England the following April); she celebrated her twenty-seventh birthday with a cake and candles and *vin rosé*; she studied German; she devised, with her husband, exercises in incantation to change the tone of her earlier descriptive poems (as in "Mussel Hunter at Rock Harbor") to a more immediate diction (as in "Mushrooms," which developed from the incantations).

Those transitional Yaddo poems which displayed her new individuality are "Blue Moles," of two dead moles she and Hughes found on the Yaddo grounds; "The Manor Garden," in which she depicts the Yaddo landscape and foretells the birth of her first child; "The Colossus," based on a dream in which she was trying to reassemble a giant, shattered, stone Colossus; at least two sections of "Poem for a Birthday" ("Flute Notes from a Reedy Pond" and "The Stones"), both generated by her own birthday; "The Burnt-out Spa," which records the ruins of a health spa near Yaddo; "Mushrooms" and "Medallion." She wrote other poems during this productive visit, but did not include them in *The Colossus*. They are "Polly's Tree," referring to Polly Hanson, a poet who served as secretary to the director; "Yaddo: The Grand Manor," an observation of the mansion; "Private Ground" and "Dark Wood, Dark Water," both based on the Yaddo landscape.[1]

To understand the dramatic change in her life and work, it is important to describe the place where it happened. Sylvia Plath wrote these poems in her West House studio, a room she described once as "low-ceilinged, painted white, with a cot, a rug, a huge, heavy darkwood table that I use as a typing and writing table with piles of room for papers and books." Of the Yaddo grounds, she told her mother: "I particularly love the scenic beauty of the estate: the rose gardens, goldfish pools, marble statuary everywhere, woodland walks, little lakes." Besides these pleasures, it is certain that she enjoyed the freedom of working undisturbed, in solitude, as well as being cared for as an artist in her own right, and meeting other artists on her own terms, after working hours.

West House, the elegant adjunct to the Yaddo mansion, has not changed considerably since 1959. When I first visited Yaddo in 1973, I found, on bookshelves just outside my West House studio, Theodore Roethke's *The Waking* and Paul Radin's *African Folktales*, two books which were essential, respectively, to Plath's earlier and later work. In the first, Roethke's vision of the natural world—a cruel, terrifying but fascinating realm—was close to Plath's view, and probably a powerful influence as well. Radin's book is filled with primitive ritual and tribal utterance, and its life-giving energy informs the celebratory voices and concerns of *Ariel*.

When I looked through the windows of the West House sitting room, where guests go often to use reference works and to meditate, I saw rows of white pines, junipers, blue spruce and Norwegian spruce trees. The white pine trunks resembled legs of a giant animal; leaves, insects, and small birds appeared distorted, as in the enlargements and diminutions found in Sylvia Plath's poems of the natural world—the "outsize hands" of "Blue Moles," the "archaic/Bones of the great trees" in "Dark Wood, Dark Water"—images which alter physical reality to convey it with more accuracy.

On a subsequent visit to Yaddo, I worked in West House again, this time in Sylvia Plath's studio. (The enormous bedroom which she and Ted Hughes had lived in is on the ground floor, near bookshelves and the sitting room with quarreled window panes.) My studio, on the top floor, had a terrace which overlooked a white pine tree with a branch that jutted toward me, bearing a starburst that changed into a mourning dove, into the limp hand of St. James the Less, a painting by El Greco I had just seen at the Hyde Collection in Glens Falls, not far from Yaddo. Objects seemed capable of change, at times because of the altering sunlight, and at other times because, during intense periods of concentration, the imagination projected its fancies upon them, dressing them in idealized garb the way the eyes can transform a lover.

The marble statues, the Tiffany vases and metal sconces in West House, the stained-glass windows of the mansion are objects which seem to flow from the imagination, and require little or no transformation. When writing about a fluted lantern, or a stereopticon with slides of the Alhambra, or trees seen through mullioned window panes, less transmutation is desirable, or even possible. In Sylvia Plath's "Yaddo: The Grand Manor," a minor poem but one that she may have had to compose to accommodate her mind to the dreamlike estate, she writes:

> Indoors, Tiffany's phoenix rises
> Above the fireplace;
> Two carved sleighs
>
> Rest on orange plush near the newel post.

The improbable scene is real, as is the ending:

The late guest

Wakens, mornings, to a cobalt sky,
A diamond-paned window,
Zinc-white snow.

Sylvia Plath was a poet of keen observation and inquiry; even when her images are distorted, or her information altered, they are so given to convey a sharper, more penetrating truth. Often she combines her precise, presentative images with strong, unusual verbs, and her lines are compressed to yield clusters of strong accents. However, when writing of Yaddo interiors, the strong verbs drop away, and her skillful molding of images is lessened. It is as though she found that simply by recording the fantastic objects in the manor houses, rather than by analyzing them or recreating them, she could convey their being.

Occasionally, this lack of meticulous precision freed her to develop ways of examining inner terrors and dreams, methods which were to become central to *Ariel*. These devices have their roots in the Yaddo period. "The Manor Garden," a Yaddo landscape poem which looks toward the birth of her child, is far more successful than "Yaddo: The Grand Manor":

The fountains are dry and the roses over.
Incense of death. Your day approaches.
The pears fatten like little buddhas.
A blue mist is dragging the lake.

You move through the era of fishes,
The smug centuries of the pig—
Head, toe and finger
Come clear of the shadow. History

Nourishes these broken flutings,
These crowns of acanthus,
And the crow settles her garments.
You inherit white heather, a bee's wing,

Two suicides, the family wolves,
Hours of blankness. Some hard stars
Already yellow the heavens.
The spider on its own string

Crosses the lake. The worms
Quit their usual habitations.

> The small birds converge, converge
> With their gifts to a difficult borning.

The first line, which could be taken for surrealism, actually has its basis in accurate observation: at Yaddo in autumn, stone fountains have a bygone quality, and the rose garden is bare. So, too, with the "blue mist," and, once again, the poet finds precisely the right verb for the lake image. The "broken flutings" and "crowns of acanthus," turning up in "The Colossus," addressed to the father, as "Your fluted bones and acanthine hair," are actual objects found among the stone and marble statuary she loved on the Yaddo ground.

This manner of observation has an interesting bearing on the imagery in *Ariel*. In earlier poems of the natural world, such as "November Graveyard," she shows a remarkable fidelity to the living object in developing the graveyard metaphor of bare trees. In later poems, such as "Elm," her images are associated but born of genuine observation, as though fantastic images have their place in reality, and dreamlike objects are genuine, existing simultaneously with natural things.

In "The Manor Garden," she writes of the child growing in her, surrounded by death, and by chilly, terrifying natural images. Further, those images of the physical universe lack their autonomy, being pressed to serve a human cause. Still, this poem has an apparent celebratory quality: the fetus is strong and alive ("Head, toe and finger/Come clear of the shadow"), and there is certainty about the birth, difficult though the borning may be. The woman, threatened by her past, is nevertheless sure of her unborn child's activity and strength ("Your day approaches" and "You move through the era of fishes"). Like many of Sylvia Plath's later poems, it is a work of praise—a fearful praise, but one that may be even stronger for its implicit faith in life despite lurking terrors.

"Blue Moles" is another of the transitional Yaddo poems which exhibits this phase of her writing at its best. Its composition was preceded by "Private Ground," a poem she excluded from *The Colossus,* and one which is considerably weaker for its discursiveness and lack of focus. In the last stanza of "Private Ground," however, she attempts what she achieves in "Blue Moles"—the unlikely identification between the speaker and dead creatures. All morning, the guest has been watching the handyman draining the goldfish ponds.

Then,

> I bend over this drained basin where the small fish
> Flex as the mud freezes.
> They glitter like eyes, and I collect them all.

In "Blue Moles," the stronger poem, she achieves that identification—an uneasy unity—with the wretched natural creatures:

(1)

> They're out of the dark's ragbag, these two
> Moles dead in the pebbled rut,
> Shapeless as flung gloves, a few feet apart—
> Blue suede a dog or fox has chewed.
> One, by himself, seemed pitiable enough,
> Little victim unearthed by some large creature
> From his orbit under the elm root.
> The second carcass makes a duel of the affair:
> Blind twins bitten by bad nature.
>
> The sky's far dome is sane and clear.
> Leaves, undoing their yellow caves
> Between the road and the lake water,
> Bare no sinister spaces. Already
> The moles look neutral as the stones.
> Their corkscrew noses, their white hands
> Uplifted, stiffen in a family pose.
> Difficult to imagine how fury struck—
> Dissolved now, smoke of an old war.

(2)

> Nightly the battle-shouts start up
> In the ear of the veteran, and again
> I enter the soft pelt of the mole.
> Light's death to them: they shrivel in it.
> They move through their mute rooms while I sleep,
> Palming the earth aside, grubbers
> After the fat children of root and rock.
> By day, only the topsoil heaves.
> Down there one is alone.
>
> Outsize hands prepare a path,
> They go before: opening the veins,
> Delving for the appendages

Of beetles, sweetbreads, shards—to be eaten
Over and over. And still the heaven
Of final surfeit is just as far
From the door as ever. What happens between us
Happens in darkness, vanishes
Easy and often as each breath.

In the first section, Plath presents, in hard, unsparing detail, two moles found dead, by the exigencies of a violent, natural order, and observed in a stony groove at Yaddo. Later, the observer finds an unexpected oneness with them ("I enter the soft pelt"), while preserving gingerly her own detachment ("while I sleep," "the topsoil heaves"). As in many of her nature poems, strong active verbs, compression, and crowded lines with heavy stresses and few light syllables convey her wonder and fascination with the victimized creatures, and also with the cruel natural world. Plath's moving, probing moles, "palming the earth aside," are akin to her own method of inquiry, her search for information, her passion for fact. These night creatures, ill-fated, shriveling in light, suggest human defeat and solitude, and are, more subtly, images of the unconscious. Death and the unconscious are quietly linked here in a way that creativity itself emerges as a creature threatened by light. The striking effect of "Blue Moles," though, is the poet's excitement and amazement, qualities enforced by the heavily stressed lines. Although what she depicts is dead and cold, her passion and wonder epitomize life, and this vitality is echoed by the music of the poem.

In "Mushrooms," another of the poems written during her Yaddo stay, Plath is so closely identified with the plants as to speak for them as "we." Again, they are objects that move at night:

Overnight, very
Whitely, discreetly,
Very quietly

Our toes, our noses
Take hold on the loam,
Acquire the air.

Nobody sees us,
Stops us, betrays us;
The small grains make room.

In the last three stanzas, the mushrooms declare their triumph:

> We are shelves, we are
> Tables, we are meek,
> We are edible,
>
> Nudgers and shovers
> In spite of ourselves.
> Our kind multiplies:
>
> We shall by morning
> Inherit the earth.
> Our foot's in the door.

"Mushrooms," written November 13 and one of the last poems she wrote at Yaddo, looks toward the new mode in which she speaks for the person or object she contemplates. It prefigures the liberating voices of *Ariel*. Here, though, the identification is with a force that is energetic and winning, but frightening and aggressive. The human character of the vegetable mushrooms seems evident in the language: "discreetly," "our toes, our noses," "nudgers and shovers." The poet is writing of a physical universe that is threatening and cold, but the prevailing tone is, again, astonishment.

According to Ted Hughes, "The Colossus" and several sections of "Poem for a Birthday" (a poem written on November 4) follow a dream she had in which she was trying to assemble a giant shattered, stone Colossus.

If a poet's use of imagery were ever predictable, it might be expected that Sylvia Plath would dwell on images of stone at the Yaddo estate. In fact, stones are everywhere in that place: there are stone fountains; stone pedestals; the fieldstone towers of West House; the turreted sandstone mansion with its stone terrace; the stone arch to a stately rose garden; "the rock garden," in which water streams from a pile of moss-covered black rocks and falls into a pool, enclosed by stones, on ground where fallen pine needles have turned amber in the sunlight; the gravestones of Spenser Trask and his wife, Katrina, who willed their estate to artists.

Nearly all of Plath's Yaddo poems incorporate images of stones, often associated with dead creatures. The dead moles are seen "neutral as the stones"; "The Manor Garden" begins with an image of dry stone fountains and an ambiance of death; in "Private Ground," the goldfish perish in drained stone basins; in "Medallion," the poet, in silent wonder, examines a dead snake, turning it in the light, and recalls: "When I split a rock one time/The garnet bits burned like that." And, of course, the overwhelming figure of the broken stone Colossus, her title poem for her first collection of poems, evokes the concluding statement: "No longer do I listen for the scrape of a keel/On the blank stones of the landing."

So it is not surprising that she dreamed of the demolished Colossus while she lived among the stones at Yaddo. Moreover, her father's actual gravestone had affected her deeply when she had visited it in Azalea Path, Winthrop, Massachusetts, on March 9 of that year. She had written:

> Three graveyards separated by streets, all made within the last fifty years or so, ugly crude black stones, headstones together, as if the dead were sleeping head to head in a poorhouse. In the third yard, on a flat grassy area looking across a sallow barren stretch to rows of wooden tenements I found the flat stone: *Otto E. Plath: 1885–1940.* Right beside the path, where it would be walked over. Felt cheated. My temptation to dig him up. To prove he existed and really was dead.

This reflection is quoted in *The Collected Poems,* in a note to "Electra on the Azalea Path," a poem she excluded from *The Colossus.* In it, she links her father's death with her own longing for extinction, and ends with a hard-edged but pitiable cry of self-loathing: "O pardon the one who knocks for pardon at/Your gate, father—your hound-bitch, daughter, friend./It was my love that did us both to death." The cry *is* pitiable, but, because of excessive emotion, less believable than her impious attitude which follows, especially in "The Colossus."

In "Sylvia Plath and Her Journals," Ted Hughes provides a gloss on the father in "The Colossus" when he writes of her dealings, in the late fifties, with a Ouija board, whose agents would bring words from Prince Otto (her father's name), an underworld force. Hughes writes:

> When she pressed for a more personal communication, she would be told that Prince Otto could not speak to her directly, because he was under orders from the Colossus. And when she pressed for an audience with The Colossus, they would say he was inaccessible.

In "Ouija" and in "Electra on the Azalea Path," both preceding the composition of "The Colossus," the male figures are powerful and remote, "a chilly god, a god of shades," in the earlier "Ouija," and a loved dead father in the later poem.

In the light of these earlier poems and events, it does seem clear that "The Colossus" represents a turning point in her poems about the father, about the gods in her mythology, and about what she spoke of as her "death," the failed suicide attempt of 1953. After "The Colossus," those themes are objectified, or developed presentatively, with minimal description. "The Colossus" itself exhibits a rather sassy, defiant attitude toward the stone ruins addressed as father. Where "Ouija" called forth a god, "The Colossus" portrays another creature entirely: "Perhaps you consider yourself an oracle,/Mouthpiece of the dead, or of some god or other." Most striking are the ironic, mock-heroic effects; antithetical to the damaged stone mass, the speaker performs small, domestic labors: "Scaling little ladders with gluepots and pails of Lysol/I crawl like an ant in mourning/Over the weedy acres of your brow . . ."

"The Colossus" is more successful than "Electra on the Azalea Path" because of its frankly unsentimental view, enforced by withheld emotion and by a preposterous, wildly humorous central image. If the massive image here is inaccessible, like the earlier figures, the speaker is irreverent, and is, in fact, weary of trying to mend the immense stone ruins. Plath is still very far from her outcry of 1962, "Daddy, daddy, you bastard, I'm through." She is, however, at this point, turning from the stone wreckage of another being to the ruins of her own. The movement is vital, for it indicates her wish to leave death—her father's actual death and her own dramatized death—for new life. That transformation took place among the stones of Yaddo in the fall of 1959.

Accordingly, "The Stones" is the final poem of the sequence "Poem for a Birthday," written at Yaddo, and it carries over the ruins of "The Colossus." In "The Stones," though, the scene is a hospital city "where men are mended," and the speaker is one who has lived in fragments, and is now reborn. The entire sequence is a departure from her concern with the cruel natural world and its victimized creatures, and from the received mythology of the earlier poems: "The wingy myths won't tug at us anymore," she writes, in "Flute Notes from a Reedy Pond," another poem in the sequence. "The Stones" is the seventh, and last:

> This is the city where men are mended.
> I lie on a great anvil.
> The flat blue sky-circle
>
> Flew off like the hat of a doll
> When I fell out of the light. I entered
> The stomach of indifference, the wordless cupboard.
>
> The mother of pestles diminished me.
> I became a still pebble.
> The stones of the belly were peaceable,
>
> The head-stone quiet, jostled by nothing.
> Only the mouth-hole piped out,
> Importunate cricket
>
> In a quarry of silences.
> The people of the city heard it.
> They hunted the stones, taciturn and separate,
>
> The mouth-hole crying their locations.
> Drunk as a foetus
> I suck at the paps of darkness.
>
> The food tubes embrace me. Sponges kiss my lichens away.
> The jewelmaster drives his chisel to pry
> Open one stone eye.
>
> This is the after-hell: I see the light.
> A wind unstoppers the chamber
> Of the ear, old worrier.
>
> Water mollifies the flint lip,
> And daylight lays its sameness on the wall.
> The grafters are cheerful,
>
> Heating the pincers, hoisting the delicate hammers.
> A current agitates the wires
> Volt upon volt. Catgut stitches my fissures.
>
> A workman walks by carrying a pink torso.
> The storerooms are full of hearts.
> This is the city of spare parts.

My swaddled legs and arms smell sweet as rubber.
Here they can doctor heads, or any limb.
On Fridays the little children come

To trade their hooks for hands.
Dead men leave eyes for others.
Love is the uniform of my bald nurse.

Love is the bone and sinew of my curse.
The vase, reconstructed, houses
The elusive rose.

Ten fingers shape a bowl for shadows.
My mendings itch. There is nothing to do.
I shall be good as new.

Ted Hughes sees this poem as the culmination of her rebuilding a new self out of her father's "ruins," her primary work up to age twenty-seven. He writes of "The Stones": "It is the birth of her real poetic voice, but it is the rebirth of herself. That poem encapsulates, with literal details, her 'death,' her treatment, and her slow, buried recovery."

In this poem she writes in the well-known voice of *Ariel*, replacing the earlier narrative, expository utterance with stark, passionate lines which cry out for life in the midst of death. It represents a great leap from her poems of the cold natural universe. "The Stones" has an associative movement, built on images she has considered and used, for some years, in descriptive contexts and in a tone of Romantic wonder. "The Stones" begins with the repair of her fallen self, her earlier "death," the stillness broken only by her voice "in a quarry of silences." It progresses in a rapid, jerky manner, the passionate outcries held in check by her skillful use of terza rima, the form of many of the Yaddo poems, and done to technical perfection in "Medallion." In "The Stones," the work of mending is given, image by image: "The jewelmaster drives his chisel to pry/Open one stone eye." Then the light that was "death" to the moles, as well as the speaker, is painfully manifest: "This is the after-hell: I see the light." The senses are opened, delicately but causing torment. The "current" is a healing one; the catgut stitches are benign.

She writes with fierce irony, with terror, but with praise, for a hospital that will substitute human qualities—hearts, eyes—for the ruins of a toppled being. "The Stones" is a poem of hard praise for life:

> Love is the bone and sinew of my curse.
> The vase, reconstructed, houses
> The elusive rose.

That life, however anguished, is the inevitable goal, the outcome of her passionate inquiry into tormented existence around her. The inquiry, the wonder, dazzles her into knowing she will survive in any way she can. "I shall be good as new" is her conclusion, her solemn promise.

NOTE

1. The information that these poems were written at Yaddo in autumn 1959 is from "Notes on the Chronological Order of Sylvia Plath's Poems," by Ted Hughes, in which the dates are approximate, and from the groupings, with exact dates, in Sylvia Plath, *The Collected Poems*, edited by Ted Hughes (New York: Harper & Row, 1981).

Anne Sexton

The Barfly Ought to Sing

I can add, for Sylvia, only a small sketch and two poems—one poem written for her at the news of her death and the other, written a year later, written directly for both of us and for that place where we met . . . "balanced there, suicides sometimes meet. . . ."

I knew her for a while in Boston. We did grow up in the same suburban town, Wellesley, Massachusetts, but she was about four years behind me and we never met. Even if we had, I wonder if we would have become close friends, back then—she was so bright, so precocious and determined to be special while I was only a pimply boy-crazy thing, flunking most subjects, thinking I was never special. We didn't meet, at any rate, until she was married to Ted Hughes and living in Boston. We met because we were poets. Met, not for protocol, but for truth. She heard, and George Starbuck heard, that I was auditing a class at Boston University given by Robert Lowell. They kind of followed me in, joined me there and so we orbited around the class silently. If we talked at all then we were fools. We knew too much about it to talk. Silence was wiser, when we could command it. We tried, each one in his own manner; sometimes letting our own poems come up, as for a butcher, as for a lover. Both went on. We kept as quiet as possible in view of the father.

Then, after the class, we would pile into the front seat of my old Ford and I would drive quickly through the traffic to, or near, The Ritz. I would always park illegally in a LOADING ONLY ZONE, telling them gaily, "It's okay, because we are only going to get loaded!" Off we'd go, each on George's arm, into The Ritz to drink three or four or two martinis. George even has a line about this in his first book of poems, *Bone Thoughts*. He wrote, "I weave with two sweet ladies out of The Ritz." Sylvia and I, such sleep mongers, such death mongers, were those two sweet ladies.

In the lounge bar of The Ritz, not a typical bar at all, but very plush, deep dark red carpeting, red leather chairs around polite little tables and with waiters, white coated and awfully hushed, where one knew upon stepping down the five velvet red steps that he was entering *something*, we entered. The waiters knew their job. They waited on the best of Boston, or at least, celebrities. We always hoped they'd make a mistake in our case and think us some strange Hollywood types. There had to be something to explain all our books, our snowboots, our clutter of poems, our oddness, our quick and fiery conversations—and always the weekly threesome hunched around their small but fashionable table.

Often, very often, Sylvia and I would talk at length about our first suicides; at length, in detail, and in depth between the free potato chips. Suicide is, after all, the opposite of the poem. Sylvia and I often talked opposites. We talked death with burned-up intensity, both of us drawn to it like moths to an electric light bulb. Sucking on it! She told the story of her first suicide in sweet and loving detail and her description in *The Bell Jar* is just the same story. It is a wonder that we didn't depress George with our ego-centricity. Instead, I think, we three were stimulated by it, even George, as if death made each of us a little more real at the moment. Thus we went on, in our fashion, ignoring Lowell and the poems left behind. Poems left behind were technique—lasting but, actually, over. We talked death and this was life for us, lasting in spite of us, or better, because of us, our intent eyes, our fingers clutching the glass, three pairs of eyes fixed on someone's—each one's gossip. I know that such fascination with death sounds strange (one does not argue that it isn't sick—one knows it *is*—there's no excuse), and that people cannot understand. They keep, every year, each year, asking me, "Why, why?" So here is the Why-poem, for both of us, those sweet ladies at The Ritz. I do feel somehow that it's the same answer that Sylvia would have given. She's since said it for me in so many poems—so I try to say it for us in one of mine. . . .

Wanting to Die

Since you ask, most days I cannot remember.
I walk in my clothing, unmarked by that voyage.
Then the almost unnameable lust returns.

Even then I have nothing against life.
I know well the grass blades you mention,
the furniture you have placed under the sun.

But suicides have a special language.
Like carpenters they want to know *which tools.*
They never ask *why build.*

Twice I have so simply declared myself,
have possessed the enemy, eaten the enemy,
have taken on his craft, his magic.

In this way, heavy and thoughtful,
warmer than oil or water,
I have rested, drooling at the mouth-hole.

I did not think of my body at needle point.
Even the cornea and the leftover urine were gone.
Suicides have already betrayed the body.

Still-born, they don't always die,
but dazzled, they can't forget a drug so sweet
that even children would look on and smile.

To thrust all that life under your tongue!—
that all by itself becomes a passion.
Death's a sad bone; bruised, you'd say,

and yet she waits for me, year after year,
to so delicately undo an old wound,
to empty my breath from its bad prison.

Balanced there, suicides sometimes meet,
raging at the fruit, a pumped up moon,
leaving the bread they mistook for a kiss,

leaving the page of the book carelessly open,
something unsaid, the phone off the hook
and the love, whatever it was, an infection.

And balanced there we did meet and never asking *why build*—
only asking *which tools.* This was our fascination. I neither could nor

would give you reasons why either of us wanted *to build*. It is not my place to tell you Sylvia's why nor my desire to tell you mine. But I do say, come picture us exactly at our fragmented meetings, consumed at our passions and at our infections, as we ate five free bowls of potato chips and consumed lots of martinis.

After this we would weave out of The Ritz to spend our last pennies at the Waldorf Cafeteria—a dinner for seventy cents. George was in no hurry. He was separating from his wife. Sylvia's Ted was either able to wait or was busy enough with his own work and I had to stay in the city (I live outside of it) for a 7 P.M. appointment with my psychiatrist. A funny three.

I have heard since that Sylvia was determined from childhood to be great, a great writer at the least of it. I tell you, at the time I did not notice this in her. Something told me to bet on her but I never asked it why. I was too determined to bet on myself to actually notice where she was headed in her work. Lowell said, at the time, that he liked her work and that he felt her poems got right to the point. I didn't agree. I felt they really missed the whole point. (These were early poems of hers—poems on the way, on the working toward way.) I told Mr. Lowell that I felt she dodged the point and did so perhaps because of her preoccupation with form. Form was important for Sylvia and each really good poet has one of his own. No matter what he calls it—free verse or what. Still, it belongs to you or it doesn't. Sylvia hadn't then found a form that belonged to her. Those early poems were all in a cage (and not ever her own cage at that). I felt she hadn't found a voice of her own, wasn't, in truth, free to be herself. Yet, of course, I knew she was skilled—intense, skilled, perceptive, strange, blonde, lovely, Sylvia.

From England to America we exchanged a few letters. I have them now, of course. She mentions my poems and perhaps I sent her new ones as I wrote—I'm not sure. The time of the LOADING ONLY ZONE was gone as now we sent aerograms back and forth, now and then. George was in Rome. He never wrote. He divorced and remarried over there. Sylvia wrote of one child, keeping bees, another child, my poems—happy, gossip-letters, and then, with silence between us, she died.

After her death, with the printing of her last poems, I read that she gave me credit on a BBC program, credit as an influence upon her work. Certainly she never told me anything about it. But then, maybe she wouldn't have—nothing that ordinary, nothing that direct. She gave me and Robert Lowell (both in a rather casual lump, Sylvia!) credit for our breakthrough into the personal in poetry. I suppose we might have shown her something about daring—daring to tell it true. W. D. Snodgrass showed me in the first place. Perhaps he influenced Robert Lowell too—I can't speak for him. But let's get down to facts. I'm sure Sylvia's influences are hidden, as with most of us, and if one feels compelled to name an influence then let us begin with Theodore Roethke. I remember writing to Sylvia in England after *The Colossus* came out and saying something like, "if you're not careful, Sylvia, you will out-Roethke Roethke," and she replied that I had guessed accurately and that he had been a strong influence on her work. Believe me, no one ever tells one's real influences—and certainly not on the radio or the TV or in interviews, if he can help it. As a matter of fact, I probably guessed wrong and she was lying to me. She ought to. I'd never tell anyone and she was smarter than I am about such hidden things. Poets will not only hide influences. They will bury them! And not that her lines reminded me of Roethke—but the openness to metaphor, the way they both have (and Sylvia even more so in her last work) of jumping straight into their own image and then believing it. No doubt of it—at the end, Sylvia burst from her cage and came riding straight out with the image-ridden-darer, Roethke. But maybe she buried her so-called influence deeper than that, deeper than any one of us would think to look, and if she did I say good luck to her. Her poems do their own work. I don't need to sniff them for distant relatives of some sort. I'm against it. Maybe I did give her a sort of daring, but that's all she should have said. That's all that's similar about our work. Except for death—yes, we have that in common (and there must be enough other poets with that theme to fill an entire library). Never mind last diggings. They don't matter. What matters is her poems. These last poems stun me. They eat time. As for death—

Sylvia's Death

for Sylvia Plath

O Sylvia, Sylvia,
with a dead box of stones and spoons,

with two children, two meteors
wandering loose in the tiny playroom,

with your mouth into the sheet,
into the roofbeam, into the dumb prayer,

(O Sylvia, Sylvia,
where did you go
after you wrote me
from Devonshire
about raising potatoes
and keeping bees?)

what did you stand by,
just how did you lie down into?

Thief!—
how did you crawl into,

crawl down alone
into the death I wanted so badly and for so long,

the death we said we both outgrew,
the one we wore on our skinny breasts,

the one we talked of so often each time
we downed three extra dry martinis in Boston,

the death that talked of analysts and cures,
the death that talked like brides with plots,

the death we drank to,
the motives and then the quiet deed?

(In Boston
the dying
ride in cabs,
yes death again,
that ride home
with *our* boy.)

O Sylvia, I remember the sleepy drummer
who beat on our eyes with an old story,

how we wanted to let him come
like a sadist or a New York fairy

to do his job,
a necessity, a window in a wall or a crib,

and since that time he waited
under our heart, our cupboard,

and I see now that we store him up
year after year, old suicides

and I know, at the news of your death,
a terrible taste for it, like salt.

(And me,
me too.
And now, Sylvia,
you again,
with death again,
the ride home
with *our* boy.)

And I say only
with my arms stretched out into that stone place,

what is your death,
but an old belonging,

a mole that fell out
of one of your poems?

(O friend,
while the moon's bad,
and the king's gone
and the queen's at her wit's end,
the bar fly ought to sing!)

O tiny mother,
you too!
O funny duchess!
O blonde thing!

A. Alvarez

Sylvia Plath: A Memoir

As I remember it, I met Sylvia and her husband in London in the spring of 1960. My first wife and I were living near Swiss Cottage, on the unsmart edge of literary Hampstead, in a tall Edwardian building of particularly ugly red brick; it was the color of some old boiler that had been left out to rust for so long that even the brightness of decay had worn off. When we moved in the place had just been converted by one of those grab-and-get-out property companies that did so well before the Rachman scandal made life harder for extortionist landlords. Naturally, they had made a shoddy job of it: the fittings were cheap and the finish awful; the window frames seemed too small for the brickwork around them and there were large, rough gaps at every joint. But we had sanded the floors and painted the place out in bright colors. Then we bought bits and pieces from the junk-furniture dealers in Chalk Farm, and sanded and painted them, too. So in the end it seemed gay enough in a fragile, skin-deep way; just the place for the first baby, the first book, the first real unhappiness. By the time we left eighteen months later, there were gaping cracks in the outer wall where the new windows had been cut. But by that time there were gaping cracks in our lives, too, so it all seemed to fit.

Since I was the regular poetry critic for *The Observer* I saw few writers. To know whom I was reviewing seemed to make too many difficulties: nice men often write bad verse and good poets can be monsters; more often than not, both the man and his work were unspeakable. It seemed easier all around not to be able to put a face to the name, and judge solely on the printed page. I kept to my rule even when I was told that Ted Hughes was living nearby, just across

Primrose Hill, with an American wife and small baby. Three years before, he had brought out *The Hawk in the Rain,* which I admired greatly. But there was something about the poems which made me suspect that he wouldn't care what I thought. They seemed to emerge from an absorbed, physical world that was wholly his own; for all the technical skill deployed, they gave the impression that literary goings-on were no concern of the author. "Don't worry," I was told, "he never talks shop." I was also told that he had a wife called Sylvia, who also wrote poetry, "but"—and this was said reassuringly—"she's very sharp and intelligent."

In 1960 came *Lupercal.* I thought it the best book by a young poet that I had read since I began my stint on *The Observer.* When I wrote a review to say so, the paper asked for a short piece about him for one of the more gossipy pages. I phoned him and we arranged to take our kids for a walk on Primrose Hill. It seemed like a nice, neutral idea.

They were living in a tiny flat not far from the Regent's Park Zoo. Their windows faced onto a run-down square: peeling houses around a scrappy wilderness of garden. Closer to the Hill gentility was advancing fast: smart Sunday newspaper house agents had their boards up, the front doors were all fashionable colors—"Cantaloupe," "Tangerine," "Blueberry," "Thames Green"—and everywhere was a sense of gleaming white interiors, the old houses writ large and rich with new conversions.

Their square, however, had not yet been taken over. It was dirty, cracked, and rackety with children. The rows of houses that led off it were still occupied by the same kind of working-class families they had been built for eighty years before. No one, as yet, had made them chic and quadrupled their price—though that was to come soon enough. The Hughes's flat was one floor up a bedraggled staircase, past a pram in the hall and a bicycle. It was so small that everything appeared to be sideways on. You inserted yourself into a hallway so narrow and jammed that you could scarcely take off your coat. The kitchen seemed to fit one person at a time, who could span it with arms outstretched. In the living room you sat side by side, longways on, between a wall of books and a wall of pictures. The bedroom off it, with its flowered wallpaper, seemed to have room for nothing except a double bed. But the colors were cheerful, the bits and pieces pretty, and the whole place had a sense of liveliness about it, of things being done. A typewriter stood on a little table by the window, and they took turns at it, each working shifts while the other minded the baby. At night they cleared it away to make room for the child's cot. Later they borrowed a room from another American poet, W. S. Merwin, where Sylvia worked the morning shift, Ted the afternoon.

This was Ted's time. He was on the edge of a considerable reputation. His first book had been well received and won all sorts of prizes in the States, which usually means that the second book will be an anticlimax. Instead, *Lupercal* effortlessly fulfilled and surpassed all the promises of *The Hawk in the Rain*. A figure had emerged on the drab scene of British poetry, powerful and undeniable. Whatever his natural hesitations and distrusts of his own work, he must have had some sense of his own strength and achievement. God alone knew how far he was eventually going but in one essential way he had already arrived. He was a tall, strong-looking man in a black corduroy jacket, black trousers, black shoes; his dark hair hung untidily forward; he had a long, witty mouth. He was in command.

In those days Sylvia seemed effaced, the poet taking a back seat to the young mother and housewife. She had a long, rather flat body, a longish face, not pretty but alert and full of feeling, with a lively mouth and fine brown eyes. Her brownish hair was scraped severely into a bun. She wore jeans and a neat shirt, briskly American: bright, clean, competent, like a young woman in a cookery advertisement, friendly and yet rather distant.

Her background, of which I knew nothing then, belied her housewifely air. She had been a child prodigy—her first poem was published when she was eight—and then a brilliant student, winning every prize to be had, at Wellesley High School, then at Smith College: scholarships all the way, straight A's, Phi Beta Kappa, president of this and that college society, and prizes for everything. A New York glossy magazine, *Mademoiselle*, had picked her as an outstanding possibility and wined her, dined her, and photographed her all over Manhattan. Then, almost inevitably, she had won a Fulbright to Cambridge, where she met Ted Hughes. They were married in 1956, on Bloomsday. Behind Sylvia was a self-sacrificing, widowed mother, a schoolteacher who had worked herself into the ground so that her two children might flourish. Sylvia's father— ornithologist, entomologist, ichthyologist, international authority on bumblebees and professor of biology at Boston University—had died when she was eight. Both parents were of German stock and were German-speaking, academic and intellectual. When she and Ted went to the States after Cambridge, a glittering university career seemed both natural and assured.

On the surface it was a typical success story: the brilliant examination-passer driving forward so fast and relentlessly that nothing could ever catch up with her. And it can last a lifetime, provided nothing checks the momentum, and the vehicle of all those triumphs doesn't disintegrate into sharp fragments from sheer speed and pressure. But already her progress had twice lurched to a halt. Between her month on *Mademoiselle* and her last year in college she had had the nervous breakdown and desperately serious suicide attempt which became the theme of her novel, *The Bell Jar*. Then, once reestablished at Smith—"an outstanding teacher," said her colleagues—the academic prizes no longer seemed worth the effort. So in 1958 she had thrown over university life—Ted had never seriously contemplated it—and gone free-lance, trusting her luck and talent as a poet. All this I learned much later. Now Sylvia had simply slowed down; she was subdued, absorbed in her new baby daughter, and friendly only in that rather formal, shallow, transatlantic way that keeps you at your distance.

Ted went downstairs to get the pram ready while she dressed the baby. I stayed behind a minute, zipping up my son's coat. Sylvia turned to me, suddenly without gush.

"I'm so glad you picked that poem," she said. "It's one of my favorites but no one else seemed to like it."

For a moment I went completely blank; I didn't know what she was talking about. She noticed and helped me out.

"The one you put in *The Observer* a year ago. About the factory at night."

"For Christ's sake, Sylvia *Plath*." It was my turn to gush. "I'm sorry. It was a lovely poem."

"Lovely" wasn't the right word, but what else do you say to a bright young housewife? I had picked it from a sheaf of poems which had arrived from America, immaculately typed, with addressed envelope and international reply coupon efficiently supplied. All of them were polished and talented, but that in itself was not rare in those days. The late Fifties was a period of particularly high style in American verse, when every campus worth its name had its own "brilliant" poetic technician in residence. But at least one of these poems had more going for it than rhetorical elegance. It had no title, though later, in *The Colossus,* she called it "Night Shift." It was one of those poems which starts by saying what they are *not* about so strongly that you don't believe the explanations that follow:

> It was not a heart, beating,
> That muted boom, that clangor
> Far off, not blood in the ears
> Drumming up any fever
>
> To impose on the evening.
> The noise came from outside:
> A metal detonating
> Native, evidently, to
>
> These stilled suburbs: nobody
> Startled at it, though the sound
> Shook the ground with its pounding.
> It took root at my coming . . .

It seemed to me more than a piece of good description, to be used and moralized upon as the fashion of that decade dictated. The note was aroused and all the details of the scene seemed continually to be turning inward. It is a poem, I suppose, about fear, and although in the course of it the fear is rationalized and explained (that pounding in the night is caused by machines turning), it ends by reasserting precisely the threatening masculine forces there were to be afraid of. It had its moments of awkwardness—for example, the prissy, pausing flourish in the manner of Wallace Stevens: "Native, evidently, to . . ."—but compared with most of the stuff that thudded unsolicited through my letter-box every morning, it was that rare thing: the always unexpected, wholly genuine article.

I was embarrassed not to have known who she was. She seemed embarrassed to have reminded me, and also depressed.

After that I saw Ted occasionally, Sylvia more rarely. He and I would meet for a beer in one of the pubs near Primrose Hill or the Heath, and sometimes we would walk our children together. We almost never talked shop; without mentioning it, we wanted to keep things unprofessional. At some point during the summer Ted and I did a broadcast together. Afterwards we collected Sylvia from the flat and went across to their local. The recording had been a success and we stood outside the pub, around the baby's pram, drinking our beers and pleased with ourselves. Sylvia, too, seemed easier, wittier, less constrained than I had seen her before. For the first time I understood something of the real charm and speed of the girl.

About that time my wife and I moved from our flat near Swiss Cottage to a house higher up in Hampstead, near the Heath. A couple of days before we were due to move I broke my leg in a climbing accident, and that put out everything and everyone, since the house had to be decorated, broken leg or not. I remember sticking black and white tiles to floor after endless floor, a filthy dark-brown glue coating my fingers and clothes and gumming up my hair, the huge, inert plaster cast dragging behind me like a coffin as I crawled. There wasn't much time for friends. Ted occasionally dropped in and I would hobble with him briefly to the pub. But I saw Sylvia not at all. In the autumn I went to teach for a term in the States.

While I was there *The Observer* sent me her first book of poems to review. It seemed to fit the image I had of her: serious, gifted, withheld, and still partly under the massive shadow of her husband. There were poems that had been influenced by him, others which echoed Theodore Roethke and Wallace Stevens; clearly, she was still casting about for her own style. Yet the technical ability was great, and beneath most of the poems was a sense of resources and disturbances not yet tapped. "Her poems," I wrote, "rest secure in a mass of experience that is never quite brought out into the day-light. . . . It is this sense of threat, as though she were continually menaced by something she could see only out of the corners of her eyes, that gives her work its distinction."

I still stand by that judgment. In the light of her subsequent work and, more persuasively, her subsequent death, *The Colossus* has been overrated. "Anyone can see," the doctrine now runs, "that it's all there in crystalline form." There are even academic critics who prefer these elegant early poems to the more naked and brutal frontal attacks of her mature work, although when the book first appeared their reviews were cool enough. Meanwhile, hindsight can alter the historical importance but not the quality of the verse. *The Colossus* established her credentials: it contained a handful of beautiful poems, but more important was the sheer ability of the work, the precision and concentration with which she handled language, the unemphatic range of vocabulary, her ear for subtle rhythms, and her assurance in handling and subduing rhymes and half-rhymes. Obviously, she had now developed the craft to cope with anything that arrived. My mistake was to imply that at that stage she hadn't, or wouldn't, recognize the forces that shook her. It turned out that she knew them all too well: they had driven her to the thin near-edge of suicide when she was nineteen, and already in the last piece in the book, the long "Poem for a Birthday," she was turning to face them. But the echoes of Roethke in the poem obscured that for me, and I couldn't see it.

When I got back from the States in February 1961, I saw the Hugheses again, but briefly and not often. Ted had fallen out of love with London and was fretting to get away; Sylvia had been ill—first a miscarriage, then appendicitis—and I had my own problems, a divorce. I remember her thanking me for the review of *The Colossus,* adding disarmingly that she agreed with the qualifications. I also remember her enthusing about the beautiful house she had found in Devon—old, thatched, flagstoned, and with a large orchard. They moved, I moved, something was finished.

Both of them continued to send poems to *The Observer.* In May 1961 we published Sylvia's poem about her daughter, "Morning Song"; in November of that year "Mojave Desert," which remained uncollected for some years; two months later, "The Rival." The current was deepening, its flow becoming easier.

I didn't see her again until June 1962 when I dropped in on them on my way down to Cornwall for the long Whitsun weekend. They were living a few miles northwest of Exeter. By Devon standards it wasn't a pretty village: more gray stone and gloom than timber, thatch, and flowers. Where the most perfect English villages give the impression of never having been properly awakened, theirs seemed to have retired into sleep. Once it might have been a center for the surrounding countryside, a place of some presence where things happened. But not any more. Exeter had taken over, and the life of this village had drained slowly away, like a family that has come down in the world.

The Hugheses's house had once been the local manor. It was set slightly above the rest of the village, up a steep lane next to a twelfth-century church, and it seemed important. It was large and thatched, with a cobbled courtyard and a front door of carved oak, the walls and passages were stone, the rooms gleamed with new paint. We sat out in the big wild garden drinking tea while little Frieda, now aged two, teetered among the flowers. There was a small army of apple and cherry trees, a vivid laburnum swaying with blossom, a vegetable patch and, off to one side, a little hillock. Sylvia called it a prehistoric burial mound. Given the Hugheses's flair and tastes, it could hardly have been anything else. Flowers glowed everywhere, the grass was high and unkempt, and the whole luxuriant place seemed to be overflowing with summer.

They had had a new baby in January, a boy, and Sylvia had changed. No longer quiet and withheld, a housewifely appendage to a powerful husband, she seemed made solid and complete, her own woman again. Perhaps the birth of a son had something to do with this new confident air. But there was a sharpness and clarity about her that seemed to go beyond that. It was she who showed me around the house and the garden; the electric gadgets, the freshly painted rooms, the orchard and the burial mound—above all, the burial mound, "the wall of old corpses," she called it later in a poem —were *her* property.[1] Ted, meanwhile, seemed content to sit back and play with little Frieda, who clung to him dependently. Since it appeared to be a strong, close marriage, I suppose he was unconcerned that the balance of power had shifted for the time being to her.

I understood why as I was leaving. "I'm writing again," she said. "Really writing. I'd like you to see some of the new poems." Her manner was warm and open, as though she had decided I could be trusted.

Some time before, *The Observer* had accepted a poem by her called "Finisterre." We finally published it that August. In the meantime she sent a beautiful short poem, "Crossing the Water," which was not in *Ariel*, although it is as good as many that were. It arrived with a formal note and a meticulously stamped-addressed envelope. She seemed to be functioning as efficiently as ever. Yet when I saw Ted sometime later in London, he was tense and preoccupied. Driving on her own, Sylvia had some kind of accident; apparently, she had blacked out and run off the road onto an old airfield, though mercifully without damaging herself or their old Morris station wagon. His dark presence, as he spoke, darkened an even deeper shade of gloom.

When August came, I went abroad for a few weeks, and by the time I got back autumn had already started. Although it was not yet mid-September, the leaves had begun to blow about the streets and the rain came down. That first morning, when I woke up to a drowning London sky, summer seemed as far away as the Mediterranean itself. Automatically, I found myself huddling into my clothes; the London crouch. We were in for a long winter.

At the end of September *The Observer* published "Crossing the Water." One afternoon soon after, when I was working and the charlady was banging around upstairs, the bell rang. It was Sylvia, smartly dressed, determinedly bright and cheerful.

"I was just passing, so I thought I'd drop in," she said. With her formal town clothes and prim bun of hair, she had the air of an Edwardian lady performing a delicate but necessary social duty.

The little studio I rented had been converted from an old stable. It lay down a long passage, behind a garage, and was beautiful in its crumbling way, but uncomfortable; there was nothing to lounge on—only spidery Windsor chairs and a couple of rugs on the blood-red uncarpeted lino. I poured her a drink and she settled in front of the coal stove on one of the rugs, like a student, very much at her ease, sipping whiskey and making the ice clink in her glass.

"That sound makes me homesick for the States," she said. "It's the only thing that does."

We talked about her poem in *The Observer*, then chatted about nothing in particular. Finally, I asked her why she was in town. She replied, with a kind of polished cheerfulness, that she was flat-hunting, and then added casually that she and the children were living on their own for the time being. I remembered the last time I had seen her, in that overflowing Devon garden, and it seemed impossible that anything could have disrupted the idyll. But I asked no questions and she offered no explanations. Instead, she began to talk about the new drive to write that was upon her. At least a poem a day, she said, and often more. She made it sound like demonic possession. And it occurred to me that maybe this was why she and her husband had, however temporarily, parted: it was a question not of differences but of intolerable similarities. When two genuinely original, ambitious, full-time poets join in marriage, and both are productive, every poem one writes probably feels to the other as though it had been dug out of his, or her, own skull. At a certain pitch of creative intensity it must be more unbearable for the Muse

to be unfaithful to you with your partner than for him, or her, to
betray you with a whole army of seducers.

"I'd like to read you some of the new poems," she said, and
pulled a sheaf of typescript from her shoulder bag on the floor beside
her.

"Gladly," I said, reaching over for them. "Let's see."

She shook her head: "No. I don't want you to read them to
yourself. They've got to be read out loud. I want you to *hear* them."

So sitting cross-legged on the uncomfortable floor, with the
charlady clanking away upstairs, she read me "Berck-Plage":

> This is the sea, then, this great abeyance. . . .

She read fast, in a hard, slightly nasal accent, rapping it out as
though she were angry. Even now I find it a difficult poem to
follow, the development indirect, the images concentrated and elid-
ing thickly together. I had a vague impression of something injuri-
ous and faintly obscene, but I don't think I understood much. So
when she finished I asked her to read it again. This time I heard it
a little more clearly and could make some remarks about details. In
some way, this seemed to satisfy her. We argued a bit and she read
me more poems: one of them was "The Moon and the Yew Tree";
"Elm," I think, was another; there were six or eight in all. She would
let me read none to myself, so I didn't get much, if anything, of their
subtlety. But I did at least recognize that I was hearing something
strong and new and hard to come to terms with. I suppose I picked
on whatever details and slight signs of weakness I could as a kind
of protection. She, in her turn, seemed happy to read, argue, and be
heard sympathetically.

"She's a poet, isn't she?" asked my charlady the next day.

"Yes."

"I thought so," she said with grim satisfaction.

After that, Sylvia dropped in fairly often on her visits to London,
always with a batch of new poems to read. This way I first heard,
among others, the bee poems, "A Birthday Present," "The Applicant," "Getting There," "Fever 103°," "Letter in November," and
"Ariel," which I thought extraordinary. I told her it was the best
thing she had done and a few days later she sent me a fair copy of
it, carefully written out in her heavy, rounded script, and illuminated like a medieval manuscript with flowers and ornamental
squiggles.

One day—I'm not sure when—she read me what she called "some light verse." She meant "Daddy" and "Lady Lazarus." Her voice, as she read them, was hot and full of venom. By this time I could hear the poetry fairly clearly, without too great a time lag and sense of inadequacy. I was appalled. At first hearing, the things seemed to be not so much poetry as assault and battery. And because I now knew something about her life, there was no avoiding how much she was part of the action. But to have commented on that would have been to imply that the poems had failed as poetry, which they clearly had not. As always, my defense was to nag her about details. There was one line I picked on in particular:

> Gentlemen, ladies
>
> These are my hands
> My knees.
> I may be skin and bone,
> *I may be Japanese . . .*

"Why *Japanese?*" I niggled away at her. "Do you just need the rhyme? Or are you trying to hitch an easy lift by dragging in the atomic victims? If you're going to use this kind of violent material, you've got to play it cool. . . ." She argued back sharply, but later, when the poem was finally published after her death, the line had gone. And that, I think, is a pity: she did need the rhyme; the tone is quite controlled enough to support the apparently not quite relevant allusion; and I was overreacting to the initial brutality of the verse without understanding its weird elegance.

In all this time the evidence of the poems and the evidence of the person were utterly different. There was no trace of the poetry's despair and unforgiving destructiveness in her social manner. She remained remorselessly bright and energetic: busy with her children and her beekeeping in Devon, busy flat-hunting in London, busy seeing her novel *The Bell Jar* through the press, busy typing and sending off her poems to largely unreceptive editors (just before she died she sent a sheaf of her best poems, most of them now classics, to one of the national British weeklies; none was accepted). She had also taken up horse-riding again, teaching herself to ride on a stallion called Ariel, and was elated by this new excitement.

Cross-legged on the red floor, after reading her poems, she would talk about her riding in her twangy, New England voice. And perhaps because I was also a member of the club, she talked, too, about suicide in much the same way: about her attempt ten years before which, I suppose, must have been very much on her mind as she corrected the proofs of her novel, and about her recent incident with the car. It had been no accident; she had gone off the road deliberately, seriously, wanting to die. But she hadn't, and all that was now in the past. For this reason, I am convinced that at this time she was not contemplating suicide. On the contrary, she was able to write about the act so freely because it was already behind her. The car crash was a death she had survived, the death she sardonically felt herself fated to undergo once every decade:

> I have done it again.
> One year in every ten
> I manage it—
>
> A sort of walking miracle . . .
> . . . .
> I am only thirty.
> And like the cat I have nine
> times to die.
>
> This is Number Three.

In life, as in the poem, there was neither hysteria in her voice, nor any appeal for sympathy. She talked about suicide in much the same tone as she talked about any other risky, testing activity: urgently, even fiercely, but altogether without self-pity. She seemed to view death as a physical challenge she had, once again, overcome. It was an experience of much the same quality as riding Ariel or mastering a bolting horse—which she had done as a Cambridge undergraduate —or careening down a dangerous snow slope without properly knowing how to ski—an incident, also from life, which is one of the best things in *The Bell Jar*. Suicide, in short, was not a swoon into death, an attempt "to cease upon the midnight with no pain"; it was something to be felt in the nerve ends and fought against, an initiation rite qualifying her for a *life* of her own.

God knows what wound the death of her father had inflicted on her in her childhood, but over the years this had been transformed into the conviction that to be an adult meant to be a survivor. So, for her, death was a debt to be met once every decade: in order to stay alive as a grown woman, a mother, and a poet, she had to pay —in some partial, magical way—with her life. But because this impossible payment involved also the fantasy of joining or regaining her beloved dead father, it was a passionate act, instinct as much with love as with hatred and despair. Thus in that strange, upsetting poem "The Bee Meeting," the detailed, doubtless accurate description of a gathering of local beekeepers in her Devon village gradually becomes an invocation of some deadly ritual in which she is the sacrificial virgin whose coffin, finally, waits in the sacred grove. Why this should happen becomes, perhaps, slightly less mysterious when you remember that her father was an authority on bees; so her beekeeping becomes a way of symbolically allying herself to him, and reclaiming him from the dead.

The tone of all these late poems is hard, factual, and, despite the intensity, understated. In some strange way, I suspect she thought of herself as a realist: the deaths and resurrections of "Lady Lazarus," the nightmares of "Daddy" and the rest had all been proved on her pulses. That she brought to them an extraordinary inner wealth of imagery and associations was almost beside the point, however essential it is for the poetry itself. Because she felt she was simply describing the facts as they had happened, she was able to tap in the coolest possible way all her large reserves of skill: those subtle rhymes and half-rhymes, the flexible, echoing rhythms and offhand colloquialisms by which she preserved, even in her most anguished probing, complete artistic control. Her internal horrors were as factual and precisely sensed as the stallion on which she was learning to ride or the car she had tried to smash up.

So she spoke of suicide with a wry detachment, and without any mention of the suffering or drama of the act. It was obviously a matter of self-respect that her first attempt had been serious and nearly successful, instead of a mere hysterical gesture. That seemed to entitle her to speak of suicide as a subject, not as an obsession. It was an act she felt she had a right to as a grown woman and a free agent, in the same way that she felt it to be necessary to her development, given her queer conception of the adult as a survivor, an imaginary Jew from the concentration camps of the mind. Because of this there was never any question of motives: you do it because you do it, just as an artist always knows what he knows.

Perhaps this is why she scarcely mentioned her father, however clearly and deeply her fantasies of death were involved with him. The autobiographical heroine of *The Bell Jar* goes to weep at her father's grave immediately before she holes up in a cellar and swallows fifty sleeping pills. In "Daddy," describing the same episode, she hammers home her reasons with repetitions:

> At twenty I tried to die
> And get back, back, back to you.
> I thought even the bones would do.

I suspect that finding herself alone again now, whatever the pretense of indifference, all the anguish she had experienced at her father's death was reactivated: despite herself, she felt abandoned, injured, enraged, and bereaved as purely and defenselessly as she had as a child twenty years before. As a result, the pain that had built up steadily inside her all that time came flooding out. There was no need to discuss motives because the poems did that for her.

These months were an amazingly creative period, comparable, I think, to the "marvellous year" in which Keats produced nearly all the poetry on which his reputation finally rests. Earlier she had written carefully, more or less painfully, with much rewriting and, according to her husband, with constant recourse to *Roget's Thesaurus*. Now, although she abandoned none of her hard-earned skills and discipline, and still rewrote and rewrote, the poems flowed effortlessly until, at the end, she occasionally produced as many as three a day. She also told me that she was deep into a new novel. *The Bell Jar* was finished, proofread and with her publishers; she spoke of it with some embarrassment as an autobiographical apprentice-work which she had had to write in order to free herself from the past. But this new book, she implied, was the genuine article. Considering the conditions in which she worked, her productivity was phenomenal. She was a full-time mother with a two-year-old daughter, a baby of a few months, and a house to look after. By the time the children were in bed at night she was too tired for anything more strenuous than "music and brandy and water." So she got up very early each morning and worked until the children woke. "These new poems of mine have one thing in common," she wrote in a note for a reading she prepared, but never broadcast, for the BBC, "they were all written at about four in the morning—that still blue, almost eternal hour before the baby's cry, before the glassy music of the milkman, settling his bottles." In those dead hours between night and day, she was able to gather herself into herself in silence and isolation, almost as though she were reclaiming some past innocence and freedom before life got a grip on her. Then she could write. For the rest of the day she was shared among the children, the housework, the shopping, efficient, bustling, harassed, like every other housewife.

But this dawn sense of paradise temporarily regained does not explain the sudden flowering and change in her work. Technically, the clue is in her insistence that she herself should always read the poems out loud. In the early Sixties, this was a rare procedure. It was, after all, still a period of high formalism, of Stevensesque cadences and Empsonian ambiguities at which she herself was, as her earlier work proved, particularly adept. Essentially, this was the style of the academies, of self-imposed limitations of feeling and narrow devotion to the duties of craftsmanship which were echoed in thumping iambics and painfully analyzable imagery. But in 1958 she had made the vital decision to abandon the university career for which she had so carefully prepared herself all through her adolescence and early twenties. Only gradually over the next four years did that total commitment to her own creative life emerge in the fabric of her verse, breaking down the old, inert molds, quickening the rhythms, broadening the emotional range. The decision to abandon teaching was the first critical step toward achieving her identity as a poet, just as the birth of her children seemed, as she described it, to vindicate her as a woman. In these last poems the process was complete: the poet and the poems became one. What she wrote depended on her voice in the same way as her children depended on her love.

The other crucial element in her poetic maturity was the example of Robert Lowell's *Life Studies*. I say "example" rather than "influence" because, although Sylvia had attended Lowell's classes at Boston University in the company of Anne Sexton and George Starbuck, she never picked up his peculiarly contagious style. Instead of a style, she took from him a freedom. She told a British Council interviewer: "I've been very excited by what I feel is the new breakthrough that came with, say, Robert Lowell's *Life Studies*. This intense breakthrough into very serious, very personal emotional experience, which I feel has been partly taboo. Robert Lowell's poems about his experiences in a mental hospital, for example, interest me very much. These peculiar private and taboo subjects I feel have been explored in recent American poetry. . . ." Lowell provided her with an example of the quality she most admired outside poetry and had herself in profusion: courage. In its way, *Life*

Studies was as brave and revolutionary as *The Waste Land*. After all, it appeared at the height of the tight-lipped Fifties, the era of doctrinaire New Criticism, of the Intentional Fallacy and the whole, elaborate iron dogma by which poetry was separated utterly from the man who made it. In his time, Lowell had been the darling of the school with his complex Catholic symbolism, thickly textured Eliot–Elizabethan language, and his unwavering ability to stamp every line with his own individual rhythm. Then, after nearly ten years' silence, he turned his back on it all. The symbols disappeared, the language clarified and became colloquial, the subject matter became intensely, insistently personal. He wrote as a man who had had breakdowns and was haunted at every crisis by family ghosts; and he wrote without evasions. All that was left of the former young master of Alexandrian complexity was the still unanswerable skill and originality. Even more strongly than before, it was impossible to avoid the troubled presence of Lowell himself, but now he was speaking out in a way that violated all the principles of New Criticism: there was immediacy instead of impersonality, vulnerability in place of exquisitely dandified irony.

Sylvia derived from all this, above all, a vast sense of release. It was as though Lowell had opened a door which had previously been bolted against her. At a critical moment in her development there was no longer any need to be imprisoned in her old poetic habits, which despite their elegance—or maybe because of it—she now felt to be intolerably constricting. "My first book, *The Colossus*," she told the man from the British Council, "I can't read any of the poems aloud now. I didn't write them to be read aloud. In fact, they quite privately bore me." *The Colossus* was the culmination of her apprenticeship in the craft of poetry. It completed the training she began as an eight-year-old and continued through the tensely stylish verse of her undergraduate days, when each poem seemed built up grudgingly, word by word, like a mosaic. Now all that was behind her. She had outgrown the style; more important, she had outgrown the person who had written in that oblique, reticent way. A combination of forces, some chosen deliberately, others chosen for her, had brought her to the point where she was able to write as from her true center about the forces that really moved her: destructive, volatile, demanding, a world apart from everything she had been trained to admire. "What," asked Coleridge, "is the height and ideal of mere association? Delirium." For years Sylvia had apparently agreed, pursuing formal virtues and finger-tip detachment, contemptuous of the self-pity, self-advertisement and self-indulgence of the beatniks. Now, right on cue, came *Life Studies* to prove that the violence of the self could be written about with control, subtlety, and a dispassionate but undefended imagination.

I suspect that this is why she had first come to me with the new poems, although she knew me only glancingly. It helped that I had reviewed *The Colossus* sympathetically and had got *The Observer* to publish some of her more recent things. But more important was the introduction to my Penguin anthology, *The New Poetry*, which had been published the previous spring. In it I had attacked the British poets' nervous preference for gentility above all else, and their avoidance of the uncomfortable, destructive truths both of the inner life and of the present time. Apparently, this essay said something she wanted to hear; she spoke of it often and with approval, and was disappointed not to have been included among the poets in the book. (She was later, since her work, more than anyone else's, vindicates my argument. But in the first edition I had stuck to British poets, with the exception of two older Americans, Lowell and Berryman who, I felt, set the tone for the postwar, post-Eliot period.) Perhaps it made things easier for her to know that someone was making a critical case for what she was now trying to do. And perhaps it made her feel less lonely.

Yet lonely she was, touchingly and without much disguise, despite her buoyant manner. Despite, too, the energy of her poems, which are, by any standards, subtly ambiguous performances. In them she faced her private horrors steadily and without looking aside, but the effort and risk involved in doing so acted on her like a stimulant: the worse things got and the more directly she wrote about them, the more fertile her imagination became. Just as disaster, when it finally arrives, is never as bad as it seems in expectation, so she now wrote almost with relief, swiftly as though to forestall further horrors. In a way, this is what she had been waiting for all her life, and now that it had come she knew she must use it. "The passion for destruction is also a creative passion," said Mikhail Bakunin, and for Sylvia also this was true. She turned anger, implacability, and her roused, needle-sharp sense of trouble into a kind of celebration.

I have suggested that her cool tone depends a great deal on her realism, her sense of fact. As the months went by and her poetry became progressively more extreme, this gift of transforming every detail grew steadily until, in the last weeks, each trivial event became the occasion for poetry: a cut finger, a fever, a bruise. Her drab domestic life fused with her imagination richly and without hesitation. Around this time, for example, her husband produced a curious radio play in which the hero, driving to town, runs over a hare, sells the dead animal for five shillings, and with the blood money buys his girl two roses. Sylvia pounced on this, isolating its core, interpreting and adjusting it according to her own needs. The result was the poem "Kindness," which ends:

> The blood jet is poetry,
> There is no stopping it.
> You hand me two children, two roses.

There was, indeed, no stopping it. Her poetry acted as a strange, powerful lens through which her ordinary life was filtered and refigured with extraordinary intensity. Perhaps the elation that comes of writing well and often helped her to preserve that bright American façade she unfailingly presented to the world. In common with her other friends of that period, I chose to believe in this cheerfulness against all the evidence of the poems. Or rather, I believed in it and I didn't believe. But what could one do? I felt sorry for her, but she clearly didn't want that. Her jauntiness forestalled all sympathy and, if only by her blank refusal to discuss them otherwise, she insisted that her poems were purely poems, autonomous. If attempted suicide is, as some psychiatrists believe, a cry for help, then Sylvia at this time was not suicidal. What she wanted was not help but confirmation: she needed someone to acknowledge that she was coping exceptionally well with her difficult routine life of children, nappies, shopping, and writing. She needed, even more, to know that the poems worked and were good, for although she had gone through a gate Lowell had opened, she was now far along a peculiarly solitary road on which not many would risk following her. So it was important for her to know that her messages were coming back clear and strong. Yet not even her determinedly bright self-reliance could disguise the loneliness that came from her almost palpably, like a heat haze. She asked for neither sympathy nor help but, like a bereaved widow at a wake, she simply wanted company in her mourning. I suppose it provided confirmation that, despite the odds and the internal evidence, she still existed.

One gloomy November afternoon she arrived at my studio greatly excited. As usual, she had been trudging the chill streets, house-hunting despondently and more or less aimlessly. A block away from the square near Primrose Hill where she and Ted had lived when they first came to London, she saw a "To Let" notice up in front of a newly refurbished house. That in itself was something of a miracle in those impossible, overcrowded days. But more important, the house bore a blue plaque announcing that Yeats had once lived there. It was a sign, the confirmation she had been looking for. That summer she had visited Yeats's Tower at Ballylee and wrote to a friend that she thought it "the most beautiful and peaceful place in the world." Now there was a possibility of finding another Yeats tower in her favorite part of London which she could in some way share with the great poet. She hurried to the agent's and found, improbably, that she was the first to apply. Another sign. On the spot she took a five-year lease of the flat, although the rent was more than she could afford. Then she walked across dark, blowy Primrose Hill to tell me the news.

She was elated not just because she had at last found a flat, but because the place and its associations seemed to her somehow preordained. In varying degrees, both she and her husband seemed to believe in the occult. As artists, I suppose, they had to, since both were intent on finding voices for their unquiet, buried selves. But there was, I think, something more to their belief than that. Ted has written that "her psychic gifts, at almost any time, were strong enough to make her frequently wish to be rid of them." That could simply have been her poet's knack of sensing the unspoken content of every situation and, later, her easy, instinctive access to her own unconscious. Yet although both of them talked often enough about astrology, dreams, and magic—enough, anyway, to imply that these were not just a casually interesting subject—I had the impression that at heart their attitudes were utterly different. Ted constantly and carefully mocked himself and deflated his pretensions, yet there was always a sense of his being in touch with some primitive area, some dark side of the self which had nothing to do with the young literary man. This, after all, was what his poems were about: an immediate, physical apprehension of the violence both of animal life and of the self—of the animality of the self. It was also part of his physical presence, a quality of threat beneath his shrewd, laconic manner. It was almost as though, despite all the reading and polish and craftsmanship, he had never properly been civilized—or had, at least, never properly believed in his civilization. It was simply a shell he sardonically put up with for the sake of convenience. So all that astrology, primitive religion, and black magic he talked about, however ironically, was a kind of metaphor for the shaking but obscure creative powers he knew himself to possess. For this reason those dubious topics took on for him an immediacy which may not have implied any belief but which certainly transformed them into something beyond mere fad. Perhaps all I am describing is, quite simply, a touch of genius. But it is a genius that has little to do with the traditional Romantic concept of the word: with Shelley's canny otherworldliness or Byron's equally canny sense of his own drama. Ted too, is canny and practical, like most Yorkshiremen, unwillingly fooled and with a fine, racing-mechanic's ear for the rumblings of the literary machine. But he is also, in a curiously complete way, an original: his reactions are unpredictable, his frame of reference different. I imagine the most extreme example of this style of genius is Blake. But there are also many people of genius—perhaps the majority—who have almost nothing of that dislocating and dislocated quality: T. S. Eliot, for example, the Polish poet Zbigniew Herbert, John Donne, and Keats—all men whose unusual creative intelligence and awareness seem not essentially at odds with the reality of their everyday worlds. Instead, their particular gift is to clarify and intensify the received world.

Sylvia, I think, belonged with these latter. Her intensity was of the nerves, something urban and near screaming point. It was also, in its way, more intellectual than Ted's. It was part of the fierceness with which she had worked as a student, passing exam after exam brilliantly, effortlessly, hungrily. With the same intensity she immersed herself in her children, her riding, her beekeeping, even her cooking; everything had to be done well and to the fullest. Since her husband was interested in the occult—for whatever clouded personal reasons—she threw herself into that, too, almost out of the desire to excel. And because her natural talents were very great, she discovered she had "psychic gifts." No doubt the results were genuine and even uncanny, but I suspect they were a triumph of mind over ectoplasm. It is the same in the poems: Ted's gain their effect by expressing his sense of menace and violence immediately, unanswerably; in Sylvia's the expression, though often more powerful, is a by-product of a compulsive need to understand.

On Christmas Eve 1962, Sylvia telephoned me: she and the children were finally settled into their new apartment; could I come over that evening to see the place, have a meal, and hear some new poems? As it happened, I couldn't, since I had already been invited to dinner by some friends who lived a few streets away from her. I said I'd drop in for a drink on my way.

She seemed different. Her hair, which she usually wore in a tight, school-mistressy bun, was loose. It hung straight to her waist like a tent, giving her pale face and gaunt figure a curiously desolate, rapt air, like a priestess emptied out by the rites of her cult. When she walked in front of me down the hall passage and up the stairs of her apartment—she had the top two floors of the house—her hair gave off a strong smell, sharp as an animal's. The children were already in bed upstairs and the flat was silent. It was newly painted, white and chill. There were, as I remember, no curtains up yet and the night pressed in coldly on the windows. She had deliberately kept the place bare: rush matting on the floor, a few books, bits of Victoriana and cloudy blue glass on the shelves, a couple of small Leonard Baskin woodcuts. It was rather beautiful, in its chaste, stripped-down way, but cold, very cold, and the oddments of flimsy Christmas decoration made it seem doubly forlorn, each seeming to repeat that she and the children would be alone over Christmas. For the unhappy, Christmas is always a bad time: the terrible false jollity that comes at you from every side, braying about good will and peace and family fun, makes loneliness and depression particularly hard to bear. I had never seen her so strained.

We drank wine and, as usual, she read me some poems. One of them was "Death & Co." This time there was no escaping the meaning. When she had written about death before it was as something survived, even surpassed: "Lady Lazarus" ends with a resurrection and a threat, and even in "Daddy" she manages finally to turn her back on the grinning, beckoning figure—"Daddy, daddy, you bastard, I'm through." Hence, perhaps, the energy of these poems, their weird jollity in the teeth of everything, their recklessness. But now, as though poetry really were a form of black magic, the figure she had invoked so often, only to dismiss triumphantly, had risen before her, dank, final, and not to be denied. He appeared to her in both his usual shapes: like her father, elderly, unforgiving, and very dead, and also younger, more seductive, a creature of her own generation and choice.[2] This time there was no way out for her; she could only sit still and pretend they hadn't noticed her:

> I do not stir.
> The frost makes a flower,
> The dew makes a star,
> The dead bell,
> The dead bell.
>
> Somebody's done for.

Perhaps the bell was tolling for "somebody" other than herself; but she didn't seem to believe so.

I didn't know what to say. The earlier poems had all insisted, in their different ways, that she wanted nobody's help—although I suddenly realized that maybe they had insisted in such a manner as to make you understand that help might be acceptable if you were willing to make the effort. But now she was beyond the reach of anyone. In the beginning she had called up these horrors partly in the hope of exorcising them, partly to demonstrate her omnipotence and invulnerability. Now she was shut in with them and knew she was defenseless.

I remember arguing inanely about the phrase "The nude/Verdigris of the condor." I said it was exaggerated, morbid. On the contrary, she replied, that was exactly how a condor's legs looked. She was right, of course. I was only trying, in a futile way, to reduce the tension and take her mind momentarily off her private horrors —as though that could be done by argument and literary criticism! She must have felt I was stupid and insensitive. Which I was. But to have been otherwise would have meant accepting responsibilities I didn't want and couldn't, in my own depression, have coped with. When I left about eight o'clock to go on to my dinner party, I knew I had let her down in some final and unforgivable way. And I knew she knew. I never again saw her alive.

It was an unspeakable winter, the worst, they said, in a hundred and fifty years. The snow began just after Christmas and would not let up. By New Year the whole country had ground to a halt. The trains froze on the tracks, the abandoned trucks froze on the roads.

The power stations, overloaded by million upon pathetic million of hopeless electric fires, broke down continually; not that the fires mattered, since the electricians were mostly out on strike. Water-pipes froze solid; for a bath you had to scheme and cajole those rare friends with centrally heated houses, who became rarer and less friendly as the weeks dragged on. Doing the dishes became a major operation. The gastric rumble of water in outdated plumbing was sweeter than the sound of mandolins. Weight for weight, plumbers were as expensive as smoked salmon and harder to find. The gas failed and Sunday joints were raw. The lights failed and candles, of course, were unobtainable. Nerves failed and marriages crumbled. Finally, the heart failed. It seemed the cold would never end. Nag, nag, nag.

In December *The Observer* had published a long poem by Sylvia called "Event"; in mid-January we published another, "Winter Trees." Sylvia wrote me a note about it, adding that maybe we should take our children to the zoo and she would show me "the nude verdigris of the condor." But she no longer dropped into my studio with poems. Later that month I met a literary editor of one of the big weeklies. He asked me if I had seen Sylvia recently.

"No. Why?"

"I was just wondering. She sent us some poems. Very strange."

"Did you like them?"

"No," he replied, "too extreme for my taste. I sent them all back. But she sounds in a bad state. I think she needs help."

Her doctor, a sensitive, overworked man, thought the same. He prescribed sedatives and arranged for her to see a psychotherapist. Having been bitten once by American psychiatry, she hesitated for some time before writing for an appointment. But her depression did not lift and finally the letter was sent. It did no good. Either her letter or that of the therapist arranging a consultation went astray; apparently the postman delivered it to the wrong address. The therapist's reply arrived a day or two after she died. This was one of several links in the chain of accidents, coincidences, and mistakes that ended in her death.

I am convinced by what I know of the facts that this time she did not intend to die. Her suicide attempt ten years before had been, in every sense, deadly serious. She had carefully disguised the theft of the sleeping pills, left a misleading note to cover her tracks, and hidden herself in the darkest, most unused corner of a cellar, rear-ranging behind her the old firelogs she had disturbed, burying her-self away like a skeleton in the nethermost family closet. Then she had swallowed a bottle of fifty sleeping pills. She was found late and by accident, and survived only by a miracle. The flow of life in her was too strong even for the violence she had done it. This, anyway, is her description of the act in *The Bell Jar;* there is no reason to believe it false. So she had learned the hard way the odds against successful suicide; she had learned that despair must be counter-poised by an almost obsessional attention to detail and disguise.

By these lights she seemed, in her last attempt, to be taking care not to succeed. But this time everything conspired to destroy her. An employment agency had found her an *au pair* girl to help with the children and housework while Sylvia got on with her writing. The girl, an Australian, was due to arrive at nine o'clock on the morning of Monday, February 11. Meanwhile, a recurrent trouble, her sinuses were bad; the pipes in her newly converted flat froze solid; there was still no telephone and no word from the psychother-apist; the weather continued monstrous. Illness, loneliness, depres-sion, and cold, combined with the demands of two small children, were too much for her. So when the weekend came she went off with the babies to stay with friends in another part of London. The plan was, I think, that she would leave early enough on Monday morning to be back in time to welcome the Australian girl. Instead, she decided to go back on the Sunday. The friends were against it but she was insistent, made a great show of her old competence and seemed more cheerful than she had been for some time. So they let her go. About eleven o'clock that night she knocked on the door of the elderly painter who lived below her, asking to borrow some stamps. But she lingered in the doorway, drawing out the conversa-tion until he told her that he got up well before nine in the morning. Then she said good night and went back upstairs.

God knows what kind of a sleepless night she spent or if she wrote any poetry. Certainly, within the last few days of her life she wrote one of her most beautiful poems, "Edge," which is specifically about the act she was about to perform:

> The woman is perfected.
> Her dead

Body wears the smile of accomplishment,
The illusion of a Greek necessity

Flows in the scrolls of her toga,
Her bare

Feet seem to be saying:
We have come so far, it is over.

Each dead child coiled, a white serpent,
One at each little

Pitcher of milk, now empty.
She has folded

Them back into her body as petals
Of a rose close when the garden

Stiffens and odors bleed
From the sweet, deep throats of the night flower.

The moon has nothing to be sad about,
Staring from her hood of bone.

She is used to this sort of thing.
Her blacks crackle and drag.

It is a poem of great peace and resignation, utterly without self-pity. Even with a subject so appallingly close she remains an artist, absorbed in the practical task of letting each image develop a full, still life of its own. That she is writing about her own death is almost irrelevant. There is another poem, "Words," also very late, which is about the way language remains and echoes long after the turmoil of life has passed; like "Edge," it has the same translucent calm. If these were among the last things she wrote, I think she must in the end have accepted the logic of the life she had been leading and come to terms with its terrible necessities.

Around 6 A.M. she went up to the children's room and left a plate of bread and butter and two mugs of milk, in case they should wake hungry before the *au pair* girl arrived. Then she went back down to the kitchen, sealed the door and window as best she could with towels, opened the oven, laid her head in it and turned on the gas.

The Australian girl arrived punctually at 9 A.M. She rang and knocked a long time but could get no answer. So she went off to search for a telephone kiosk in order to phone the agency and make sure she had the right address. Sylvia's name, incidentally, was not on either of the doorbells. Had everything been normal, the neighbor below would have been up by then; even if he had overslept, the girl's knocking would have aroused him. But as it happened, the neighbor was very deaf and slept without his hearing aid. More important, his bedroom was immediately below Sylvia's kitchen. The gas seeped down and knocked him out cold. So he slept on through all the noise. The girl returned and tried again, still without success. Again she went off to telephone the agency and ask what to do; they told her to go back. It was now about eleven o'clock. This time she was lucky: some builders had arrived to work in the frozen-up house, and they let her in. When she knocked on Sylvia's door there was no answer and the smell of gas was overpowering. The builders forced the lock and found Sylvia sprawled in the kitchen. She was still warm. She had left a note saying, "Please call Dr. _____," and giving his telephone number. But it was too late.

Had everything worked out as it should—had the gas not drugged the man downstairs, preventing him from opening the front door to the *au pair* girl—there is little doubt she would have been saved. I think she wanted to be; why else leave her doctor's telephone number? This time, unlike the occasion ten years before, there was too much holding her to life. Above all, there were the children: she was too passionate a mother to want to lose them or them to lose her. There were also the extraordinary creative powers she now unequivocally knew she possessed: the poems came daily, unbidden and unstoppable, and she was again working on a novel about which, at last, she had no reservations.

Why, then, did she kill herself? In part, I suppose, it was "a cry for help" which fatally misfired. But it was also a last desperate attempt to exorcise the death she had summoned up in her poems. I have already suggested that perhaps she had begun to write obsessively about death for two reasons. First, when she and her husband separated, whether she was willing or not, she went through again the same piercing grief and bereavement she had felt as a child when her father, by his death, seemed to abandon her. Second, I believe she thought her car crash the previous summer had set her free; she had paid her dues, qualified as a survivor and could now write about it. But as I have written elsewhere, for the artist himself art is not necessarily therapeutic; he is not automatically relieved of his fantasies by expressing them. Instead, by some perverse logic of creation, the act of formal expression may simply make the dredged-up material more readily available to him. The result of handling it in his work may well be that he finds himself living it out. For the artist, in short, nature often imitates art. Or, to change the cliché, when an artist holds up a mirror to nature he finds out who and what he is; but the knowledge may change him irredeemably so that he becomes that image.

I think Sylvia, in one way or another, sensed this. In an introductory note she wrote to "Daddy" for the BBC, she said of the poem's narrator, "She has to act out the awful little allegory once over before she is free of it." The allegory in question was, as she saw it, the struggle in her between a fantasy Nazi father and a Jewish mother. But perhaps it was also a fantasy of containing in herself her own dead father, like a woman possessed by a demon (in the poem she actually calls him a vampire). In order for her to be free of him, he has to be released like a genie from a bottle. And this is precisely what the poems did: they bodied forth the death within her. But they also did so in an intensely living and creative way. The more she wrote about death, the stronger and more fertile her imaginative world became. And this gave her everything to live for.

I suspect that in the end she wanted to have done with the theme once and for all. But the only way she could find was "to act out the awful little allegory once over." She had always been a bit of a gambler, used to taking risks. The authority of her poetry was in part due to her brave persistence in following the thread of her inspiration right down to the Minotaur's lair. And this psychic courage had its parallel in her physical arrogance and carelessness. Risks didn't frighten her; on the contrary, she found them stimulating. Freud has written, "Life loses in interest, when the highest stake in the game of living, life itself, may not be risked." Finally, Sylvia took that risk. She gambled for the last time, having worked out that the odds were in her favor, but perhaps, in her depression, not much caring whether she won or lost. Her calculations went wrong and she lost.

It was a mistake, then, and out of it a whole myth has grown. I don't think she would have found it much to her taste, since it is a myth of the poet as a sacrificial victim, offering herself up for the sake of her art, having been dragged by the Muses to that final altar through every kind of distress. In these terms, her suicide becomes the whole point of the story, the act which validates her poems, gives them their interest and proves her seriousness. So people are drawn to her work in much the same spirit as *Time* featured her at length: not for the poetry but for the gossipy, extra-literary "human interest." Yet just as the suicide adds nothing at all to the poetry, so the myth of Sylvia as a passive victim is a total perversion of the woman she was. It misses altogether her liveliness, her intellectual appetite and harsh wit, her great imaginative resourcefulness and vehemence of feeling, her control. Above all, it misses the courage with which she was able to turn disaster into art. The pity is not that there is a myth of Sylvia Plath but that the myth is not simply that of an enormously gifted poet whose death came carelessly, by mistake, and too soon.

I used to think of her brightness as a façade, as though she were able, in a rather schizoid way, to turn her back on her suffering for the sake of appearances, and pretend it didn't exist. But maybe she was also able to keep her unhappiness in check because she could write about it, because she knew she was salvaging from all those horrors something rather marvelous. The end came when she felt she could stand the subject no longer. She had written it out and was ready for something new.

> The blood jet is poetry,
> There is no stopping it.

The only method of stopping it she could see, her vision by then blinkered by depression and illness, was that last gamble. So having, as she thought, arranged to be saved, she lay down in front of the gas oven almost hopefully, almost with relief, as though she were saying, "Perhaps this will set me free."

On Friday, February 15, there was an inquest in the drab, damp coroner's court behind Camden Town: muttered evidence, long silences, the Australian girl in tears. Earlier that morning I had gone with Ted to the undertaker's in Mornington Crescent. The coffin was at the far end of a bare, draped room. She lay stiffly, a ludicrous ruff at her neck. Only her face showed. It was gray and slightly transparent, like wax. I had never before seen a dead person and I hardly recognized her; her features seemed too thin and sharp. The room smelled of apples, faint, sweet but somehow unclean, as though the apples were beginning to rot. I was glad to get out into the cold and noise of the dingy streets. It seemed impossible that she was dead.

Even now I find it hard to believe. There was too much life in her long, flat, strongly boned body, and her longish face with its fine brown eyes, shrewd and full of feeling. She was practical and candid, passionate and compassionate. I believe she was a genius. I sometimes catch myself childishly thinking I'll run into her walking on Primrose Hill or the Heath, and we'll pick up the conversation where we left off. But perhaps that is because her poems still speak so distinctly in her accents: quick, sardonic, unpredictable, effortlessly inventive, a bit angry, and always utterly her own.

On Sunday, February 17, 1963 I published a brief obituary of Sylvia in *The Observer:*

> Last Monday, Sylvia Plath, the American poetess and wife of Ted Hughes, died suddenly in London. She was thirty. She published her first and highly accomplished book of poems, *The Colossus,* in 1960. But it was only recently that the particular intensity of her genius found its perfect expression. For the last few months she had been writing continuously, almost as though possessed. In the last poems, she was systematically probing that narrow, violent area between the viable and the impossible, between experience which can be transmuted into poetry and that which is overwhelming. It represents a totally new breakthrough in modern verse, and establishes her, I think, as the most gifted woman poet of our time. . . . She leaves two small children. The loss to literature is inestimable.

NOTES

1. The "burial mound" was, in fact, a prehistoric fort; and I am told that "the wall of corpses" probably refers to the wall between the Hugheses' garden and the adjacent churchyard.

2. In her own note on the poem, which she wrote for the BBC, she said: "The poem—'Death & Co.'—is about the double or schizophrenic nature of death—the marmoreal coldness of Blake's death mask, say, hand in glove with the fearful softness of worms, water and other katabolists. I imagine these two aspects of death as two men, two business friends, who have come to call."

Aurelia S. Plath

Letter Written in the Actuality of Spring

Sessions at the typewriter tire me, and I am no longer the accurate typist I once was. I have started many pieces for you, then realized that they were not at all appropriate as essays. They are autobiographical, rough notes of our family life—particularly mine. Today is a spring day and gives promise of summer. I want to enjoy it— not sit indoors at the typewriter or delve back into the tragic transformation of my daughter, whose loss is a constant pain, one that no critic of her writing has ever seemed to sense fully.

The only Sylvia we—my son and I, for example—knew was the Sylvia revealed in her own letters and in my commentary of *Letters Home.* We were a close, affectionate family, supportive of each other, and Sylvia required the most consideration. We all adored her and catered to our "prima donna," as we teasingly called her. She was merry and witty, refreshingly original. Her skills in drawing, painting, writing—also in dramatics—resulted in her being in great demand at school, so we freed her from her share of home chores most of the time.

One observation I can make, however, involves Sylvia's tendency to fuse characters and manipulate events to achieve her own artistic ends. Richard Wilbur refers to this tendency in his own work as a "violation of actual circumstances," a phrase which seems particularly appropriate to describe the process of transformation

---

NOTE: While compiling this anthology, I asked Aurelia Plath if she would contribute an essay. Her response to me, written in letter form, seemed more public than private; consequently, after providing the current title, I asked and received her permission to include her letter herein. It is, according to Mrs. Plath, the final public statement she will make regarding her daughter or her daughter's work.—*PA*

Sylvia used in her writing. With Sylvia, this need to "violate the actual circumstances" is dominant and is present even in works in which she tries to hold to the autobiographical—as in an essay like "Ocean 1212-W," for instance—where truth is still often rearranged for the sake of art.

Because many times I knew the real-life character or event, I was much more aware of this manipulation than other people could be. Two good examples occur in the poem "The Disquieting Muses." Introducing this poem on a BBC radio program, Sylvia said that the poem, which is addressed to me, was inspired by a painting by Giorgio de Chirico. For me, however, it is also the description of a moment of recognition she had when she knew that she was to be a serious writer. To describe this occasion, she reports accurately some biographical information in the first three stanzas while transforming biographical information in the remainder of the poem.

In the fourth stanza of "The Disquieting Muses," the reader is given the picture of an ambitious mother sending her protesting, awkward child to ballet school. The fact is Sylvia never took ballet lessons. I did—and told her about my delight, especially during the ballet recital, when, at nine, I was a member of the chorus of about thirty other "fireflies." On the dimly lit stage as, in our winged costumes, we danced, tiny "blinking flashlights" in each hand, I felt myself exalted, for I knew that in the front row my parents were sitting with eyes for me alone—I was for *them* the prima ballerina! But the tone of Sylvia's poem gives an entirely different (and certainly more artistic) form and meaning:

> When on tiptoe the schoolgirls danced,
> Blinking flashlights like fireflies
> And singing the glowworm song, I could
> Not lift a foot in the twinkle-dress
> But, heavy-footed, stood aside
> In the shadow cast by my dismal-headed
> Godmothers, and you cried and cried . . .

Then in the fifth stanza the ambitious mother sends her tone-deaf daughter to take piano lessons. It is true that when we lived in Winthrop, Sylvia took piano lessons from a friend of mine, a talented pianist and teacher, who found that Sylvia enjoyed the half hour they spent together weekly. After we moved to Wellesley, these lessons were discontinued. A year or so later, Sylvia read in the newspaper of afternoon courses at the New England Conservatory of Music and eagerly asked if she might take lessons there. Commuting was easy, for a bus from Wellesley stopped right in front of the Boston School. And Sylvia did well enough to be offered a half scholarship. She continued this for two years and made good progress, enjoying Mozart, Beethoven, Brahms—the usual classical schedule—plus some "boogie-woogie." How misleading, then, autobiographically, are the following lines:

> Mother, you sent me to piano lessons
> And praised my arabesques and trills
> Although each teacher found my touch
> Oddly wooden in spite of scales
> And the hours of practicing, my ear
> Tone-deaf and yes, unteachable.

There are similar instances of fusion and of the "violation of actual circumstances" in other poems which involve the mother figure as the whipping boy, so characteristic of the Fifties. Sylvia achieved release when troubled by writing things out, thereby dissipating her frustration, even her fury, by the act. But nowhere is this violation more evident than in her novel *The Bell Jar*, where, through her creative process, she transformed personalities into cruel and false caricatures, misleading though artistically more convincing than the truth would be.

I was warned by the famous Dr. Lindeman that after shock treatment (which was considered necessary for Sylvia who showed suicidal tendencies after her return from the intense working session at *Mademoiselle*) patients' personalities were sometimes totally altered. It seemed to us that Sylvia became her "own double," and I believe she realized this in herself and was thus led so strongly to Dostoyevsky and chose the subject of the double for her senior thesis at Smith.

After her marriage, I never visited without an invitation from both Ted and Sylvia. In 1961, following Frieda's birth in London, I received urgent invitations from Sylvia and Ted to come to England. This I did, right after I turned in my grades for the year of teaching at Boston University, and took up the care of Frieda and that little household, so that Ted and Sylvia could be free to visit the Merwins in France and have additional time for their writing. I had faith in their genius.

How do I feel now about her writing? She became a master, and in form and language the later poems show the development of a constantly maturing genius. Yet in her writing the toll of the death bell frightened me, as did the obsessive return to the period of emotional confusion and the horror of that first shock treatment. I so longed for her to free herself from these memories. I thought it best not to recall them to her, but to *listen* to any references she might make. I wanted us to make the present as good and wholesome as possible and to look courageously toward our future. . . .

In the last several years I have replied to hundreds of understanding, appreciative letters from readers of my daughter's work and of *Letters Home,* but now must cease that practice of written response. All I can say is that it is now I miss Sylvia most. Her children, so dear to me, are grown; for years after her death, Frieda and Nick were my first consideration and I spent time with them each of ten summers—four times they came here. However, even while her loss is constantly with me, I find some measure of solace in the thought that her genius, evident in both her poetry and prose, will endure.

April 1983
Wellesley, Massachusetts

Copyright Acknowledgments